USAAF FIGHTERS
OF WORLD WAR TWO
IN ACTION

A factory-fresh P–51D breaks away from the camera plane, illustrating how the laminar flow wing had been filled and painted to maintain the desired airflow. At this point, Mustangs were being delivered without camouflage but the wings were always painted (although many times just the first third of the wing was filled and painted) as can be seen from the contrast between the silver paint and the bare metal of the gear doors and stress panels. Note the ejection chutes for spent shells and drop tank/bomb shackles. (NAA)

USAAF FIGHTERS

OF WORLD WAR TWO

IN ACTION

Volume One P-35 to P-39

Michael O'Leary

HTI

Historical Times INC.

Harrisburg

First published in the UK 1986 by
Blandford Press
Link House, West Street, Poole, Dorset BH15 1LL

First published in the USA 1986 by
Historical Times Inc,
2245 Kohn Road,
P.O. Box 8200,
Harrisburg, PA 17105–8200
by arrangement with Blandford Press

Typeset by Keyspools Ltd, Golborne, Lancs.
Printed in Great Britain by
R.J. Acford, Chichester

Contents

Introduction

United States Army Air Forces Fighters of World War Two shows not only the amazing growth of the American aeronautical industry but also outlines the development of the nation. In 1939, the aviation industry was a rather sleepy, backwater activity – only just beginning to respond to the frantic visits of the British and French Aircraft Commissioning Committees who were desperate to purchase combat aircraft. Fully aware of the growing German menace, both countries realized the American aeronautical effort was behind the times when compared to the very rapid developments on the Continent and in Europe.

Quantity, rather than quality, became the order of the day as massive orders were placed for a variety of combat aircraft – most of which were really obsolete when compared to what was coming from the German factories. This is not to say these were bad aircraft – some machines like the Lockheed Hudson and Curtiss Hawk 75 were rugged, dependable machines but they did not offer enough in the way of performance or armament. Some aircraft, like the Brewster Buffalo, were unmitigated disasters (see *United States Naval Fighters of World War Two*).

Huge orders from abroad, coupled with increased American government fear that the war which was obviously brewing in Europe would lead to American involvement, caused a rapid expansion in the country's aeronautical plants as unprecedented orders demanded construction of new plant space and the hiring of thousands of new workers. This increase in military development did not proceed smoothly since much of the American population (and government) favored the curious policy of isolationism. Protected by vast stretches of ocean to the east and west and with friendly neighbors to the north and south, Europe was perceived by Americans as a vague and distant place – best left to carry out its own affairs with a minimum of American aid or interference.

With the start of World War Two, vicious aerial fighting took place which quickly pointed out how unwise it had been for industry to ignore German developments. Soon, just Britain remained and that island nation began churning out thousands of Hurricanes and Spitfires to help stem the projected Nazi invasion. Drawing upon combat experience, an order was placed by the British with an upstart American company for a new fighter – and the North American Mustang was born. Other companies employed visionary designers, such as Lockheed's Kelly Johnson, who saw the shapes of future fighters and were fully capable of translating their ideas into fighting machines. Once started, the flow of new American designs was truly staggering: Lightning, Thunderbolt, and Mustang – aircraft with high performance and capable of seeking and destroying the enemy in any location. Adopting the mass production techniques developed by Henry Ford in his automobile factories, tens of thousands of new warplanes were on the way to the fighting fronts – aircraft not only superior to what the enemy could put in the air but also available in overwhelming numbers. As the aircraft industry developed, so did the American populace. The Great Depression was now at an end, high-technology aeronautical industries forecast the way of the future as huge numbers of Americans left farms to be employed in industry for the first time, and, most importantly, the average American citizen began to perceive the size and importance of the world around him.

As with any volume of this size, the number of individuals who offered assistance and information would fill up several pages of closely-packed type. However, I would like to make mention of a few individuals who went out of their way to provide assistance: USAF Major William Austin of the USAF's Magazine and Book branch; Mr Gene Boswell, now retired from Rockwell; Mr Robert Ferguson of Lockheed-California; Mr Larry Gann of McDonnell Douglas; and Ms Lois Lovisolo of the Grumman Corporation. Special thanks is also due to Barry Gregory and Michael Burns who got the project on its feet and offered guidance towards completion. Also, I would like to thank my parents for their continued interest and support.

Michael O'Leary
Los Angeles, January 1986

Seversky P-35
The Army's First Modern Fighter

Seversky's stubby fighter introduced modern features to the Army but was a disaster in combat.

Modern is a relative term. When the Seversky P-35 entered service with the Army Air Corps in 1937, the popular press made a great deal of the 'aerial superiority' of the new fighter. However, to pilots of the 34th Pursuit Squadron stationed in the Philippines on 10 December 1941, the burning hulks of their shattered P-35s did not live up to their press.

During the 1930s, a one-legged former Czarist Russian aristocrat had a very profound effect on American military aircraft design. Alexander P. de Seversky had been born in Tiflis, Russia, to a wealthy family. During the start of World War One, he entered the Imperial Russian Naval Air Service but on his first combat mission he had the misfortune to have his aircraft hit by anti-aircraft fire during an attack on German naval units in the Gulf of Riga. Seversky managed to bring his burning aircraft down for a rough crash-landing in the open sea but a bomb had hung up on its rack and detonated upon impact with the water. The explosion instantly killed Seversky's observer and blew his own right leg off. Rescued by friendly forces, Seversky was rushed to a hospital and his life was saved. While recuperating from his wounds Seversky demanded an artificial limb so that he could get back into the air! His superiors figured that the mad

A beautiful view of Army Air Corps peacetime flying. This Seversky P-35, assigned to the 27th Pursuit Squadron of the 1st Pursuit Group, is seen in flight near its home base of Selfridge Field. The P-35 was the Army's first 'modern' fighter which meant that it was all-metal, had an enclosed cockpit, and featured retractable landing gear. These innovations did little for the fighter since it had poor performance and limited armament. Note the unit's diving eagle insignia on the side of the fuselage. (USAF)

Seversky's P–35, in an incredibly complex aeronautical evolutionary process, had its beginnings in this aircraft – the SEV–3. Painted a gaudy metallic gold, the design of the SEV–3 seemed ultra-modern when it appeared during the Depression year of 1933. Seversky was an advocate of the streamline school of design that was flourishing during this period and the SEV–3 embodied the theory perfectly. (Seversky)

Russian's flying days were over but they had yet to come under the full influence of the persuasive Seversky. Once he had mastered the use of his new leg, Seversky took a training aircraft aloft to renew his piloting skills and then assaulted his superiors with requests to be returned to combat status. They finally gave in, and Seversky found orders to report to a combat unit.

Entering combat with an enthusiasm that bordered on mania, Seversky attacked every German aircraft that he spotted with a wild abandon. His score of enemy aircraft confirmed destroyed mounted, and he soon had thirteen to his credit and was ranked as Russia's third highest ace. During 1917, Seversky was ordered to travel to the United States on a fact-finding mission to check on that country's supply of raw and finished war materials. Seversky crossed the country, visiting war plants and talking to high-placed officials. While Seversky was in the United States, the depressing news of the Russian Revolution reached him. Deciding not to return to a country dominated by the hated Communists, a type that he detested even more than the Germans, Seversky made the choice to stay in the United States and work to become a citizen of the country that he had quickly learned to admire.

During the early 1920s, Seversky met General Billy Mitchell and the friendship that developed between the two airmen was to have a profound effect on Seversky's views of airpower. Mitchell was the outspoken advocate of the superiority of airpower but he was fighting against the old school of Naval and Army officers who viewed aircraft as little more than wasteful playtoys. Mitchell's views eventually led to his court martial but Seversky passionately agreed with the General's view that a nation, to be strong and independent, had to have an air arm that could disable enemy forces at will.

Along with his new citizenship, Seversky had acquired a fanatical patriotism that many found cloying but his fervor was honest and it drove Seversky on in an attempt to produce the world's most modern combat aircraft. Seversky was also a prolific writer and began a series of magazine articles and books that served as his forum for the development of airpower.

Seversky began to design features that he considered essential for modern aircraft and, during the 1920s, patented various devices that included an anti-spin parachute, advanced wing flaps, gyroscopic bombsight and a method for mid-air refueling. Seversky also assisted Elmer Sperry with the development of the autopilot. Seversky had developed friends in many high places in the military and one of his proudest moments came during 1926 when he was commissioned as a major in the Army Air Corps Reserve, a rank that he proudly used for the rest of his life.

Seversky felt that, in order adequately to develop his aeronautical ideas, he should try to raise capital to open his own aircraft factory. In 1931, during the height of the American Depression, Seversky, with his enthusiastic personality, managed to bring together enough funds from investors to rent a hangar at the Edo Aircraft Company's College Point, Long Island, New York, factory, and there he set to work on developing his ideas into the design of an actual aircraft. Two years later, Seversky found that he was growing out of his small space and moved to Farmingdale nearby in Long Island.

After his move, Seversky added another fellow Russian to his small working staff. Alexander Kartveli became chief designer and his brilliance was to lead to the P-47 Thunderbolt of World War Two fame. Kartveli had the ability to take Seversky's ideas and form them into working blueprints from which construction of the company's first aircraft could begin.

The first effort from the Seversky factory embodied all the elements of the streamlining craze that permeated the 1930s. The SEV-3 (also the first of Seversky's rather complex designation system) was a bulky yet sleek twin-float amphibian that carried three and flew for the first time in 1933. Made entirely of metal, the monoplane design appeared to the public to be the most modern thing in the air. Beside the gold-painted aircraft with the bold Seversky insignia emblazoned on the fuselage, the contemporary biplanes looked absolutely primitive.

The SEV-3 featured an unusual float system that pivoted about the end of a built-up cantilever strut and was able to travel up and down in the vertical plane. The wheels were recessed directly into the floats and attached, via the main strut, to the wing structure – thus making them completely independent of the floats. When the wheels were retracted for aquatic operation, the floats were automatically locked at the correct angle while small wheels mounted in the water rudders at the rear of the floats could once again adjust the floats for ground operations when the regular tail wheel, enclosed in a large fairing, would be

The SEV-3 on the ground, illustrating its unique adjustable amphibious gear. Registered X-2106, the aircraft carried a crew of three. The canopy was built especially low to reduce drag and considerable glazing was added to the sides of the fuselage to help improve the very limited visibility. The Seversky logo, which could also be read 'Sever the Sky', was emblazoned on the side of the fuselage. (Collect-Air Photos)

employed. The SEV-3 had a very low streamlined canopy which hampered vision but added to top speed. A window was added on each side of the fuselage by the pilot's feet so that he had some form of downward vision – essential during landing and take off.

Seversky was anxious to establish the company's name in the aeronautical world so he took the metallic gold aircraft on a number of record runs, the first being on 9 October 1933 when he piloted the aircraft from Roosevelt Field for an amphibian speed record of almost 180 mph. After this record flight and a number of promotional visits to East Coast military and civil airfields, the SEV-3 was taken back to the Farmingdale factory where the amphibious landing gear was removed and a conventional gear was installed, the two main legs being wrapped in huge streamlined fairings. In the landplane configuration, the SEV-3 demonstrated a top speed of 210 mph which quickly brought attention from the military.

Probably due to Seversky's close association with the military over the years and his many high-ranking friends, it was not a great surprise when the Army Air Corps issued a requirement for a basic trainer that had a great deal of resemblance to what the SEV-3 had to offer. Once again, the SEV-3 was returned to the factory and a number of modifications were undertaken so that the aircraft could compete in the Air Corps' evaluation program for a new trainer. Visibility is one of the prime requirements for a training aircraft and that was not a feature which the SEV-3 could claim, so the rear fuselage decking was cut down while a larger canopy with a much better view was added. The dual control system and dual instrument panels were installed

and the third crew position was deleted, while the engine mount was lengthened to compensate for the changes in the center of gravity.

The modified aircraft was redesignated SEV-3XAR (the added letters standing for Experimental Army). Flown by Army pilots, the SEV-3XAR was quickly accepted (could there have been any doubt as to the outcome?), and a production order was given for 30 aircraft to be designated BT-8. Seversky had achieved his first production contract and now he felt that he could conquer new fields in aviation. The ability of the basic SEV-3 design to be molded and adapted to new mission requirements was just beginning and such a history of modification to a basic design was not to be equaled.

The BT-8 trainers were not world beaters in looks but apparently they performed their role competently although there is little remaining history surviving as to their operation, and it is interesting to note that there were no follow-on orders.

Kartveli took the SEV-3XAR back into the shop soon after the Army testing trials and the aircraft once again emerged as an amphibian but with a new designation and powerplant. Now the SEV-3M (for military), the aircraft carried a 715 hp Wright R-1820-F3 in the nose. Seversky was soon stumping the country with the aircraft and set an impressive speed record of just over 230 mph on 15 September

Here, the SEV–3 is seen fitted with its ground only landing gear which was enclosed in huge hand-formed aluminum spats. In this form, the SEV–3 was capable of speeds up to 210 mph and performed better than virtually all aircraft of the period, and the aircraft attracted considerable interest from the Army Air Corps. Note the folding hatch on the side of the pilot's cockpit.

At this stage, the Army demanded a number of changes in the Seversky design and X–2106 emerged from the Farmingdale factory with a greatly enlarged canopy and a new designation. SEV–3XAR. The third seat was eliminated as was most of the fuselage glazing. This became the basis for the AAC's BT–8 contract. Within three months the SEV–3XAR was back on its amphibious gear, giving an idea of the changes that the aircraft could handle. The aircraft wound up its life when it was sold illegally to Spain for use in that country's Civil War. The machine arrived in Spain during 1938 in float plane configuration but the floats were soon removed and land gear was fitted. It was assigned to the Republicans' Group 71 in company with

French Dewoitines where it served as a communications aircraft and did not receive any armament. It was generally flown by a veteran of the Lacalle Squadron, Augusto Lecha. On the morning of 6 February 1939, the squadron received orders to regroup on a field at Banolas (province of Genoa). The SEV–3 took more than half an hour to get off and when it arrived at Benolas, Group 71 did not exist – it had been destroyed by a surprise bombing attack. Lecha tried to land, but without wind indication, and he turned the aircraft over on the bombed airfield. The Seversky was abandoned on the spot. It is not known if it still retained the metallic gold paint scheme.

The SEV-3XAR resulted in the rather grotesque BT-8 basic trainer. Seversky's contacts in the military resulted in his first production order for an aircraft that the Army did not really need. Seen here in its blue and yellow training colors, this BT-8 carries the Wright Field badge on the side of the fuselage.

1935. The South American country of Colombia was impressed with the aircraft and ordered six (which were built as SEV-3MWW) for the Colombian Naval Air Service which used them as reconnaissance amphibians.

During 1934, work had begun on a second prototype in the Farmingdale factory that was completed as an SEV-3M. However, before the second aircraft could be completed, Kartveli decided to modify the prototype to yet another new configuration . . . this time as a single-seat pursuit.

In the meantime, while work was progressing on the conversion of the first aircraft, the second prototype was finished as the SEV-2XP (which, in Seversky terminology, equated to two-seat experimental pursuit). This aircraft featured the huge spatted landing gear of the SEV-3XAR and the engine of the SEV-3M. The two crew-members sat under a sliding canopy and the rear occupant had a .30 caliber machine gun on a swivel at his disposal. Making its first flight in the spring of 1935, the SEV-2XP once again impressed Army officials who felt that a specification should be drafted which would call for production of a fighter in the prototype's category.

Seversky felt that the aircraft would make a good fighter for the Army and an excellent replacement for the outmoded Boeing P-26 but little did he know that Curtiss had been very busy designing and building a new fighter, the Model 75. The new Curtiss design was

submitted to the Army at Wright Field during May and proved to have impressive performance along with the added benefit of retractable landing gear.

Doubts ran high at the Seversky factory as to whether their new design could best the aircraft from Curtiss. The SEV-2XP was to arrive at Wright Field for testing during June but it had to be withdrawn due to an accident during the journey. History has revealed that the accident was a fabrication on Seversky's part in order to gain more time to modify the two-place fighter. Working around the clock, Kartveli redesigned the SEV-2XP into a single-seat aircraft that had rather crude retractable landing gear which folded straight back into the wing, leaving large fairings covering the strut and wheel. A quick redesignation of SEV-1XP, and the aircraft was off to Wright Field for evaluation during August.

The SEV-1XP followed the lines of the previous Seversky machines and was not a bad looking aircraft. The engine of the SEV-2XP had been replaced with a 950 hp Wright R-1820-G5 Cyclone with a new three-blade propeller. This combination gave a top speed of 289 mph, which was below the performance specifications issued by Seversky. Examination of the engine revealed that it was not developing full power. However, this drop in speed was not a serious problem since the Curtiss Model 75 was suffering similar engine troubles. Army officials were about to issue a contract to Seversky when Curtiss lodged an official com-

plaint relating to the fact that the Seversky entry had more time since the 'accident' to undergo modifications.

The Material Division, afraid to enter into a contract that might end in a law suit, decided to delay the selection until April 1936, at which time another fly-off would take place between the competitors. By that time, two other aircraft had entered the arena. These machines were the Consolidated Special and the Vought V-141, but neither aircraft was really in the running as they failed to meet a number of Air Corps specifications.

In the time leading up to the April fly-off, Kartveli had been busy reworking the SEV-1XP. The aircraft was fitted with a new engine, the 950 hp Pratt & Whitney R-1830-9 Twin Wasp. A smaller cowling was installed while the tail area was redesigned and the Air Corps armament of one .30 and one .50 caliber machine gun was installed in the upper fuselage decking. The aircraft received yet another designation change to SEV-7 by the time it reached Wright Field for the fly-off. Curtiss had also been busy improving the Model 75.

Once again, both the Model 75 and the SEV-7 were plagued by a number of minor but

*S*ticking to the same basic theme, Seversky came up with the SEV–X–BT, a retractable gear version of the BT–8 trainer. The project did not progress past the prototype X189M. (Seversky)

*S*een as the SEV–1XP, the form of the future P–35 is virtually jelled in X18Y (which started out life as the two-place fixed gear SEV–2XP). In competition with the Curtiss Hawk 75, it became very clear that the Army favored Seversky's design even though the aircraft was having troubles with its engine. The SEV–1XP won out over the Model 75 although the Model 75 was the winner in the long run. (USAF)

performance-degrading problems. The SEV–7 came out on top in the Army's point system, and a contract was awarded on 16 June 1936 for the construction of 77 fighters with the new Army designation of P–35.

Seversky began work on a company-funded prototype for the series that was designated AP–1 (for Army prototype). Given the civil registration of NR1390, the aircraft served as a test bed for a number of Kartveli modifications. Problems plagued the P–35 and by the time the first prototype reached the Army during July 1937, top speed had fallen to a very disappointing 281 mph.

In order to promote the P–35, Seversky came up with the very clever idea of sending some of his 'near' P–35 products to the Cleveland National Air Races, an event that was immensely popular with the 1930s public. Millionaire Frank Fuller flew an SEV–S2 (later, just S–2) in the 1937 Cleveland event and came in first while Frank Sinclair took fourth place in the Bendix Trophy Race with the S–1, which was the rebuilt SEV–1XP! Seversky also intended to enter the AP–2 NR1250, which was similar to the P–35 but had a new canopy and a new wing center section that incorporated inward, flush-retracting landing gear. While en route to Cleveland, and being flown by Seversky, the AP–2 had a landing gear failure and had to be withdrawn from competition.

Seversky found that the publicity gained at the air races was extremely useful so a number

of other aircraft built on the same basic design as the P–35 were put together. During this time period, American oil companies were very interested in promoting aviation and most usually had a stable of high-performance aircraft and famous aviators. Shell Oil Company contracted with Seversky to build a racing aircraft designated DS (Doolittle Special) for Jimmy Doolittle. The DS followed basic P–35 lines and was powered by an 850 hp Wright R–1820–G5 Cyclone. Doolittle was quite pleased with the speedy aircraft and flew it as his own personal mount for the next three years.

The AP–7 was built from the wreckage of the AP–2 and was powered by a Pratt & Whitney R–1830 Twin Wasp of 1,200 hp. Given the registration of NX1384, the AP–7 was flown by Jacqueline Cochran. While delivering the AP–7 to Miss Cochran at Burbank, California, Seversky set a new speed record by covering the continent in ten hours, three minutes and seven seconds. After racing in the Bendix Trophy Race of 1938, the aircraft was returned to the factory and modified with a new wing leading edge, inward retracting landing gear and a number of other small modifications in preparation for the 1939 Bendix but the aircraft was completely destroyed in a hangar fire at Miami before the race.

Seversky also kept a close eye on the export market and sold his aircraft whenever a likely customer appeared. One example each of the

After winning the Army contract, the amazing career of 18Y continued. Redesignated S–1, the aircraft was flown by Seversky test pilot Frank Sinclair to fourth place in the 1937 Bendix Trophy Race. These races served as a billboard for the flamboyant Seversky to display his wares.

two-seat SEV–2XP and the SEV–2PA–A and the SEV–2PA–1 amphibians were sold to the Soviet Union which, after a brief testing period, re-shipped them to the Spanish Republican forces for use in that country's Civil War. Two SEV–3XARs, fixed gear land aircraft, were sold to the Mexican government. Seversky also made a very controversial sale to the Japanese government when he supplied that nation with 20 SEV–2PA–B3 two-seat fighters in 1939. The Imperial Japanese Navy intended to employ the SEV–2PA–B3 as a long-range fighter to escort their bombers deep into China. The Japanese designated the type as A8–V1, but quickly found that the aircraft did not live up to its performance claims and was inferior to Japanese types currently in service. The SEV–2PA–B3 was relegated to reconnaissance duties over central China.

The contract with the Japanese had a disastrous effect on future business for Seversky. The secret nature of the Seversky negotiations with the Japanese angered the American government who, in turn, apparently exerted considerable pressure on the Air Corps not to order any more P–35s and, instead, to concentrate on the loser of the contest, the Curtiss Model 75!

Using much of the wrecked airframe of the AP–2, the AP–7 (registered N X 1384) was built. The aircraft was an attempt to get as much performance out of the basic P–35 design without radical modifications. Fitted with a Pratt & Whitney R–1830 Twin Wasp of 1,200 hp, the aircraft was flown to victory in the 1938 Bendix Race by Jacqueline Cochran. Before this event the plane had been flown by Seversky on a cross-country speed dash for a record ten hour, three minute and seven second crossing. After the Bendix the AP–7 was returned to the factory for drastic modification.

While no actual evidence was uncovered that Seversky acted illegally, his sale of aircraft to Japan was extremely unpopular with the public and the company quickly began to experience severe financial difficulties. While Seversky was in England trying to convince the British that the P–35 was just what they wanted (fortunately, they knew better), the Board of Directors ousted Seversky and re-organized the company in order to avoid bankruptcy. The new organization became known as the Republic Aircraft Corporation.

During the transition between the two companies, negotiations had started with Sweden for the purchase of a modified version of the P–35. During February 1939, Sweden placed

an order with Republic for 100 EP–106s (the company designation of EP–1 was also used), and 50 SEV–2PA–204A two-place fighters that were to be equipped as dive bombers. The first batch of EP–1s was completed during January and was shipped to Sweden where they arrived the following month, and were delivered to *Flygflottilj* 8 where they replaced Gloster Gladiator biplanes. The Swedes, in dire need of new aircraft, signed another order for a further 60 EP–1s.

Events soon turned sour for Sweden when the United States placed an embargo on all military goods to that country and, on 24 October 1940, claimed all the completed and uncompleted Swedish aircraft in the United

States. At this time 40 EP–1s had been delivered. The embargoed aircraft were given the designation P–35A and 17 were immediately crated and shipped to the Philippines to bolster that area's defenses. The Swedish version of the P–35 was equipped with a 1,050 hp Pratt & Whitney R–1830–45 radial and had a greater armament of two .30 caliber machine guns in the upper cowling and two .50 caliber machine guns in the wings. Only two of the SEV–2PA–204A dive bombers had been delivered and the remaining machines were taken over by the Army Air Force (redesignated the previous June) and assigned to training units as AT–12 Guardsmen advanced trainers.

When initial deliveries of the P–35 to Air Corps units began with the first aircraft going to Wright Field during May 1937. It was found that the aircraft had dangerous spinning and stalling characteristics while performing aerobatics and a modification was undertaken that added several degrees of dihedral to the outer wing panels which helped the situation but the P–35 remained placarded against certain aerobatics during its military life. The P–35 (the fighter was never given a popular name) took up active service with the famous 1st Pursuit Group at Selfridge Field, Michigan, with final aircraft delivery taking place during August 1938, months behind time. Before the last P–35 had been delivered to the 17th, 27th and 94th Pursuit Squadrons that made up the Group, an order was received instructing that the unit would receive the Curtiss P–36 as replacement. This meant that the 1st would have P–35s and P–36s serving at the same time while one new fighter was phased out and the other new fighter was phased into service. Pilots found the P–35 a pleasant aircraft to fly but quickly realized that it was no combat machine. Sluggish in performance and undergunned, the P–35 was woefully outdated by the new aircraft coming into service in Europe and Japan.

The bulky fuselage of the Seversky had enough room for the crew chief to go along for a ride during check flights, locking himself in the spacious baggage compartment – access to which was gained by a large door in the side of the fuselage. During the P–35's brief combat career, the large fuselage held several people as P–35s were evacuated in the face of advancing enemy forces.

The P–35As that were sent to the Philippines were assigned to the 21st and 34th

Reappearing from the Farmingdale plant, NX1384 had a new look. A new, more modern wing had been fitted with landing gear that retracted flush towards the center line. The modified AP–7 was to participate in the 1939 Bendix with Jacqueline Cochran at the controls once again. However, the plane was destroyed in a hangar fire before the event. Note that the Seversky logo has been replaced with that of the new Republic Aviation Corporation. (Republic)

The aircraft that cost Seversky his future in military aviation. Completely unmarked except for the letter R on the fin and under the left wing, the SEV-2PA-1 was built for Russia, who ordered one example along with two other Seversky aircraft. These planes also found their way to Spain after a brief testing period by the Russians. The next export order was from Japan who purchased 20 SEV-2PA-B3 two-place fighters (almost identical to the SEV-2PA-A) during 1939. This contract was carried out with a great deal of secrecy on Seversky's part and was so unpopular with the military and the public alike that Seversky was booted from the controlling position of his company which reorganized as the Republic Aviation Corporation. Used by the Japanese Navy in China, the Seversky's were not particularly well liked but the fact remains that they were the only American-built aircraft to serve in squadron strength with Japan during World War Two.

Pursuit Squadrons. The first 17 aircraft were reinforced by a further 31 machines shipped from Farmingdale. When the aircraft arrived in the Philippines it was found that all instructions and manuals were in Swedish as were all the instruments and cockpit notes. Mechanics struggled with primitive facilities to erect the fighters and make them airworthy. Long-range plans called for the P-35As to be transferred to the Philippine Air Corps where they would replace the antiquated Boeing P-26 while the Army Air Force units in the area would be equipped with new Curtiss P-40s. However, the Japanese were to have other plans.

For being such a strategic area, the Philippines had been greatly neglected as the United States tried to build up its strength in other

parts of the Pacific. The admittedly obsolete P-35As and P-26s were absolutely no deterrent to Japanese aggression as the Army soon discovered.

Throughout 1941, a number of frantic changes were made in the organization of the defense of the Philippines. The Philippine Department Air Force was comprised of a single group, the 4th Composite Group, that included the 28th Medium Bombardment Group, the 2nd Observation Squadron (both based at Clark Field, 60 miles North of Manila), and the 3rd, 17th, and 20th Pursuit Squadrons based at Nichols Field which was located just south of the city. Lt Boyd D. 'Buzz' Wagner was given the command of the 17th PS and this young and innovative fighter pilot whipped the poorly-equipped P-35A unit into fighting shape as they received new P-40s. Along with the diverted Swedish P-35As, the Philippine Department Air Force gained another bit of international flavor when they received 11 A-27s that had originally been intended for delivery to Siam before that country was overrun by the Japanese. The pursuit squadrons received these aircraft for training and the pilots had to puzzle once again over instructions and instruments in Siamese.

Staffing the pursuit squadrons was a problem; most of the ground staff was on hand but pilots were in short supply and, for a time, the squadrons could only muster half strength. On 4 December, the squadrons began to receive

new-in-the-crate Curtiss P-40Es. The new fighters were eagerly assembled just as fast as the ground crews could work. At this time, the 34th, commanded by Lt Samuel W. Marrett, was moved to a newly prepared field with the rather romantic name of Del Carmen. However, Del Carmen was no tropical paradise – rather it was a stinking hell hole that the pilots and ground crew instantly began to detest. The raw dirt strip was located near the small town of Floridablanca which, in itself, had little to offer except for impoverished Filipinos. The dirt and dust that was kicked up as each Seversky took off from Del Carmen caused a hazard by greatly reducing visibility and taking two or three minutes to settle. The dirt also played havoc with the worn-out systems and engines of the P-35As; overhauls were needed but the facilities were so primitive and the lack of parts so critical that the pilots had to keep flying machines that probably would have been grounded at Stateside bases. Radio communication between Del Carmen with Nichols and Clark was poor at best and the one radio set was prone to breakage.

The moment of truth for the American air arm in the Philippines came at 12:00 pm on 8 December 1941 (7 December Hawaiian time) when the Japanese, in coordinated attacks, quickly swept across the main bases. At 4:00 am that morning, messages had arrived at Clark signalling Pearl Harbor had been attacked by the Japanese. The airmen were

During February 1939, the Swedish government placed an order for 100 improved P–35s, designated EP–1, (known as the J9 in Swedish service) and 50 SEV–2PA–204A two-place fighters to be equipped as dive bombers. One of the two-seaters is seen here after undergoing flight tests and before being shipped to Sweden.

The EP–106s were delivered to the Swedish Air Force in natural metal finish with national crown insignia in six positions. The aircraft was powered by the Pratt & Whitney R–1830–45 of 1,050 hp which gave a top speed of just over 300 mph. The Swedish aircraft were more heavily armed than their American counterparts, two .30 caliber machine guns in the nose and two .50 caliber weapons in the wing. Sixty of the fighters had been delivered to Sweden by May 1939 when the American government put a complete embargo on military sales to that country. The remaining aircraft plus a further order for 20 went to the Army as P–35As.

assembled and told of the news; they were surprised that Pearl had been hit but not surprised that the Japanese were finally on the move against America. Bombs were taken out to the operational aircraft to be loaded for a strike against Formosa, the most likely enemy target. However, it was decided that the bombs would not be loaded in case a special strike was called and a different bomb load would be needed. It was also thought that having the bombed-up aircraft sitting on the field would not be safe in case of an enemy air raid. The bombs were left by the aircraft where they could be quickly loaded. Communications were extremely poor and many pilots did not know of the attack on Pearl until several hours later. The pilots at Del Carmen were totally unaware as nobody bothered to radio the field.

A morning patrol of P–40s was launched as soon as there was enough light while a Douglas B–18 Bolo rattled aloft for patrol duty with a load of bombs. At Nielson Field the staff of the Far East Air Force (FEAF) gathered to discuss the critical situation. A number of divergent opinions were voiced but there was a consensus that the limited supply of Boeing B–17 Flying Fortresses should be immediately

Opposite

The third service P–35, 36–356, seen shortly after delivery but before the application of squadron markings. The P–35 suffered from a poor production delivery which set squadron introduction considerably back.

Right

Beautifully maintained P–35 carrying the markings of the 94th Pursuit Squadron of the 1st Pursuit Group with the designator PA–88. The P–35 was the first USAAF fighter to be left in natural metal finish. Tests with bare aluminum had shown that the metal was prone to structure-damaging corrosion so a 1.5 percent layer of pure aluminum (Alclad) was applied over the aircraft's aluminum alloy skin and the resulting surface was much more impervious to the elements. The bare metal finish also resulted in slightly higher speeds because the weight of paint was eliminated while costs of stripping and painting aircraft were greatly reduced. (E. Strasser)

Right

Seversky P–35 36–383 photographed on 14 April 1938 in the markings of the 1st Pursuit Group with the Group's green, black, yellow, white and blue insignia on the side of the fuselage. The designator (PA 1) was a coordinated system for aircraft markings that was adopted on 15 November 1937 to readily identify aircraft and the units to which they were assigned. The 1st PG was assigned the PA 1 designator and this was applied to the aircraft with black paint. (E. Strasser)

Opposite

Another view of P–35 36–356, this time in full squadron regalia. Taken at Selfridge Field, Michigan, this photograph illustrates the entire strength of the 27th Pursuit Squadron. It also shows to advantage the manner in which the designator PA 54 was applied to the top of the left wing of 356. The Army was rather fond of parking its combat aircraft in close groups such as this – it looked good and made the aircraft easy to get at. All this would change when eager Japanese aircraft decimated the rows of packed-in American aircraft at Pearl Harbor. (USAF/14441AC)

launched on a reprisal raid against Japanese-held Formosa. The assembled group of officers was shocked to a man when General Brereton announced 'No, We can't attack till we're fired on'. Major General Lewis H. Brereton had recently been appointed commander of the American air arm in the Philippines and his decision to avoid a direct attack on the enemy was not popular.

On 8 December 1941, the inventory of the 24th Pursuit Group was not particularly impressive: the 3rd PS, 18 P–40s in tactical commission at Iba; the 17th PS, 18 P–40s in tactical commission at Nichols Field; the 21st PS, 18 P–40s in tactical commission at Nichols Field; the 20th PS, 18 P–40Bs in tactical commission at Clark Field; and the 34th PS, 18 P–35As in tactical commission (22 in actual commission) at Del Carmen. This gave the 24th Pursuit Group a total of 90 first-line combat aircraft with which to oppose an enemy of unknown, but probably considerable, strength. Also, to be included with the inventory of combat aircraft, were a number of Boeing B–17C Flying Fortresses and obsolete Bolo bombers and various communication and light transport aircraft.

P–35 of the 17th Pursuit Squadron of the 1st PG with the unit's famous black and white eagle proudly displayed on the side of the fuselage. Squadron color was white and the cowl ring was thus painted. This view of the P–35 gives a good idea of the aircraft's large canopy and the pilot's positioning on the highest point of the fuselage for the best visibility. Note the polished face of the propeller while the rear portion of the blades were Flat Black. While in military service the P–35s suffered from a number of maintenance problems, including leaking fuel tanks. The fuel tank system in the P–35 was rather interesting since the entire wing center section formed a gas tank, there were no bladders or metal tanks as the wing structure formed the basis for the fuel container. When the aircraft were delivered to the 1st PG, tiny leaks of fuel from the center section were apparent. However, after some time in the air and a number of hard landings, the rivets began to loosen up and fuel began to cascade in quantity. This situation had to be rectified and the fix fell to unfortunate airmen who had to remove the small center section access plates and paint the entire inside of the unit with a sealer. This unpleasant job had to be repeated three or four times before the unit was sealed but then, with time, the sealer began to crack and shrink and the fuel once again began leaking. Another maintenance problem concerned itself with the engines which threw off excessive amounts of oil when running. It was not uncommon for a 1st PG crew chief to be standing at his aircraft's parking spot with a bucket full of gasoline, waiting for 'his' P–35 to return from a flight. Sometimes, if the aircraft had been on a high-altitude mission, the entire accessory section of the engine was awash with oil. The crew chief would remove the cowling of the P–35 and begin sloshing in the gasoline in an effort to remove the oil and return the fighter to the pristine shape of the pre-War Army aircraft. (E. Strasser)

Although the P–35As were listed as operational, they were, in fact, only marginally so. The aircraft had been poorly maintained and many were in need of engine and airframe overhaul while spare barrels for the machine guns were in such short supply that many of the aircraft were forced to fly with worn out guns. The fact that many of the manuals for maintaining the P–35s were written in Swedish did not help. Many of the P–40s were also marginally combat ready because they had just been uncrated and some had not even been air tested. The P–40s of the 18th did not have an average of over three flight hours each. The pilots were unfamiliar with their aircraft and had little chance to practise aerial maneuvers or test the guns of the P–40s.

Between the hours of two and three pm, the primitive American radar set located at Iba picked up a large formation of aircraft coming in towards the main Philippine island of Luzon (on which the important American bases were located). The aircraft were presumed to be Japanese and their intentions hostile. In the early sunlight of the morning of 8 December, P–40s of the 3rd Pursuit Squadron roared aloft with the orders to attack the incoming forma-

tion if it came within 20 miles of the coast. However, the poorly equipped P–40s had not been fitted with any form of oxygen equipment which limited operations to around 15,000 ft and, in any event, the Allison engines performed very poorly above that altitude. The radar operators saw the tracks of the two groups of aircraft converge. The pilots of the P–40s never saw the Japanese who were at much greater height. Oddly, the Japanese formation turned back and the P–40s returned to land.

The Americans had mistakenly presumed that the Philippines would be the first objective of the Japanese and confusion among the military units in the Philippines was rampant as word spread of the attack on Pearl Harbor. How had the enemy ventured over 5,000 miles from the Philippines without being spotted? When would an actual strike on Luzon come and where would it come from?

Confusion was in the extreme that morning as the 17th PS climbed into the humid air to fly a covering patrol over Clark. Fearing a surprise Japanese attack, the B–17 Flying Fortresses, which were sitting targets, were ordered into the air and the crews began taking the four-engine bombers aloft at 8:30 am. A number of mechanical problems kept some of the bombers on the field and the launching of the fleet took some time. The Fortresses had arrived in the Philippines, for the most part, in the shiney natural metal finish that typified the aircraft of the peacetime Army. An attempt was made to camouflage the B–17s as the chances of open conflict grew. There was only one paint spray gun available at Clark (another interesting oversight in the supply of the American forces in the Philippines) and it took a considerable time to camouflage each of the large bombers.

Initial Japanese bombing attacks took place at Baguio and Tuguegaro while the 20th tried to engage the marauding enemy formation that was flying at 22,000 ft. Most of the P–40s had an impossible time struggling to this altitude but a few of the pilots (presumably with huge lung capacity) managed to get their fighters to the bombers' height but the few shots fired were inconclusive. The first act of overt Japanese aggression had been committed against the Philippines and the FEAF was now officially at war.

Through confusion and extremely poor military planning which had the high-ranking Army ground officers and high-ranking Army air officers almost quarreling in their differing opinions, the B–17s began to return to Clark at around 10:30 after aimlessly circling the immediate area. As the Fortresses landed, ground crews frantically began the lengthy refueling process with Clark's limited equipment. Many of the bombers needed minor repairs and adjustments and all of the servicing procedures took time. Some officers wanted the B–17s to get into the air as soon as possible to avoid being on the ground in case of attack. To this day a controversy still exists as to why the bombers remained on the ground during this critical time period. General Hap Arnold stated after the war that he had never been able to get the real story of what happened but, as common with American thinking of the period, the Far East Air Force had woefully underestimated the strength and ability of the Japanese armed forces'.

At about noon Iba was hit by Japanese bombers just as aircraft of the 3rd PS were coming in to land for refueling after a patrol. Some of the P–40s managed to struggle back into the air as enemy bombs were demolishing the field. The few P–40s that became airborne spotted what they thought to be a formation of P–35As, but, upon investigation, the 'P–35As' turned out to be a pack of Zeke fighters. The Zekes began a textbook strafing attack on Iba. The airfield, through the effects of the highly accurate bombing and strafing, was completely destroyed and the flyable aircraft headed for the small strip at Rosales. Casualities at Iba were as high as 50 per cent.

At 12:40 it was Clark's turn for the attentions of the Japanese. It was a disaster for the FEAF. Over 50 enemy aircraft hit Clark with little warning. The first indication of an air raid for many of the airmen was the sight of bombs exploding on the field. There were no American fighters in the air as most were on the ground refueling (again another glaring example of military incompetence). The enemy bombers came over in perfect formation at high altitude and only four P–40s of the 20th PS managed to get into the air among the explosions. Clark was devastated by the severity and accuracy of the attack. Many of the major buildings were demolished and communication with other bases was cut. Zeke strafers came in after the bombers and increased the toll of American men and aircraft. Most of the B–17s had escaped destruction in the initial bombing attack but the Zekes quickly took care of that and soon many of the Fortresses were in flames. Anti-aircraft protection at Clark was inadequate with old-fashioned weapons that were so slow on their mounts that they could not track the fast, low-flying fighters. Crewmen ran to their Fortresses and tried to put up a defensive fire from the bombers' machine guns and many of the gunners died at their positions. Only a few enemy aircraft were destroyed or damaged but the Zekes that fell to the P–40s were among the first confirmed and credited American kills of the war.

Back at Del Carmen, the men of the 34th PS were ignorant of the rapid happenings at Iba and Clark but at the sight of the huge smoke clouds billowing from Clark, the pilots ran to the P–35As and the crew chiefs had the engines running in short order. As soon as the P–35As were airborne and gaining altitude, they tangled with a pack of Zekes that had been strafing Clark. Several of the Zekes were hit as were the P–35As but no aircraft were lost in the P–35A's first taste of action. The out of the way location of Del Carmen made it an ideal target for local fifth columnists, called Sakdalistas, who lit fires in the bush and cane fields around the airstrip in an attempt to attract Japanese aircraft. Patrols sent out to stop the fire-setting never found any traces of the Sakdalistas, who always managed to slip away after starting their fires. After the brief skirmish, the P–35As returned to Del Carmen to regroup and try to figure out what was happening. Del Carmen's thick, choking dust did the tired P–35A engines no good and the strain of the mass launching caused several of the engines to break down.

Mechanics worked frantically on the tired P–35As as the depressing news from Clark and Iba – as well as other Luzon locations – began to filter in to Del Carmen. Through heroic efforts, almost all of the P–35As were made airworthy and stood ready for missions on 9 December against the very powerful enemy but the Japanese did not show up because of storms over their bases on Formosa. On 10 December, the Japanese began to make landings at Vigan and the FEAF made a maximum effort to get every available aircraft into the air. The B–17s that escaped destruction at Del

*A*lthough the P–35 was basically a rugged machine problems arose because of a great deal of hand fitting of parts on individual machines, resulting in non-interchangeable parts. This caused many maintenance problems but the P–35 was unique in Army history as being declared obsolete while aircraft were still being delivered to the Army. (Collect-Air Photos)

Only two Swedish machines had been delivered before the embargo, and the remaining two-seat aircraft were impressed into the US Army as AT-12 Guardsmen. This particular example is seen at Wright Field where it is being tested with a fin of greatly increased area.

Monte and a couple that had been patched up at Clark were bombed up while the remaining P–40s were armed as escorts. The patched and damaged aerial armada set out to Vigan but the P–35As, which were to escort the bombers, could not make the rendevous point because of their slow speed. The tired engines of the Severskys began to malfunction and, one after another, the stubby fighters began to turn back to Del Carmen. However, Lt Sam Marrett stubbornly continued on with the remaining fighters and attacked the landing enemy with extreme vigor and determination. The Japanese had not expected any aerial opposition and the casualties on the ships and ground were heavy. If more aircraft had been available there would have been a good chance that the enemy landings could have been completely routed. Unfortunately, Lt Marrett was killed by anti-aircraft fire as he pressed his attacks home at ship mast height.

The surviving P–35As headed back to Del Carmen but luck was just not with the Severskys. While landing at Del Carmen, the P–35As were hit by 12 strafing Zekes and a dozen of the fighters were destroyed and six more were damaged. The Squadron, now commanded by Lt Brown, was almost instantly reduced to a ground unit. The Japanese began to make many more landings in the face of dwindling American airpower and the P–35A squadron did not get aircraft airborne again until the 25 of December when they acquired a few P–40s.

The confusion and rapidly changing events that followed the Japanese landings on Luzon saw the squadrons break apart from their rigid pre-war order into loose-knit units that began operating from any airstrip they could find. The part played by the Severskys (individual aircraft were scattered at several fields) in the last days before Japanese victory in the Philippines was small, their performance made contact with raiding bombers difficult and they were at the mercy of the Zekes. However, the P–35As did participate in strafing attacks on enemy shipping and troop concentrations. The number of serviceable P–35As varied from day to day as the ground crews made heroic efforts to patch together flyable aircraft out of wrecks. The engines of the P–35As gave considerable trouble because of the effects of the clouds of thick choking dust thrown up at the primitive airstrips from which they were operating. Fighting in conjunction with the rapidly decreasing numbers of P–40s and B–17s, the remains of American air power in the Philippines managed to make life for the Japanese difficult.

As the Americans were forced to move from one temporary airstrip to the next, the spacious aft fuselage of the P–35A allowed several men or extra parts to be accommodated with ease. The P–35As were usually flown at treetop heights during these reshuffling flights to avoid the attentions of prowling enemy fighters. Many of the P–35As had been given crude camouflage paint schemes to help avoid detection. As the situation in the Philippines became more and more desperate and evacuations were beginning, the active role of the P–35A in combat had basically come to an end. However, two patched-up P–35As managed to make it to Bataan on 5 March. It is thought that these aircraft were used for supply and reconnaissance work as the island made a last-ditch stand against hordes of Japanese. Captain Hank Thorne made the last P–35A flight out of Cabcaben airstrip with two pilots in the rear fuselage and a small load of bombs to drop on the Japanese after takeoff as he headed for safer territory. Thus the brief and not very heroic saga of the Philippine Severskys came to an end as all American resistance in the Philippines collapsed in surrender on 6 May with the fall of Corregidor.

The P–35s that were left in the United States were dispersed to training units or used as base hacks. Since the type was not a particularly loved aircraft, the P–35 soon became a rare sight at an operational base and most were scrapped or sent to mechanic training schools. The Severskys in Sweden did not see action but were used by that air force until the early 1950s when the last of the type was retired. Today, the United States Air Force Museum has on display an EP–1 (donated by Sweden) and an authentic P–35 that was discovered in a trade school. Thus Seversky's portly and much modified basic design can now stand beside the more famous fighters of World War Two, showing how it pointed the way towards the high-performance propeller-driven combat aircraft of that conflict.

SAM MARRETT – FORGOTTEN HERO

The heroic actions of many American fighter pilots during the early days of the fighting in the Philippines have gone largely unrecorded.

Lieutenant Sam Marrett viewed his new command and their airstrip with a great deal of distaste. Firstly, Del Carmen was not his idea of a well-maintained fighter base. Situated in Philippine agricultural land not far from Clark Field, Del Carmen consisted of a rough dirt strip with dust so thick that the slightest movement stirred up clouds of choking intensity. The facilities at Del Carmen were almost non-existent. Electricity was minimally provided by one small generator and quarters for the officers and men consisted of rows of tents. There were no eating, sanitary, or operational facilities and the supplies of fuel and ammunition were miniscule. Secondly, the aircraft that had been assigned to Marrett's 34th Pursuit

Squadron were a cruel joke – worn-out Seversky P–35As, much like the aircraft that they had been trained on back in the States. They had been promised brand-new Curtiss P–40Es.

Marrett, a lanky native of New Braunfels, Texas, was as green as the other pilots of his squadron. They had arrived in Manila aboard the ss *Coolidge* on 20 November 1941 with great hopes of setting up a modern pursuit unit, yet the young pilots only had training time entered in their log books. Marrett and his men were ordered to Nichols Field where they were greeted by the sight of 25 P–35As, their 'new' fighters. Some of the aircraft had been given a coat of drab camouflage paint but most were still finished in their natural metal skin and bright Army Air Corps markings. Everyone in the Philippines seemed to believe that war was coming and coming soon but Marrett and his men assembled their ground crews and began working on the almost impossible task of forming a combat unit within what most military officials figured would be a very short period of time.

Rather than center all aircraft at the few main bases on the island of Luzon, it was decided to transfer fighter and bomber units to more primitive 'hidden' airstrips that would not be well-known to the Japanese. Del Carmen certainly filled the primitive aspect but Marrett busied himself in setting up his unit in the best possible manner. Little could be done to make Del Carmen more palatable to the men, but a few temporary sheds were erected along with a crude control tower that gave the field a bit more presence as an operational military organization. The P–35As, however, proved to be a more difficult matter. The clouds of dust that were thrown up each time an engine started did little good for the engines or the airframes and systems. The dust penet-

Through poor communications and bad military leadership, American forces in the Philippines were caught with their proverbial pants down. These destroyed P–35A fighters were gleefully photographed by the victorious Japanese after the capture of American airfields. Note that aircraft 25 has been camouflaged, which was a difficult operation since only a couple of spray guns were available on the island of Luzon.

rated everything and played havoc with the radial engines which were long overdue for overhaul to begin with. The mechanics had to labor under additional difficulties since the aircraft were originally built for Sweden and many of the servicing instructions and manuals were in Swedish.

A limited amount of practice flying was carried out along with gunnery practice but the pilots soon discovered that the gun barrels were almost worn out and firing results were wildly inaccurate. Cut-off from activity at Clark Field and having to rely on a primitive radio for communications the young pilots of the 34th felt completely disconnected from the outside world. Water had to be dragged by bucket from a nearby polluted stream and boiled before it could be consumed and the various ills of living in the open in a tropical environment began to play unpleasant tunes with the men's physical well-being.

When the war started on 8 December, it was almost as if Del Carmen had been forgotten, the base did not receive word of the Pearl Harbor attack until five hours after Clark Field had been notified. Marrett immediately mustered his men and explained the situation as crew chiefs topped off the fuel tanks and loaded ammunition. The Seversky's did not have self-sealing fuel tanks or armor protection and the pilots were not pleased with what they considered to be flying coffins.

The confusion that resulted from the news of the Pearl Harbor attack left many of the young pilots puzzled. Almost everyone was sure that the Philippines would be attacked first if the Japanese declared war on the United States and, after several hours and no action, some of the fliers began to feel that the news of the

Pearl Harbor attack was false and broadcasted by the Japanese as part of some elaborate plot. Still, the pilots sat in the sweltering cockpits of the P–35As, parachutes strapped on and everything ready. As the day wore on, the heat became too intense and the pilots abandoned the cockpits for the shade offered by the wing. Shortly before one in the afternoon, Marrett and the men of the 34th spotted huge clouds of black smoke pouring into the sky from nearby Clark Field. Without warning, the attack had come.

Without waiting for orders, Marrett jumped into the cockpit of his Seversky, whose engine was already ticking over courtesy of the crew chief, and led his squadron out onto the crude runway. Amazingly, all the P–35As managed to get airborne through the clouds of dust, even though the last aircraft were probably flying on instruments. With throttles to the firewall, the 34th headed towards Clark. The enemy bomber formation had passed overhead in parade-ground drill at great height, but they were followed up by low-flying Zeke fighters which were strafing everything in sight. Sam Marrett and his fighter pilots ran right into this hornet's nest but, in the ensuing dogfight, not one P–35A was lost although several suffered battle damage and a number of Zekes felt the sting of the P–35A's two .30 and two .50 caliber machine guns. The Zekes broke off contact and headed back to their bases in the Philippines, and Marrett patrolled the skies over Clark, noting with a sick feeling the many burning B–17s and P–40s on the ground. When fuel began to run low, Marrett took the 34th back to Del Carmen where the aircraft were refueled and rearmed. If the pilots had suffered low morale before the attack, then it

was even worse now for they had been completely powerless to stop the destruction of Clark Field.

Although Marrett had the P–35As prepared for instant scramble, most of the day was spent sitting by the aircraft and waiting for the enemy to return, but they did not. Communications with Clark were limited and the next day saw the 34th constantly in the air on patrol for Japanese, but a series of storm systems were keeping the Japanese on the ground in Formosa although the men of the 34th had no way of knowing this. However, fifth columnists were busy on the ground, sneaking close to Del Carmen and setting fires in the bush in hopes of directing Japanese bombers to the airfield. Ground personnel were kept busy trying to put out the fires and taking the odd pot-shot at what they thought were the fifth columnists. By the end of the day the pilots were exhausted and defects had cropped up on some of the aircraft, meaning that the mechanics would have a very long night. However, Marrett received orders late in the day that the 34th was to retreat to an equally primitive field, San Marcelino, for the night because of the threat of bombing attack.

On the morning of the 10th, the 34th was back at Del Carmen and Marrett found urgent orders awaiting him. Every Seversky was to get into the air and head for Vigan on the northern coast of Luzon where the Japanese were making their first landing. A P–40, airborne just before dawn, had spotted the enemy fleet and brought back the message to Clark. Patched-up B–17s and P–40s from Clark, joined by some of the B–17s that had escaped destruction at Del Monte, were airborne and headed for Vigan with the objective of doing as much damage to the enemy as possible.

The ground crews swarmed around the P–35As in an attempt to put fuel in the aircraft for the flight to Vigan. Time was critical and Marrett stood in the cockpit of his Seversky, surveying the sky for any sight of the enemy. Once again, the P–35As struggled through the dust cloud and became airborne. However, the time spent on the ground meant that they could not rendezvous with the aircraft from Clark which were already heading towards Vigan, and the slow speed of the P–35s prevented them from catching up.

Departing Del Carmen in two flights of eight aircraft, one flight led by Marrett and one by Lt Ben S. Brown, the Seversky's soon began encountering problems. One by one, the fighters began turning back with engine problems. The high-time powerplants and the effects of the dust were taking their toll and a nervous Marrett watched as his formation steadily decreased. When the 34th approached Vigan only seven P–35As were still in the air, two in Brown's flight and five with Marrett.

The depressing sight of a huge Japanese naval force greeted the small group of pilots. Close to shore were the transports and landing craft while farther out stood the warships, destroyers and cruisers. The B–17s and P–40s had finished their attacks and smoke was rising from where bombs and bullets had found their mark. This also meant that the Japanese were now fully alerted to the fact that American airpower in the Philippines still had some sting and anti-aircraft guns were being erected as the P–35s appeared on the horizon.

What good the lightly-armed P–35s could do against the formidable Japanese force was debatable but Marrett knew that the 34th would have to attack. The pilots knew that the Filipino troops would not be able to hold the enemy off for more than a brief period so, just like in training school, the P–35s broke formation in a perfect peel off and, with engines screaming, dived on the enemy. The little fighters roared among the shipping, sending volleys of machine gun fire into the surprised Japanese who had not expected the small force to commit themselves to battle.

Marrett, flying right above the surface of the ocean, selected a transport and held the trigger down as he watched his bullets slam into the lightly armored superstructure. Racking the Seversky around in a dangerous tight turn just a few feet above the water, Marrett went back for another firing pass as the Japanese gunners were blazing away with everything they had. Shells were kicking up water spouts around Marrett's aircraft as he centered his sights on the transport. Again he flew straight and level and poured gunfire into the middle of the ship. One of the 34th's pilots yelled to Marrett over the radio to abandon his attack because it was becoming too dangerous. Marrett persisted on his run and pulled over the ship's mast at the last possible instant. However, Marrett had waited too long. The 10,000 ton transport had apparently been carrying shells and ammunition and, just as Marrett cleared the superstructure, a violent explosion blasted the enemy vessel in two and, at the same time, blew the right wing off Marrett's P–35A which instantly flipped over and plunged into the ocean. It was all over in a second. The Japanese ship literally disappeared in the massive explosion. The surviving 34th pilots decided that

they had done all that was possible and began a hasty retreat to Del Carmen.

By the time the fighters had got back into Del Carmen, the ground crews had managed to patch together most of the fighters that had aborted but one of the P–35As returning from the strafing attack crashed into the jungle when the engine stopped, the pilot parachuting to safety. As the fighters were being rearmed, a dozen Zekes hit the strip in a surprise raid and their shooting, as had been discovered at Clark Field, was very accurate. With little in the way of anti-aircraft, the Americans were helpless and dived for cover into trenches or foxholes. After the Zekes left and after the fires and explosions had quieted down, the 34th discovered that 12 of the P–35As were smoking ruins and another six were very badly damaged. It looked like the 34th was out of the fighting business. Lt Ben S. Brown took over the unit after Marrett's death and had the men move their living quarters deeper into the jungle while they patched the wrecks together to look like operational aircraft. This deceived the Japanese who paid much time and attention to destroying the already destroyed P–35s.

To be expected, morale – already reaching bottom – really took a dive with the death of Marrett and the virtual destruction of all the Severskys. The pilots and ground crews were almost completely cut-off from any news of the war, even though Del Carmen was fairly close to Clark Field, and the young pilots felt as if they had been deserted. Even the patching up of the ruined Severskys after each bombing raid could not take up all their time and the situation was beginning to get very critical when Captain Harold Munton decided to do something about it. Munton had come to Del Carmen to set up the new Air Depot at the field and, as the men of the 34th were beginning to rebel and getting ready to take to the hills, Munton took it upon himself to take charge.

Captain Munton forced the squadron to take a hold of itself as a unit and initiated a move to Orani on the morning of the 26th; all members were able to receive a Christmas meal the night before from the operators of a nearby sugar mill. The command of the 34th was taken over by Lt Robert S. Wray and was soon flying reconnaissance missions with the P–40s that had been assigned to that base. Munton then went on to transport all Depot supplies to Bataan Field and was later in charge of supplies at that base. The few remaining P–35s left on Luzon flew reconnaissance missions until the last two flyable examples were taken to Bataan on 2 January.

Those hectic first days of America's entry into World War Two meant that records were slim and that many heroes went without the recognition that they deserved. On the day that Marrett was killed, Captain Colin Kelly in a B–17 Flying Fortress made an attack on a Japanese vessel and was awarded a posthumous Medal of Honor when he was killed trying to bring the damaged aircraft back to base. The American propaganda mill, desperate for some good news, amplified Kelly's attack on the ship to make it appear that the vessel was a carrier or a battleship and that it was sunk. The craft Kelly and his crew attacked was actually a cruiser and damage to the vessel was probably light. This event completely overshadowed Marrett's courageous attack in an obsolete aircraft but he was eventually awarded a posthumous Distinguished Flying Cross.

SEVERSKY P–35 SERIAL NUMBERS AND SPECIFICATIONS

Serial Numbers

P–35	36–354 through 36–429
P–35A	41–17434 through 41–17493

Specifications

P–35

Span	36 ft
Length	25 ft 2 in
Height	9 ft 1 in
Wing area	220 sq ft
Empty weight	4,315 lb
Loaded weight	6,295 lb
Max. speed	282 mph
Cruise speed	258 mph
Ceiling	31,000 ft
Rate of climb	2,400 fpm
Range	450 to 1,100 miles
Powerplant	Pratt & Whitney R–1830–9 of 950 hp

P35A

Span	36 ft
Length	26 ft 10 in
Height	9 ft 9 in
Wing area	220 sq ft
Empty weight	4,575 lb
Loaded weight	6,723 lb
Max. speed	290 mph
Cruise speed	260 mph
Ceiling	31,400 ft
Rate of climb	1,920 fpm
Range	600 to 950 miles
Powerplant	Pratt & Whitney R–1830–45 of 1,050 hp

Curtiss P-36
It Fought For Both Sides

The P–36 was the eventual winner in the Seversky/Curtiss fighter contest but its main claim to fame was that it would evolve into the P–40.

Lt G. H. Sterling, sweating in the cockpit of his Curtiss P–36A, was wishing that he had an aircraft with more horsepower, more guns, more maneuverability . . . more everything. It was 0855 hrs on the morning of 7 December 1941, and, over Wheeler Field, Lt Sterling was having very little time to think about much else except surviving. Sterling had managed to get off the ground at Wheeler Field with two

other 46th Pursuit Squadron P–36As. With huge columns of smoke billowing up from Pearl Harbor and the airfields in the vicinity, it was not hard for the P–36 pilots to find action. Anti-aircraft fire, now that the initial surprise of the devastating Japanese attack had somewhat passed, was pouring into the sky and any aircraft was considered a target – even if they were friendly. Just before 0800 hrs, aerial units of the Imperial Japanese Navy had staged a perfectly executed attack on American bases located on the Hawaiian island of Oahu. Dive and horizontal bombers, torpedo aircraft and a variety of fighters smashed the American

Perhaps the grandest hour for the P–36 in American skies was at the Cleveland, Ohio, National Air Races during September 1939. The P–36s of the 27th Pursuit Squadron were given individual and wildly imaginative 'camouflage' schemes on the excuse of an upcoming 'war game' but the war game was never held and it is more likely that the pilots and crews of the 27th just wanted to make a grand entrance to the Air Races, which were the most important aviation gathering in America. At the same time, the 1st PG has left a puzzle for historians that probably will never be solved – namely in defining the colors used on the P–36s. Aircraft No 59 carries the insignia of the 27th Pursuit Squadron and was probably painted in washable colors of dark green, brown, white, and orange. Many of the colors used on the P–36s were non-standard so it is impossible to match them to official color designations.

facilities with precision in the initial assault. At 0840 hrs, a second wave of enemy aircraft continued the attack. The Navy had suffered the worst losses in its long history. *Arizona, California, West Virginia* were sunk, *Oklahoma* had rolled over, and the *Nevada* was blazing from numerous hits. Smoke and explosions were filling the air over Pearl as the P–36s clawed for altitude.

About 25 bombers had hit Wheeler Field shortly after 0800, causing heavy damage to the aircraft that were parked closely together and to the facilities and hangars at the Army base. During a brief lull in the aerial attack, the three P–36As managed to get into the air with orders to proceed to Bellows Field to patrol the area and attack bombers at will. With throttles all the way to the stop, the P–36As dodged bursts of anti-aircraft fire as they headed towards Bellows. Bellows had not been hit as hard as Hickam or Wheeler but nine Zekes had strafed the field without opposition or any positive results from the limited anti-aircraft fire that the Army was able to put up. The Curtiss fighters arrived over Bellows shortly after the strafing attack and spotted the forms of nine Val dive bombers heading towards Bellows. The pilots immediately waded into the surprised enemy formation. Sterling kicked his rudder pedal over hard as he selected the fat fuselage of a Val that had broken formation. Closing rapidly against the fixed-gear bomber, Sterling quickly settled the aircraft in his sights and hit the trigger, sending off several bursts of .30 and .50 caliber machine gun fire from the two guns located in the upper forward fuselage. Although the firepower of the P–36A was anything but adequate, the well-aimed bursts from Sterling's guns were devastating against the unarmored Val. With its fuel tanks unprotected, the steel-jacketed slugs from the P–36A instantly turned the Val into an inferno and the blazing aircraft plunged to the ground – the two Japanese airmen going to meet their ancestors much sooner than they probably wished. Enemy aircraft were everywhere over Oahu so targets were not a problem but the ill-equipped hunters soon became the hunted. Superlative Mitsubishi Zeke fighters – a type unleashed with complete surprise against the Americans – were soon after the P–36As. One of the other Curtiss pilots managed to flame another bomber before being pounced upon by the fighters. Two of the three P–36As managed to get back to Wheeler but Lt Sterling – the first American pilot to score a victory over Pearl – had fallen to the guns of the avenging Zekes.

The Curtiss P–36A had had its moment of combat glory – at least in Army hands – on 7 December 1941. From that point, the woefully inadequate fighters were retired to second-line

duties or to training units. However, history books would have to record the significant fact that the first Japanese aircraft to be claimed as destroyed by the USAAF was a victim of the Curtiss P–36A and a brave pilot.

The Curtiss P–36, along with the Seversky P–35, was the bridge between biplanes and modern fighter aircraft for the USAAF. As stated in the chapter on the P–35, both aircraft were entered in a particularly hard–fought contest that was to have curious final results. Both machines were less than adequate in all categories of performance but they did manage to change the rather staid thinking of the American military and to help aircraft factories tool up for the coming conflict.

If the P–36 had served with just the US Army, then its story would have been short indeed. The build-up of war tensions meant that European nations – as well as many other smaller countries – were frantic to obtain as many combat-ready aircraft as they could as soon as possible. The Curtiss design happened to be at the right place at the right time. The P–36 design was available to be quickly mass-produced and supplied to foreign nations and it was with some of these countries that the design achieved its greatest success.

Curtiss began prototype construction of its 'Hawk 75' design as a private undertaking.

The Curtiss Model 75 (carrying the civil registration of 17Y) in flight near the Curtiss factory in Buffalo, New York. This was the aircraft with which Curtiss entered the Army pursuit aircraft competition during May 1935 but lost out to the Seversky P–35. Yet, in a curious reversal of circumstances, the Model 75 was the eventual winner. Principal designer of the Model 75 was the talented Donovan A. Berlin who had left Northrop to join Curtiss. Carrying s/n 11923, the Model 75 was originally powered by the Wright R–1670 900 hp radial, an unfortunate choice. Engine problems dogged 17Y and the first replacement engine was the Pratt & Whitney R–1535 of 700 hp but, since this was basically an obsolete powerplant, it was quickly replaced with a Wright R–1820 Cyclone. These engine problems were a major factor in the contest with the P–35 and 17Y (now designated Model 75B since the engine change) lost out in the fly-off of April 1936. This aircraft eventually gained new life when it was converted to the XP–37. Color scheme for 17Y consisted of blue fuselage and yellow flying surfaces – an evident attempt to impress the Army with an aircraft painted up in their standard color scheme.

The Army was interested in obtaining an aircraft to replace the little Boeing P–26 Peashooter and the new contract would be extremely lucrative and one that would bring prestige and fortune to the winning company. Like the P–35, the prototype Hawk 75 did not offer anything completely new in aviation terms but it did combine a number of factors, such as retractable landing gear, all-metal construction and enclosed cockpit, into a fighter that could be classified as 'modern' in appearance but not in performance – especially when one considers that the Hurri-

*C*urtiss did not completely lose out in the
fly-off contest with the Seversky P–35, for the
Army, not all that pleased with the Seversky,
decided to issue Curtiss with a contract for three
developmental YIP–36 aircraft to be powered by
the same Pratt & Whitney R–1830 that lugged the
Seversky through the air. The combination of
airframe and new engine changed the downward
slide of the Model 75's career. This YIP–36 is seen in
natural metal finish with the yellow and blue
Wright Field arrow on the side of the fuselage.

*O*ne of the three YIP–36s seen at the Buffalo,
New York, airfield. These aircraft were
extensively flown with the new engine installation
and proved quite popular with factory and Army
test pilots. Given the Curtiss factory designation of
Model H75E, the three YIP–36s were delivered
during March 1937 and carried the standard
inadequate Army armament of the time period:
one .30 and one .50 caliber machine gun firing
through the propeller and located in the upper
fuselage decking. The YIP–36s could be
distinguished from production machines by the
lack of cowl flaps on the smooth NACA cowling. It
is interesting to note that the three aircraft had
different prices: $48,432, $43,477 and $73,477. These
prices are a bit deceptive since the Army supplied
such essential items as engine and guns. Note the
cumbersome retractable landing gear which, while
being retracted, swiveled 90 degrees before
entering the wells in the wing.

cane, Spitfire and Bf 109 were all under development at the same time.

Since the Model 75 was a privately-funded
venture, the prototype had to be given a civil
registration – X17Y. Curtiss rather optimistic-
ally committed the aircraft to an Army-style
paint scheme of blue fuselage and yellow flying
surfaces. The new aircraft was powered by the
experimental XR–1670–5 radial built by
Wright (a division of Curtiss). The radial was

composed of 14 cylinders arranged into two
rows and was theoretically capable of pump-
ing out 900 hp.

Curtiss factory test pilot Lloyd Child took the
new aircraft up for its first test flight on 13 May
1935 but reported that the aircraft did not
handle all that well and power from the engine
was disappointing. The XR–1670–5 was totally unsatisfactory and it was temporarily replaced with an obsolete 700 hp P&W R–1535.

Seven hundred horsepower was not enough
for a plane like the Model 75 so the engine
mount was redesigned and the airframe was
fitted with a Wright XR–1820–39 single-row
radial of 950 hp. Child felt that the extra real
horsepower improved the handling and performance of the machine so, on 27 May, the
aircraft was submitted to the Army's Material
Division for testing.

The Army was looking for a cleanly deigned fighter (incorporating the 'modern' innovations previously listed) but they were limiting the usefulness of the design by specifying the carriage of two guns and a speed up to only 300 mph. Curtiss was in for a surprise – figuring that the fighter contest was in their pocket – for none of the other designs were ready and the Seversky entry had been mysteriously pulled out from the competition due to a questionable 'accident'. Actually, the so-called accident gave Seversky time to install crude retractable landing gear on his design and make it more competitive with the Model 75. The Army went along with the idea – feeling that the 'accident' should not deprive Seversky of his chance at the brass ring! Designer Donovan Berlin and the management of Curtiss protested at the decision but the Army felt that their action was warranted and stuck to the time extension. However, the modified Seversky entry and the Model 75 both suffered technical and engine troubles at the next gathering date and the Army once again extended the contest, this time until April 1936.

Both manufacturers took the extra time to develop and refine their fighters. The Model 75 had a new engine installed, this time an 850 hp Wright Cyclone, and the fuselage around the engine installation of X17Y was slightly redesigned while rear vision panels were placed in the fuselage behind the canopy. These modifications resulted in a designation change to H–75B. Thus modified, the aircraft entered the contest but the extra work had not completely cured the Curtiss fighter of its problems. During a short period of testing time, four engines had to be changed on the Curtiss because of failures, but all the fault was not on the side of the Curtiss entry as the Seversky was enjoying less than qualified successes. Curtiss had promised a top speed of 294 mph at 10,000 ft but the fighter was only able to produce 285 mph. The P–35, when the Army announced the results of the testing, proved to be a winner with a total of 812 points gained in the various categories (this was for the aircraft equipped with the Pratt & Whitney radial). Worse still, Seversky also took second place (792 points) with the aircraft powered by a Wright Cyclone. The H–75B dragged in at third with a not too exciting showing of 720 points.

This rather bleak picture was not all that bad for – although Seversky had many friends in the military – the Army was not satisfied with the company's ability to mass-produce a combat aircraft. To get around putting all their eggs in one basket, the Army issued a Service Test Order (AC 9045) to Curtiss for three service evaluation aircraft based on the H–75B but to be powered by the more reliable and powerful Pratt & Whitney R–1830 Twin Wasp. Since service test aircraft were assigned the Y1 designation, there never was a prototype (X) for the P–36, the designation the Army had given the new fighter. Curtiss was pleased with the contract, especially in the light of the fact that the 75 series was picking up increased export interest.

The Y1P–36 aircraft benefitted from additional detail design and clean-up work and the type was given the factory number of 75E. A new cowling housed the much more reliable P&W radial and the three aircraft, delivered in gleaming polished metal finish with Army markings, were sent to Wright Field for intensive testing. The R–1830–13 engine swung a three blade Hamilton Standard constant speed propeller and could deliver 950 hp. Since these were service test aircraft, the three machines were handed over to regular squadron pilots from the 1st Pursuit Group who put in about 60 hours of flying time, doing everything from slow flight testing to full power dives. The comments of these pilots were noted and recorded for a final summary. After the period of testing, a three-page report was carefully prepared by Colonel Frank Kennedy who summed up the test results. On the negative side, the pilots had felt that the cockpit was very hot; the heat came from defects in the firewall which, while it let in large amounts of engine heat, also allowed deadly gases to seep into the cockpit. Controls were also reported to be heavy when flying at high speeds, or at the beginning of a spin or snap roll. The combat pilots felt that the handles for the flaps and landing gear were too close together which could result in an embarrassing and expensive mistake. Engineers had noticed a structural weakness in the wing and a lack of strength in the gear attachment point. Lesser complaints included the fact that the baggage compartment was too small. On the positive side, the testing revealed that the re-engined P–36 performed aerobatic maneuvers with considerable *élan* and that vision from the cockpit was good. The Y1P–36s displayed very stable flight attitudes while ground handling and take-off characteristics were also good.

Curtiss went to work on the complaints. They reinforced the wing structure and landing gear attachment points, and modified the cowling to included cooling gills so that improved air circulation could take place while the engine was running on the ground. The controls were also modified and this was perhaps one of the most significant changes undertaken by Curtiss for the control system modification turned the P–36 into a beautifully flying aircraft with superb control harmonization. The P–36 was now able to roll at a faster rate than even the vaunted Spitfire.

Less than pleased with the delivery and performance of the Seversky P–35, the Army issued a contract, huge at the time, to Curtiss for the production of 210 P–36A fighters, costing $4,113,550 – the largest contract price for American aircraft. Curtiss was very pleased with the obvious victory over Seversky. The prestige of the Army contract would also bring foreign orders from governments who felt more confident in buying an aircraft already ordered in large quantity by the US Army.

The Curtiss P–36A was to be built entirely out of metal with a cantilever multi-spar wing that was skinned with 24ST Alclad. The fuselage was an aluminium monocoque. The retractable landing gear was of a patented Boeing design and Curtiss had to pay royalties to Boeing for each set of landing gear constructed.

The P–36A wing was built in two pieces and the wing tips were easily detachable. The airfoil was a NACA 2215 section at the root, tapering to a NACA 2209 section at the tip. The wings were joined at the centerline by a heavy ribbing and a large number of strong bolts that linked the two halves in a tight bond. The outer panels of the wing were sealed to help the aircraft to float in case it had to be ditched in the sea. Not quite sure of the merits of retractable landing gear, Curtiss built a strong skid into the forward centerline portion of the lower fuselage to reduce airframe damage in a wheels-up landing.

The hydraulically operated split flaps enabled a low landing speed of 74 mph to be achieved while also shortening the take-off run to 750 ft with a bit of wind coming over the nose. The wing area was to prove to be a weak point in the P–36. Structural wrinkles appeared around the landing gear/wing area due to hard landings or from being subjected to particularly hard g forces. Reinforcement was attempted in the form of thicker wing skinning and extra rib webs but this never entirely solved the problem.

The fuel situation was taken care of with three tanks that held a total of 162 gallons, giving a range of about 820 miles at economy cruise. Although different powerplant combinations were experimented with, the standard P–36A engine remained the Pratt & Whitney radial turning a Curtiss Electric three-blade propeller that was capable of full feathering as well as constant speed.

The tail section was also cantilever and used the NACA 0009 section and was entirely covered in Alclad except for the rudder and elevator which were finished in the traditional fabric covering as were the ailerons.

Designated P–36A, the production model of the new Curtiss fighter was not much different

The fortunes of Curtiss, concerning the P–36, dramatically improved when the Army, dissatisfied with the performance of their new Severskys, placed a contract with Curtiss for 210 P–36A fighters. This was the largest and most expensive contract that the Army had ever issued for a fighter and the cost for the original contract was $4,113,550. With this order, the P–36 became the Army's main fighter until 1941. This photograph emphasises the pre-war Army attitude of 'combat' flying. A formation of P–36As of the 20th Pursuit Group illustrate a formation that was popular in peacetime but soon proved of little use and dangerous in the hazardous skies over war-torn Europe. Upon examining the original print in detail, the letter 'E' can be distinguished on the cowlings of at least the first nine aircraft. This may have been a similar application to the Navy award of 'E' for excellence – given to units that have offered outstanding performance in various fields. The 20th PG had gratefully traded in its ageing Boeing P–26s for the P–36A and the unit comprised the 55th, 77th and 79th Pursuit Squadrons. (Barksdale AFB)

from the service test machines. The propeller was changed to a Curtiss Electric fully-feathering three-blade unit while the engine was produced to the latest modification standards, with the addition of flaps on the rear of the annular cowling to aid cooling. Brand new, the P–36A could nudge over 300 mph but it had a ridiculously inadequate armament of one .30 and one .50 caliber gun. The smaller weapon was equipped with 500 rounds while the .50 had only 200 rounds. This curious throw-back to World War One standards went in the face of effective European and Japanese cannon armament which had been developed, tested and put into service. Even the British standard .303 caliber aerial machine guns was tempered by the fact that these guns were usually installed in some number – eight guns in the early Hurricanes and Spitfires.

The first production P–36A (Curtiss Model 75L) was delivered to the Army during April 1938 but deliveries of further machines did not proceed all that smoothly. Apparent lack of design foresight and production line quality control led to a weakness in the fuselage and wing that followed the P–36A through its short career with the Army. Testing of the first P–36A (s/n 38–001) during aerobatics brought back the problem of skin wrinkling and buckling in the area of the landing gear wells and on certain sections of fuselage skinning. Curtiss tried to correct the problem with thicker skin but apparently the problem went deeper – to a poorly designed structure – and it was not resolved.

Service P–36As went to the 20th Pursuit Group and its three squadrons – the 55th, 77th and 79th – at Barksdale Field in Louisiana, but serviceability was extremely poor and groundings were frequent. Controls on the Curtiss production line apparently did little good, for the Army would usually ground a newly delivered aircraft until they had made their own modifications. The three squadrons had a hard time coming up to operational strength – they had given up their Boeing

*L*ine-up of P–36As from the 79th Pursuit Squadron of the 20th Pursuit Group. The aircraft in the lead was the mount of the squadron commander and can be identified by the two bands around the rear fuselage which were painted in yellow as was the large band around the engine cowling. Yellow was the color assigned to the 79th PS. Lightly armed and less than overpowered, the P–36 would have been a poor opponent for the Bf 109 that was flying with the Luftwaffe. (Barksdale AFB)

P–26s in anticipation of getting the P–36As. Flying hours were low as aircraft had to be grounded each time a skin wrinkle was found so that its entire airframe could be carefully inspected by Army mechanics for any signs of structural failure.

Factory changes were common for the P–36A at Buffalo and, by June 1939, Curtiss had instigated no fewer than 81 changes. These caused an increase in airframe weight and an obvious decay in performance and most factory-fresh P–36As with the new modifications would have had a hard time topping 300 mph. Pilots of the 20th PG were also having difficulties getting enough flying hours to keep current and had to borrow training aircraft to fly. The Boeing P–26s that had equipped the 20th PG were transferred to overseas units where a few later saw action in the Philippines and a number were destroyed on the ground in the initial attack on Pearl Harbor.

The Seversky P–35 and the P–36A gave the Army inadequate new fighters that were not only poorly armed to fight but were also limited in the types of combat maneuvers which they could perform. The Army, in concern for its pilots' safety, limited the top speed to 250 mph and strictly limited rough, combat-style maneuvers. One Army document lists, on 30 April 1939, the fact that 47 of the 61 P–36As based in America were grounded due to problems.

The 1st Pursuit Group, based at Selfridge Field in Michigan (and mentioned in the chapter on the P–35), was to give up its Seversky fighters for P–36As during 1938 but the problems with the Curtiss aircraft severely hampered the 1st's plans. The 17th, 27th and 94th Pursuit Squadrons made up the 1st PG but only the 94th was able to equip with the P–36A by the time the year closed. Even then, the 94th was not up to strength and had to fill in with P–35s. The 27th began taking on P–36As during 1939 but also could not come up to strength. The 17th stayed with the P–35. While operating both types, the 1st PG was able to experience the frustrations caused by the many troubles that the P–35 and P–36 generated.

Developmental work continued at the Curtiss factory on the P–36 and several other versions were produced to test armament configurations. P–36A 38–020 was modified to carry a Twin Wasp of 1,100 hp and was given the designation P–36B in November 1938. Another P–36A was fitted with a turbo-supercharger and had the airframe lightened a bit in an attempt to increase performance, but the increase was negligible and the aircraft was put back into stock configuration after testing.

The P–36D saw the conversion of P–36A 38–174 to mount a Twin Wasp R–1830–17 of 1,200 hp. The nose armament was modified to carry two .50 caliber weapons while modified outer wing panels carried two .30 calibers with 500 rpg on each side. The 147th P–36A, 38–147, became the XP–36E when the wings were modified to carry a total of eight .30 caliber guns with 500 rpg; the nose armament was eliminated. S/n 38–172 became the XP–36F when Curtiss installed one 23 mm Danish Madsen cannon with 100 rpg in a fairing under each wing panel; the XP–36F kept the standard nose armament. The increased weight and drag from the cannon pods reduced the top speed to an unimpressive 265 mph and development was discontinued.

The Army was not pleased with the performance of the P–36As that were beginning to arrive at squadron level, so the last 30 aircraft of the contract were uprated to become the P–36C. The P–36C was powered by the 1,200 hp Twin Wasp R–1830–17 radial while the outer wing panels were modified to take an additional .30 caliber gun with 500 rpg. A distinctive identifying feature of the P–36C was the cartridge container case that was mounted below the wing gun. Even with the increased drag of these units, the P–36C's speed rose a bit because of the extra horsepower. Modification of other P–36 airframes to XP–37, XP–42 and XP–40 prototypes is dealt with in the chapters concerning those aircraft.

As more P–36As became available, more units were equipped with the fighter, but it was rapidly becoming very obsolete as a result of the military developments in Europe. Curtiss fighters went to the 35th and 36th Pursuit Groups at Moffett Field, California, and Langley Field, Virginia, where, instead of arriving as operational fighters they were utilized as combat training aircraft.

America's far-flung outposts often received hand-me-down aircraft and Alaska was certainly no exception. In any upcoming threat of global conflict, Alaska was considered to be relatively safe from any enemy incursion – little did Washington know that the Japanese had mapped out a most effective invasion plan of Alaska via the long string of bleak and dismal islands known as the Aleutians.

Alaska was a vast uncharted frontier in the late 1930s and airfields capable of accepting modern military aircraft were virtually nil. Construction workers were sent to Anchorage to build a modern facility, Elmendorf Field, in 1940 but, by July 1940, when the first Army Air Force representatives arrived in Alaska, only a portion of the construction had been undertaken and completed. Since Anchorage is located at the end of a long inlet, the yearly temperatures, moderated by the influence of ocean currents, are considerably milder than in the interior of Alaska. The first temporary

hangar at Elmendorf was erected during the first months of 1941 and the officers in charge of the project decided that it was time for tactical aircraft to be transferred from the continental United States to the northern outpost. During February, the first combat aircraft arrived – 20 carefully crated P–36A fighters belonging to the 18th Pursuit Squadron. These were soon joined by 12 equally obsolete Douglas B–18A Bolo bombers of the 73rd Bombardment Squadron (Medium) and the 36th Bombardment Squadron (Heavy).

The Army Air Force effort in Alaska was consolidated under the title of Air Field Forces, Alaska Defense Command, on 29 May. The organization assumed the responsibility of training personnel, repairing and maintaining aircraft and preparing aerial defense methods for Alaska. Since the weather conditions in this part of the world were completely different to those in the United States, it was essential that pilots be fully trained to fly within the confines of Alaskan weather. Navigation aids were primitive, so it was also necessary that each

pilot become acquainted with every airfield and its surrounding points of identity. There was initially some conflict between the Navy and the Army concerning the roles of defense that each service should undertake but these differences were smoothed out by close co-operation.

As the war in Europe escalated, the importance of Alaska to America rapidly became clear. The Aleutian chain of islands provided many natural harbors for enemy landing forces who could set up temporary harbors and airfields that would be very difficult to dislodge. Ground forces in Alaska were fairly immobile because of the difficult nature of the terrain

Side-view of a P–36A assigned to the 36th Pursuit Squadron of the 8th Pursuit Group. The 36th PS could trace its history back to the 36th Aero Squadron of World War One and its P–36As carried the squadron's insignia on the sides of the fuselage, which consisted of a golden orange bordered in blue, 'a flying fiend' proper with a gutte de sang dropping from tongue, blue helmet and white goggles with black rims on an irregular cloudlike background. The 36th PS operated the P–36 from 1939 to 1940, during which time it also had on charge YP–37s and A–17s.

A P–36A from the 1st Pursuit Group shows off the aircraft's clean and simple lines to advantage. The plexiglass panels behind the sliding canopy offered a limited degree of visibility to the rear. Pre-war aircraft serving with the Army were maintained in pristine condition by individual crew chiefs and their helpers. This P–36A, carrying the group's insignia on the fuselage sides, was photographed on 22 October 1939. (E. Strasser)

and the weather, so they were basically tied to their stations and the Army felt that an intergrated system of airfields would be the only way to ensure the mobility needed in case of enemy invasion.

New airfields were rapidly put under construction during the summer of 1941 and by that fall, Elmendorf, Ladd, Kodiak, Yakutat and Nome airfields were all capable of supporting at least one fully equipped combat squadron while a dozen auxiliary landing fields were being constructed which would increase safety and the mobility of the air forces. Once the Curtiss P–36As had been uncrated and assembled, the difficult Alaskan weather did not

provide many operating problems, although preheating of the engine and oil was standard procedure during the cold months. The P–36As flew a variety of patrols, airfield scouting missions and survey flights but they were quickly phased out when newer P–40s became available. However, on 7 December 1941, the only operational combat aircraft in Alaska was the motley force of 20 P–36As and 12 Bolo bombers. The Alaska Defense Command thus became the only Army overseas air force which did not have one up-to-date combat aircraft immediately prior to the outbreak of the American entry into World War Two.

Another vital American defense location was the Panama Canal, that small but vital waterway which bisects Central America. Air defense in the Canal Zone had existed since 1917 but it was only during 1939 that the Army realized that the most likely form of attack against the Canal would come from the air. The bases in the Canal Zone had been

around for a while but were not completely finished or equipped. Personnel were also poorly trained and were usually engaged in constructing facilities rather than perfecting the tasks for which they were trained. The Canal certainly had more aircraft available than in Alaska but, once again, these machines were mostly obsolete and ineffective. New bases were being established in areas such as Puerto Rico, and the Caribbean area aerial defenses were consolidated under the command of the new Caribbean Air Force during May 1941 with the focus point of operations being the Panama Canal. Three main air bases formed the aerial defense basis of the Canal: France Field was located on the Atlantic side, Albrook Field was on the Pacific side and Howard Field was three miles from Albrook. These three bases were backed up by seven auxiliary fields and a number of emergency landing strips that had been cut out of the surrounding jungle and bush. By 7 December 1941, only 183 aircraft, out of the allotted otal of 396 planes, had been assigned to Canal Zone bases. Many of these aircraft were obsolete by any standards and included the Boeing P–26 and Northrop A–17. The start of World War Two saw P–36As operating with the 16th Pursuit Group and its 24th, 29th and 43rd Pursuit Squadrons. Located at Albrook Field, the 16th was saddled with a mixture of P–36As and P–26s. Also at Albrook was the 32nd Pursuit Group which had a mixture of P–36s, P–26s and a few P–40s for its 51st, 52nd and 53rd Pursuit Squadrons. The P–26s and P–36s were replaced with P–40s as soon as the new aircraft became available, most of the P–36s being sent back to the States. The P–36 apparently did not see any action while in the Canal Zone against the German U-Boats that occasionally slipped in close for a look, although one of the U-Boats met its end by coming to the surface at the wrong place and wrong time – just when a patrolling B–18 Bolo happened to be passing overhead (the B–18 was a contemporary of the P–36 and just as obsolete but, like the P–36, it managed to capture a brief moment of glory).

The air defense of Hawaii had reached a much more advanced level than in either Alaska or the Canal Zone, probably due to the lengthy and heavy American military presence in the Hawaiian Islands. The roster for 7 December 1941 was impressive: 754 officers

and 6,706 enlisted men formed the human component of the Hawaiian Air Force, which was concentrated on the island of Oahu. This force was broken down into the 18th Bombardment Wing at Hickham Field and the 14th Pursuit Wing with the headquarters at Wheeler Field. The 18th was made up of the 5th and 11th Bombardment Groups (Heavy), the 58th Bombardment Squadron (Light) and the 86th Observation Squadron based at Bellows Field, about 28 miles from the headquarters at Hickham. The 14th consisted of the 15th and 18th Pursuit Groups at Wheeler (one squadron was undergoing training at a small field called Haleiwa in the northern part of the island). The Hawaiian Air Force was in better physical shape than any other overseas Army Air Force command, for about half of their 231 combat aircraft could be considered modern. The modern portion consisted of 12 Boeing B–17D Flying Fortresses, 12 Douglas A–20A Havocs, 12 Curtiss P–40Cs and 87 P–40Bs. On the debit side were 33 B–18A Bolos, 14 Boeing P–26 Peashooters … and 39 P–36As along with the usual assortment of observation, training and transport aircraft.

This force had been rapidly built up since the beginning of 1941 when the total aircraft count stood at only 117 machines and all of them were considered obsolete. During February 1941, Hawaii was reinforced with 31

P–36s which, along with pilots and ground crews, arrived aboard the carrier *Enterprise*. The P–36As were rapidly supplemented with the arrival of P–40s, also transported by carrier from California.

Army pilots flew intensive practice missions from the various fields on Oahu during 1941, but a number of curious deficiencies in the air defenses persisted. Anti-aircraft defenses were primitive. The new radar that had been placed on the island's mountains was not given the full attention and respect that it deserved. The Army continued to park its highly polished aircraft in close rank formation – making perfect targets for bombing or strafing aircraft. Facilities and hangars remained uncamouflaged but some of the newly arriving aircraft such as the P–40s and some of the B–17s were wearing the new Olive Drab and Neutral Gray camouflage paints. The atmosphere at the Army and Navy bases on Oahu was almost one of an exclusive club – for good

Immediately prior to World War Two, the P–36 was a common sight on most American military airfields. This highly polished example belonged to the 79th Pursuit Squadron of the 20th Pursuit Group and the yellow diagonal stripe meant that the aircraft was assigned to B Flight Leader. The 79th PS operated the P–36 from 1938 to 1940. Insignia on the side of the fuselage was that of the 79th PS. P–36 equipped units often carried either the squadron's or unit's insignia on the sides of the fuselage. (W. T. Larkins)

reason. The pilots that made up the pre-war Army Air Corps and later the Army Air Force were just about the best to be had; add to this the lush tropical atmosphere of Hawaii and the fact that the wars in China and Europe seemed very, very far away, and one can understand this curiously detached view.

However, on 26 November, a large Japanese task force sailed from Hitakappu Bay in the Kurils; it included six aircraft carriers, two battleships, two cruisers, nine destroyers, three submarines and a train of support vessels. Plans for the attack on the American fleet and Army airfields at Oahu had been undertaken during the summer of 1940 and completed by November of that year. The Japanese picked highly qualified crews for the surface

With everything down, a P-36A comes in for a landing. This view shows off the aircraft's split flaps to advantage. Note that the pilot has the canopy slightly opened and that the air vents, located directly below the windshield, are fully open. Aircraft is in the markings of the 79th Pursuit Squadron and the band around the cowling is painted yellow. (W. T. Larkins)

vessels and aircraft and these crews trained at a breakneck pace for an attack which, the Japanese hoped, would completely eliminate American influence in the Pacific. The Japanese did not have really up-to-date information on the number of ships in the main naval base at Pearl Harbor but they hoped to sink or heavily damage at least four American carriers and four battleships. These victories would be accomplished by a fleet of Val and Kate bombers acting in the roles of horizontal, dive and torpedo bombers. The new Zeke fighters would provide protection and would attack targets of opportunity. At 0600 on the morning of 7 December from a location 200 miles away, the Japanese fleet launched the first strike force of 50 Zekes, 50 horizontal bombers, 40 torpedo planes and 50 dive bombers. Just 45 minutes later, the second wave of aircraft – 50 horizontal bombers, 80 dive bombers and 40 fighters – launched towards Oahu.

One of the six Oahu radar stations remained operational on that sleepy Sunday morning

and reported a large force of aircraft at 0702 about 130 miles away. Apparently, after some consideration as to what was the correct procedure to follow, the radar station operator telephoned the news to the main information gathering center. Since Navy aircraft were expected to be participating in maneuvers and Army B–17s would be arriving over Oahu that morning, the information was shuttled aside, especially since the Army officer on duty that morning was there for training and observation and did not feel that it was his duty to pass the information to operational units. The radar unit continued to track the enemy force towards Oahu where it lost them. At 0755, a force of aircraft heading toward the huge base at Pearl was seen near the Hickham Field hangar line. A minute late both bases came under devastating attack.

The attack on Pearl Harbor was savage and decimating. The pre-war American military was particularly sleepy on Sunday mornings, and 7 December was no exception. The Japanese could not have wished for a better

cenario. There were about 169 naval vessels in the Oahu area that morning and 87 of them were destroyed. The Navy and Marine Corps suffered 2,086 officers and men killed and 749 wounded. The one bright point in the attack was the fact that the carriers – a particularly valuable target that the Japanese wanted to destroy – were not at Pearl Harbor. The American carrier force had departed Pearl a few days previously on other missions and their escape from certain destruction at Pearl meant that the Japanese had to pay very heavily in the days to come for their sneak attack on Pearl.

The heavy clouds of smoke from the burning battleships and installations covered the sun and obscured the fact that a few American fighters were managing to get off the ground to engage the Japanese. Along with the pre-war habit of lining aircraft in close rank formation, the fear of sabotage (Oahu had a large Japanese population, thought to be sympathetic with the homeland) had caused the Army to issue an order on 27 November that all aircraft

would be grouped in tight units rather than being widely dispersed and ready for immediate action. The Japanese could not believe their eyes as they saw the tightly packed concentrations of fighters and bombers and the Zekes raked the aircraft with machine gun fire and cannon shells. Sometimes the aircraft were so close together that if one exploded, it stood a good chance of taking the remaining aircraft with it. However, at about 0830, four P–40s and two P–36s managed to get into the air from Wheeler. Three P–36As of the 46th Pursuit Squadron were in the air at 0850 while six pilots of the 47th PS, in training at Haleiwa, managed to get to their aircraft by automobile and roar aloft. Haleiwa was probably not known to the enemy or not considered a strategic target since it did not come under attack. These pilots managed to carry out a number of sorties between 0815 and 1000, with some enemy aircraft claimed as destroyed or damaged. Lt George Welch (later to become a test pilot for North American Aircraft and die in the crash of a prototype F–100 Super Sabre)

claimed four enemy aircraft destroyed while flying a P–40. Lt John L. Dains alternately flew three sorties in P–40s and P–36s but was shot down on the third sortie by American anti-aircraft fire.

After the enemy attacks were concluded, some form of order was attempted – which was difficult since virtually every military base appeared either to be destroyed or burning. Every available aircraft was put into the air – there were not many left airworthy – to avoid further Japanese attacks and to search with vengeance for the enemy carriers. The P–36As, along with P–40s, O–47s, A–20s, B–17s and B–18s patrolled to the limits of their

Dressed in their 1930s 'Bowery Boys' overalls and floppy hats, a trio of mechanics wait for the pilot of this 77th Pursuit Squadron, 20th Pursuit Group, P–36A. Note how the designator 'PT99' has been applied under the left wing. Location of the designator was rather capricious – the amount of space under the wing usually specifying location. Squadron color was bright red. The straight up and down red band around the rear fuselage signified that this aircraft was the 'A' Flight Leader.

Banking for the benefit of the camera plane, this P–36C of the 27th Pursuit Squadron displays its highly individual water-based camouflage acquired for the 1939 National Air Races. This aircraft, thought to be PA 44, shows off the cowl flaps to advantage. The YIP–36s did not have the flaps which were used to cool the engine. Also note that part of the rear fuselage plexiglass panels have been painted over.

endurance for the enemy fleet, but with no success. The Japanese fleet had arrived and left completely unseen by the Americans. The Roberts Commission, set up to investigate the raid, stated on 26 December: 'A total of ninety-six Army planes were lost as a result of enemy actions, this figure including aircraft destroyed in depots and those damaged planes which were subsequently stripped for parts.' A total of 600 Army personnel were killed or wounded.

The Pearl Harbor attack spelled the end for a strange decade of American isolationism. The blackened hulks of the great ships and the flattened hangars testified to the fact that the American awakening to what was happening in the rest of the world was sudden and painful. The elite Army Air Force and its proud polished aircraft were a thing of the past. The Curtiss

P–36, after 7 December, was relegated to second-line and training duties – they even disappeared quickly from these roles – and American began to tool up for a new air force equipped with aircraft that would smash back at the enemy.

The Curtiss P–36 and its brief moment of glory were forgotten in the following four years of war but, during the 1950s, a civilian example of a P–36 turned up at a small airfield in Florida. Seldom flown by its owners, the little fighter was eagerly acquired by the United States Air Force Museum who restored the craft with a colorful war game camouflage. Proudly on display at Wright Patterson AFB, the Curtiss P–36 stands as a reminder of the dark days of 1941 and the price that was paid for the lack of vigilance.

The Curtiss 75 series achieved its greatest success while in the service of other nations. Although it is outside the scope of this volume to give full histories of each, these are important episodes in the P–36 story and the following summary outlines the service of the aircraft with a number of different nations.

ARGENTINA Occupying the 'boot' of South America, Argentina maintained a strategic position during World War Two for shipping or submarines attempting to cross into the Pacific by the long and arduous route around South America. The Argentinian government, during the late 1930s, was being courted by both German and American interests who realized the importance of the nation. Accordingly, the air arm of Argentina began to acquire a distinctly cosmopolitan look with Focke Wulf Fw 44J *Stieglitz* trainers being license-built, beginning in 1937, as negotiations were going on with Curtiss to license-build Hawk fighters. The government had acquired the second demonstrator Hawk – with the US civil registration NR1277 – and, after having some of the country's top pilots test the aircraft, placed an order for 30 H–75O fighters. At the same time as the order was placed, a request for license manufacture of the type was also lodged.

The H–75O had the fixed landing gear

deemed more suitable for less sophisticated nations, and was similar to the Thai Hawk but had a redesigned exhaust system, 875 hp Cyclone powerplant and four .30 caliber machine guns – two in the nose and two in the wing. License manufacture was undertaken by the government factory *Fabrica Militar de Aviones* at Cordoba and a total of 20 Hawks were completed with the first being delivered on 16 September 1940. The Hawks were supplied to the *I, II* and *III Regimientos de Caza* where they became the nation's first modern fighter. The accident rate was fairly low and 45 of the total of 50 Hawks remained in service by 1945. Serving well into the 1950s, the H–75O was well-liked by pilots, the more senior of whom were known for putting on flashing aerobatic displays over local towns and bases. Several continued to fly into the 1960s as well-maintained pets of high-ranking officers. It is thought at least one H–75O still survives in Argentina. Construction numbers of the Curtiss-built H–75Os were c/n 12769 through 12797.

BRAZIL It was decided to supply Brazil, another large South American country of strategic importance, with ex-Army P–36As as part of an attempt to bolster that country's defenses. Beginning in 1942, ten P–36As were supplied to the *Fôrça Aérea Brasileria* by whom

*A*ircraft 46 at Cleveland, with the empty bleachers in the background. The Army and Navy always liked to display their new aircraft at the National Air Races, which were attended by virtually all of the American aeronautical community, and the Army apparently thought that they could get a step up on the Navy by applying these eccentric camouflage schemes. The original tail number and the insignia have been painted around, rather than freshly applied. Pilots found the P–36 a pleasant, sportsman-like aircraft with few bad vices but it certainly was not a combat aircraft. Note how the rudder stripes are showing through the lighter colored camouflage. (E. Strasser)

they were used as first-line fighters along with a small number of Curtiss P–40Es. As more P–40s became available, the P–36As were assigned to the advanced trainer role. The following list gives an account of the P–36As supplied to Brazil:

FAB Serial	Army Serial	Curtiss C/N
FAB 1	38–054	12468
FAB 2	38–039	12453
FAB 3	38–043	12457
FAB 4	38–159	12573
FAB 5	38–051	12465
FAB 6	38–158	12572
FAB 7	38–175	12589
FAB 8	38–106	12520
FAB 9	38–060	12474
FAB 10	38–053	12467

These two views of the 27th PS's No 50 P–36C illustrate that the water-based camouflage was applied with completely different patterns on both sides of the fuselage – thus confounding current aero historians even further. This aircraft was flown by John C. Kilborn during the races but normally was the mount of the squadron's executive officer, Capt Israel. Note that the 'B' Flight Leader stripe is still visible. This particular aircraft was painted in shades of black, medium grey, tan, white, and dark green. (E. Strasser)

P–36C No 67 was known by the 27th PS as 'Old Barber Pole' because of its striped appearance. This P–36C was flown by Lt William J. Feallock. Colors, from cowl to tail, ran black, grey, dark green, white, brown, chrome yellow and then began to repeat with the last color being white. The supposedly easily removable paint proved to be a surprise for the ground crews when they found that repeated scrubbings were necessary to remove the 'temporary' camouflage.

Interesting because of its excellent detail of a pre-war Army Air Corps pilot's flight gear, this photograph shows the commander of the 27th PS, Major Willis R. Taylor, in a rather dramatic pose as he issues orders to the squadron prior to a mass take off at Cleveland. (Selfridge Field)

BRITAIN The Royal Air Force became the depository of a considerable number of Hawks, many arriving as a result of the fall of France. However, in RAF service, the Hawk (or Mohawk as it was named by the British) did not, in common with several other American aircraft ordered in quantity, see any action in the North-West European theatre of war, being rated as a second-line aircraft and not really suitable for combat over Europe; it did, however, see action in less-known combat zones.

During June 1941, as the fortunes of France went from bad to worse, some French pilots decided to set course on their own – seeing the fall of France as an imminent fact – and headed for Britain with their *Armée de l'Air* Hawks. The British were certainly not puzzled by their arrival for that country had become a landing ground for aircraft of many nations since Hitler's *Blitzkreig* had begun to move upon Europe. With the collapse of France and the setting up of the pro-Nazi Vichy government, the remainder of the Hawk contracts placed with Curtiss were transferred to the Royal Air Force.

Britain received about 225 Hawk fighters, both escaping aircraft from France and aircraft supplied new from the Buffalo factory. The Hawk became the first American fighter in service with the RAF with the arrival of the first French H–75A1s, which were given the

During the many pre-war tests involving the correct use and application of camouflage, this P–36C was drawn from the 23rd Composite Group to test an Olive Drab and Neutral Gray scheme. Serial number 38–202 was one of 30 P–36Cs, being the last group of aircraft on the P–36A contract, modified to the C version after P–36A 38–85 was fitted with a single .30 caliber gun in each wing. Production P–36Cs were powered by R–1830–17 radials of 1,200 hp.

British designation Mohawk Mk 1 while the H–75A2s and 3s became Mohawk Mks II and III. The first three marks of Mohawks came directly from France, but the Mohawk Mk IV was the Cyclone version designated A4 which was delivered new from Buffalo after the transfer of the contract to Britain from France. These aircraft had been modified at the factory to fit British specifications, including the fitting of six .303 caliber machine guns, two in the nose and four in the wing, British throttles, instruments, and other miscellaneous equipment. The first five Mohawk Mk IVs to arrive from Curtiss were uncrated in July 1941 and two of them, allotted RAF serials AR644 and AR645, were sent to the Aeroplane and Armament Experimental Establishment at Boscombe Down for intensive testing. A French Hawk 75A–2, No 188 had been borrowed by the British for testing before the fall of that country, so the type was not entirely new. The

Hawks were found to be very maneuverable aircraft but in no way were they comparable to the Messerschmitt Bf 109Es and Fs that were roaming the skies of Europe at will. The borrowed French Hawk was test flown against a Supermarine Spitfire Mk I, K9944. At slower speeds, the Hawk could outmaneuver the Spitfire because of its excellent aileron response and, at higher speeds in a dive, the Hawk could break away from the Spitfire by executing a rapid aileron turn that the Spitfire could not follow due to its much heavier aileron pressures. However, the Spitfire's superior speed allowed it to run away from the Hawk. Take-offs and climbs for the Hawk were found quite good compared to the early model of Spitfire with its two-pitch propeller, and torque from the Hawk's engine was much less pronounced on take-off. The Spitfire's speed was much better and the aircraft had a great development potential compared to the Hawk.

When Mohawk Mk IVs began to arrive in considerable numbers in Britain they were assembled and flown to Maintenance Units away from possible German bombing attack and held in reserve against the German invasion which was thought to be coming soon. However, with the possibility of invasion rapidly diminishing as the months passed,

Mohawk Mk IVs were disassembled and transferred to other countries.

The Mohawk Mk IV did see some combat with the RAF, but in a rather unlikely location. No 5 Squadron, RAF, was based at Dum Dum, Calcutta, India, and, in late 1941, began receiving some Mohawk Mk IVs to replace their totally antiquated biplanes. Another RAF squadron stationed in India, No 146, also began converting from biplanes to Mohawk Mk IVs but these aircraft were soon transferred to No 5 Squadron, leaving No 146 to re-equip with the notorious Brewster Buffalo and wonder what they had done wrong. No 5 Squadron took its Mohawks into combat for the first time on 17 June 1942 as bomber escorts. After their debut, the Curtiss fighters were used for just about every combat role possible and it was not until June 1943 that the antiquated Curtiss fighters were replaced with Hurricanes. Another squadron, No 155, was also equipped with Mohawks during July 1942 at Peshawar. This squadron saw considerable action with their Hawks – from interception of Japanese aircraft to dive bombing in Burma. The Mohawks were grounded several times due to oil distribution trouble with the Cyclone engines. No 155 Squadron saw heavy action at Imphal during February and March 1943 as it worked in conjunction with the British Army and the squadron soldiered on with its tired and obsolete Mohawks until January 1944 when they were replaced with Spitfire Mk VIIIs. Mohawks in service with No 155 included AR649, AR677, AX889, BJ451, BS731, BS798, and BT470.

CHINA During the first part of 1938, the Chinese government placed an order with Curtiss for 112 H–75M fighters, the production version of the 75H. Armed with four .30 caliber machine gunes, the Chinese felt that the H–75M would be a match for the fixed-gear Mitsubishi Type 96 Claude which, at that time, was the most advanced Japanese fighter in China. The Chinese order for 112 aircraft was to be supplied to that country in major component form for assembly by the Central Aircraft Manufacturing Company at Loi-Wing. Chinese pilots were notoriously poor

and Hawks were wrecked almost faster than CAMCO could assemble them. In order to save oriental face, the Chinese accused Curtiss field representatives of incorrectly aiding in the assembly of the machines but Curtiss counter-ed with an explanation that the faults were directly the result of Chinese incompetence. A typical incident occurred during one forma-tion flight when six out of the 13 Hawk fighters crashed and were destroyed while attempting to land. Japanese bombing attacks also man-aged to take their toll of H–75Ms. Madame Chiang Kai-shek once bemoaned her pilots' ability by saying: 'What can we do, what can we do? We buy them the best planes money can buy, spend so much time and money training them, and they are killing themselves before my eyes. What can we do?' Claire Lee Chennault had been hired to shape up the Chinese air arm but it was a hard job and eventually had to be done with mercenaries.

Chennault, as a gift, had been presented with H–75H demonstrator NR1276 and found the aircraft a delight.

'I fell in love with the Hawk Special the first time I flew it and asked Madame Chiang to buy it for my personal plane. She paid Curtiss Wright $55,000 for the plane. It was in the Hawk Special that I got my first taste of Jap flak and fighter tactics, and that I learned some of the lessons that later saved many an American pilot's life over China.

'The difference between Japanese and American equipment was crystal clear in the air over the Yangtze Valley. Japanese had featherweight monoplanes and twin-float

View of a P–36C that illustrates to advantage the fairing mounted under each wing to accommodate the installation of the .30 caliber guns. Note the retractable air scoop immediately behind the lower cowl ring. Photographed on 8 June 1940. (E. Strasser)

seaplane fighters that sacrificed everything else for incredible maneuverability. In a turning, tail-chasing dogfight they were poisonous. Even then it was evident that Japan was thoroughly committed to building planes as expendable items, counting on a short combat life and depending on production for replacement rather than on field repair and maintenance to put damaged planes back into action.

'My Hawk was built ruggedly with maeuverability sacrificed for heavy firepower (this is Chennault's own statement – from a man used to pre-war Army biplanes with two guns – and not quite accurate since the soon to be encountered Zeke carried a cannon), dura-

bility, and diving speed. To get the last mile of straightaway speed we stripped the Hawk of every bit of the non-essential "hardware" so dear to American manufacturers. Since there were no air-to-ground communications in China, the radio was removed, and I generally carried my thick, heavy bedroll in the radio compartment directly behind the pilot's seat. On more than one occasion when I unrolled this pack for the night, Japanese bullets fell from the blanket folds.

'Surviving ten months of combat and operational flying under the roughest field conditions, the Hawk Special finally met an ignominious end in a ground loop caused by a hamhanded American test pilot. The cowling had been bent by Japanese bullets and the test pilot was taxiing out for a trial hop with the repaired cowling when he wrapped up the Hawk on the ground.'

The completion of the H–75M order led to interest in the more advanced retractable gear Hawks and the H–75A5 Cyclone-engined fighter was built under license in China by CAMCO after the delivery of one complete aircraft and sets of parts from Curtiss. Powered

by the GR–1820–G205A, the fighter was armed with six .30 caliber guns. Plans for mass production collapsed when, on 26 October 1940, a heavy Japanese bombing attack destroyed the CAMCO plant at Loi-Wing. Surviving jigs and material were later transferred to India.

FINLAND The Finnish people suffered greatly in the war with the Russians which began with a massive Soviet invasion on 30 November 1939. After 104 days of costly fighting, a peace treaty was signed on 12 March 1940 and the Finns soon began to rebuild their badly depleted armed forces. Peace was to be a short-lived commodity and, in June 1941, what became known as the 'Continuation War' broke out with Russia. Previous to this the Finns had purchased 21 ex-*Armée de l'Air* H–75A3s from the Nazis. These aircraft had been overhauled by the Germans and fitted with German equipment, instruments and radios by *Espenlaub Flugzeugbau*. This marked an era of cooperation between the Finns and the Germans in an effort to expel the Soviet invaders and regain captured Finnish soil. The Finns also obtained eight ex-Norwegian

▲ *French Hawk H75–A2. One hundred of these aircraft were delivered, beginning during May 1939. These aircraft were powered by the R–1830–S1C3G radial of 1,050 hp and were armed with six 7.5 machine guns, two in the nose and four mounted in the wing.*

75A6s and seven 75A4s. Small numbers of ex-French Hawks were also acquired during the coming years. The Finnish Hawks enjoyed considerable success and several aces came from the ranks of Hawk pilots.

FRANCE France was the best customer for the export 75s but it was also with this country that the Hawk would see action against Allied forces in one of the most regrettable incidents of World War Two. During the late 1930s the French were frantically rearming but their industry seemed incapable of logical production – airframes would be ready but engines would be incomplete, complete aircraft would be parked at the manufacturer's airfields ready to go except for some vital missing part which a subcontractor could not supply on time. The French were also building some of the most grotesque aircraft ever to take wing during this period, especially bombers. However, lessons were being learned but time was at an absolute premium and there was not enough of it.

A French pilot familiar to American aviators for his winning 1936 Thompson Trophy performance in a Caudron racer, Michel Detroyat, flew the Hawk 75B demonstrator at the Cleve-

land National Air Races and reported back to French military officials that the aircraft had superior handling qualities, creating official interest in the purchase of the aircraft to supplement the fighter forces of the *Armée de l'Air*.

The French Purchasing Commission filed an order for 100 H–75A1 fighters during May 1938, to supplement the Morane Saulnier 406 in French service. Powered by a Twin Wasp radial capable of producing up to 1,050 hp and armed with four 7.7 mm machine guns and French instruments, throttle and radio, the French Hawk was also equipped with rudimentary armor protection, a feature lacking in the American P–36As. The four guns gave the 75A1 a heavier armament than the P–36A but a lighter gun load than any other operational French fighter of the time. The French Hawks would be built with airframe jigs and tools purchased by the French.

Assembly of the first French Hawks proceeded rapidly, as did all the Hawk 75s, (especially since the French were demanding early delivery as a contractual obligation) and the first two aircraft were test flown at Buffalo during December before being disassembled for

sea shipment via the SS *Paris* to Le Havre. A further 14 Hawks were shipped to France as testing aircraft while the first two were retained to become pattern aircraft for license manufacture. The remainder of the Hawk order was sent in broken-down sub-assemblies and these were put together by the French. All aircraft of the initial contract for 100 machines had been assembled and flown by 12 May 1939.

The French had been particularly alarmed by the victories achieved by the Junkers Ju 87 *Stuka* during the Spanish Civil War. The *Armée de l'Air* wanted a fighter that could catch and destroy the dread *Stuka*, even when the bomber was in its infamous dive. If facts and results had been studied more closely the French would have found out that the *Stuka*, courtesy of excellent dive brakes, was extremely slow in its bombing dive, allowing the pilot considerably more time to aim his bomb accu-

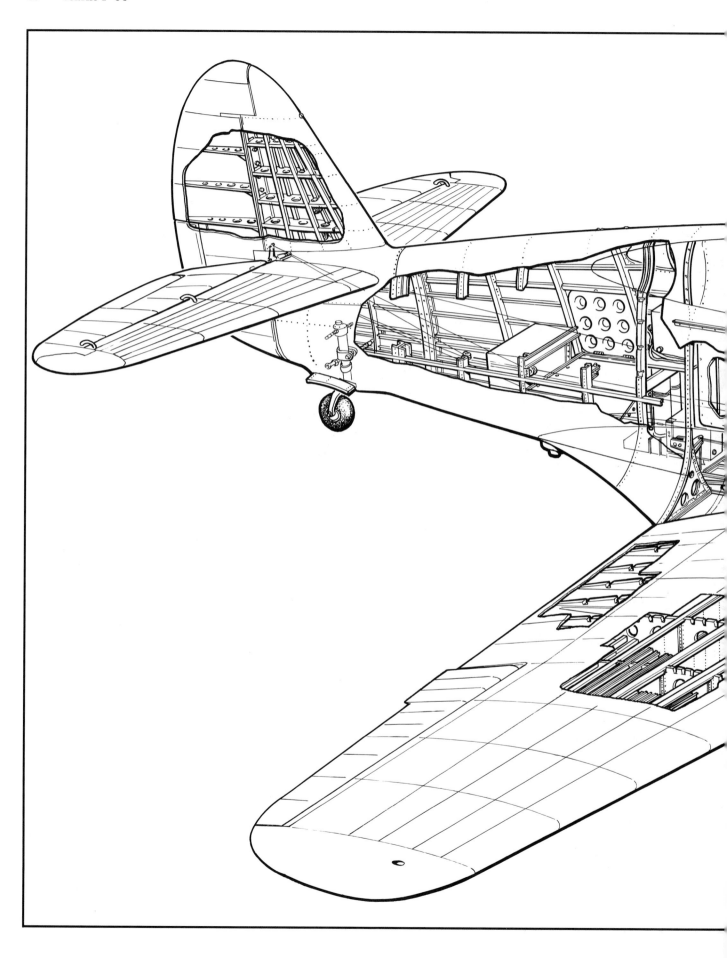

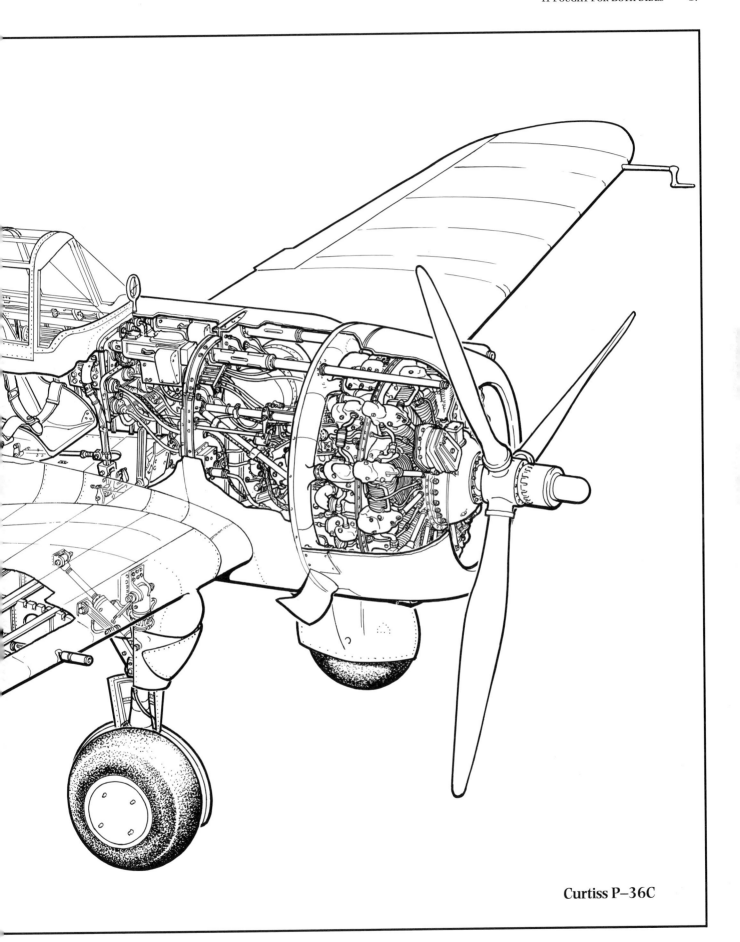

Curtiss P–36C

rately. In all truth, the *Stuka* was only a useful weapon for bombing roads clogged with fleeing civilians or for attacking targets that lacked fighter or anti-aircraft protection.

Proof was wanted of the Hawk's diving capabilities so factory test pilot Lloyd Child was assigned to fly the first French Hawk for diving tests on 9 December 1938. Child proceeded to take the Hawk up to 22,000 ft and in a power dive he brought the aircraft to within 1,500 ft of the ground. The French were quite pleased with the results and released a news bulletin stating that the Hawk had set a world diving speed record of 575 mph. Viewed in cold and analytical light, the figure was probably erroneous because of the lack of precision of the aircraft's instruments. During World War Two it became rather common for test pilot's to

The Curtiss designation of Model 75A was given to one of the research and development aircraft which was registered NX22028. This aircraft was flown in a number of different configurations as it tested a variety of equipment, including the ungainly supercharger on the side of the fuselage as seen in this photograph. The aircraft crash-landed following an engine failure and was scrapped.

claim that they had broken the sound barrier during power dives. Yet this was far from the truth as the recording instruments were sometimes as much as 200 mph off the mark. It would have been impossible for the airframe of a propeller-driven World War Two fighter to penetrate, much less break, the sound barrier. The Curtiss performance had impressed the French to such a degree that another batch of Hawks was ordered.

In the meantime, testing of the aircraft assembled in France revealed a number of weaknesses. Along with the inadequate armament, the guns tended to freeze when at high altitude and the fuel transfer system was considered too complex, but the lack of self-sealing fuel tanks drew the loudest complaints from pilots. Even with these negative testing results, Hawks were rapidly beginning to enter service with the *Armée de l'Air*, with the *4éme* and *5e Escadre de Chasse* converting during March 1939.

The second batch of Hawks, designated H–75A2, had a further machine gun in each wing panel and some of the fuselage structural modifications that had been adopted for the

Army P–36As. The first 75A2s began arriving in France during May 1939 and 100 aircraft of this type were ordered. September 1939 found the *Armée de l'Air* equipped with the 200 Hawks it had originally ordered. The Hawks were in service alongside the MS 406 which was similar in many ways to the British Hurricane. The closing possibility of war led the French to order more Hawks – 135 75A3 and 285 75A4 fighters. The A3 was equipped with a more powerful Twin Wasp while the A4 had the Wright GR–1820–G205A Cyclone 9 radial of 1,200 hp. When France surrendered, 110 A3s had been taken on strength but a smaller number was actually ready for combat because of late delivery of French systems. Only a few A4s arrived in France before the surrender. After the fall of France, 17 A4s that were en route by ship were disembarked in Martinique and six were dropped off at Guadeloupe. These aircraft had been on the French carrier *Bearn*. The fighters sat in crates for over two years before being shipped to Morocco and assembled, their unreliable Cyclones being discarded in favor of Twin Wasps.

The combat career of the Hawk in French

ervice was violent and brief. On 8 September 1939, French Hawks intercepted a force of Luftwaffe Bf 109s and claimed two destroyed. This initial victory for the Hawk elated the French pilots but, unfortunately for the *Armée de l'Air* aviators, the victories were not to be a sign of future fortunes. The French army began to make small attacks in the Saar River area in an effort to prevent the Germans from applying total military strength against Poland and to test out French equipment. The Germans took great umbrage at these military forays and launched their Messerschmitt fighters against the French aircraft supporting the army with telling effect.

At the start of the war, the Hawk fighter equipped four *Groupes de Chasse*: I/4, II/4, I/5 and II/5. Curtiss fighters were assigned to protect bomber and reconnaissance aircraft flights during the early days of the war and losses began to mount as the formations were attacked by Bf 109Es, but the French pilots did manage to score a number of victories so the aerial fights were not completely lopsided, especially since the Bf 109E was superior to the Hawk in all aspects of combat.

The winter of 1939/40 was extremely cold and, during the period that became known as the Phoney War, aerial combats were restricted. Hawks would occasionally attempt to intercept and destroy high-altitude German reconnaissance flights, usually undertaken by the unattractive Ju 86P, but the fighter's lack of performance virtually guaranteed that the photo missions would be a success for the Germans. During the Phoney War, the French made efforts to increase their military strength but the government acted a bit like a chicken with its head cut off and considerable military advantage was lost by the time the Germans launched their massive all-out *Blitzkreig* against France on 10 May 1940.

The German *Panzers* poured into the Benelux countries and France like a sharp knife slicing through the weakest of substances. The French and the British Expeditionary Force went into action but communications soon collapsed and, for all intents, both armies were soon involved in a rout. The Germans had smashed through the front-line defenses and, in a bold stroke, made a rush to the Channel coast, avoiding combat with the best Allied divisions and being able to advance on them from their weak rear positions.

The Hawks were soon engaged in heavy action, taking off from their bases to intercept enemy bomber formations and to defend their own runways. GC I/5 ran into a large force of vaunted *Luftwaffe Stukas* that was in the process of attacking French ground forces and the fighters fell on the dive bombers with vengeance. The *Stukas* were slaughtered, 16 being claimed as destroyed. Strangely, this decisive encounter did little to stem the fear of the *Stuka* and its myth of incredible power continued well into the Battle of Britain. The Hawks were also given additional duties of supporting land forces: GC I/4 was assigned to the 2nd Army in the Ardennes, and II/4 and II/5 patrolled the eastern section of France and covered the 2nd and 3rd Armies.

The French and British forces were pushed with great speed toward the coast where Hitler figured they could be annihilated, but he did not figure on the amazing rescue from the beaches of Dunkirk. Hawks hurriedly flew off to protect Paris but Paris was soon occupied and the Hawk pilots attempted to fight a rear-guard action as they retreated from one base to another. Parts were in short supply and the supply system itself had been completely destroyed as the Germans cut the country to pieces. By June the military situation was virtually hopeless, the RAF had all but ceased to exist over France and the Italian *Regia Aeronautica*, convinced that France had just a short time left, gallantly joined the battle with their Nazi allies. Hawks began to break down as their unreliable Cyclone 9 engines failed under the pressure of combat and many Curtiss fighters were withdrawn from combat because of the lack of engine parts. On 10 June, the fifth and final Hawk equipped group, GC III/2, joined the war after suffering heavy losses with their MS 406 fighters.

The surviving Curtiss fighters were ordered to withdraw to North Africa during June but some pilots did not like the idea and headed for England instead, giving the RAF their first Mohawks. When the surrender, or armistice depending on viewpoint, took effect on 25 June, the five Curtiss-equipped fighter groups were in North Africa, having made the journey between 18 and 20 June. As per the armistice, these fighters were ordered to be disarmed – especially when some of the French pilots indicated that they wanted to head to the RAF base at Gibraltar and continue the fight.

One of the strangest periods in the history of World War Two began after the fall of France. This was the establishment of the French Vichy Government, an administration of Frenchmen who were to 'rule' the country while obeying their new German masters. The French quickly settled into this arrangement with a speed which astonished the Germans. Paris became a must tourist spot for German soldiers and *Luftwaffe* aviators and the French citizenry responded with extraordinary zeal in the turning in of Jews and other 'undesirables' to the Germans.

The British were now standing with their backs to the wall. Their European allies had been efficiently demolished one by one by the German war machine which seemed to be unstoppable. The British made a direct appeal – or threat – to the French to attack the Germans with their fleet of warships at Mers el Kebir, or scuttle them. The French did not seem in a mood to sink their ships nor to attack the Germans with them (the French fleet could have posed a major problem for the rapidly expanding German forces). The Royal Navy launched a carrier-borne attack against the French warships on 3 July 1940, causing considerable damage and casualties – enraging the French into action to attack the primitive Royal Navy aircraft, which included Fairey Swordfish biplanes and Blackburn Skuas. The Hawks were able to repel some of the attacks and were credited with the destruction of two Skuas. The Germans were impressed, from a propaganda viewpoint, in the fact that ancient hatreds had been stirred in the clash with the aerial forces of Britain and France. The Germans also quickly moved in large numbers of fighters to protect their newly acquired French 'friends' against future attacks. French pilots were rewarded for their exploits by being given a greater degree of freedom and having their monthly flying hours allotment raised.

The Hawks added the colorful yellow and red tail stripes to their regular earth tone camouflage schemes to display the fact that they now obeyed orders from the Vichy government. Hawk units were moved to different bases as the need arose or as new threats were felt in French North Africa. When Charles De Gaulle's soldiers – supported by the Royal Navy – attempted to invade Senegal, Hawks of GC I/4 added a distasteful chapter to French history when they attacked and strafed their own countrymen. The Hawks were instrumental in repulsing six different landing attempts. In order to punish the British and the Free French for their transgressions, the Vichy government sent a heavy bombing attack against the British garrison on Gibraltar.

Perhaps the oddest episode in the already strange career of the French Hawks was the pitched battle with the US Navy that took place during Operation Torch – the invasion of North Africa – on 8 November 1942. Operation Torch was one of the first large-scale American military moves and one that was vitally important to the war in Europe. A rather motley invasion force had been assembled by the Americans for the attack but the invasion (including the carrier *Ranger*) went to schedule, going in favor of the Americans from the start. However, Hawks of GC I/5 and II/5 were scrambled to intercept incoming American aircraft and they did just that. The Grumman F4F Wildcats that were protecting the American dive bombers met the enemy

with considerable strength and élan. The French were also bent on extracting a high price from the invaders but the outcome was never really in doubt although the costs were high. Fifteen Hawks and eight French pilots were lost while at least seven Wildcats were destroyed in a fight that saw pilots machine-gunned while hanging from their parachutes. American pilots were full of zeal to retaliate against the Axis for Pearl Harbor and the 'turn-coat' French were treated with little respect. The end of the day's fighting had virtually finished off the Hawk in French service while opening a new front in the war against Italy and German.

HOLLAND The Netherlands originally placed an order for the Cyclone-powered H–75A7 fighter during 1939. The original order was for 35 aircraft but this number was cut down to 20 fighters after political haggling. Armed with four machine guns (two in the nose, two in the wing) these fighters had yet to arrive in Holland when the Germans poured across the border on 10 May 1940. The fighters were sent instead to the extensive Dutch holdings in the Netherlands East Indies which were in danger of imminent invasion from the Japanese who had their eyes trained on the islands' excellent natural resources. The fighters were assembled and local modifications were undertaken, including an attempt to improve the reliability of the Cyclone 9. When the war in the Pacific began, the Dutch were quickly equipping their Hawks to carry small underwing bombs for the ground attack role and the aircraft began missions against the rapidly advancing Japanese. The Dutch fighters were quickly eliminated either through accidents or by enemy fighters and Dutch Hawks had ceased to exist by the middle of February.

INDIA Since India had received a great deal of the residue from the damaged Chinese Hawk production line, including many jigs and partially completed airframe components, it was natural that India would attempt to build Hawks for its air force. Accordingly, an order was issued to Hindustan Aircraft Ltd that called for the construction of 48 H–75A fighters to be powered by Cyclone 9 radials. India had obtained a licensing agreement with Curtiss and the first Royal Indian Air Force Hawk

Hawk H75–A7s put up an heroic fight when the Japanese invaded the Netherlands East Indies. The Japanese invaded Java on 2 March 1942 and landed 85,000 troops while another large invasion fleet was just offshore. Some of the Hawks had been destroyed on the ground while others managed to oppose the overwhelming enemy forces, but it was just a short few days until most were destroyed and Java surrendered on 5 March. This patrol of Hawks was photographed from a Lockheed 212 bomber.

flew on 31 July 1942 from the Hindustan factory. Hindustan had acquired an enviable reputation for high-quality aircraft workmanship and it was not surprising that USAAF activity, which was increasing at a break-neck pace in India, would require additional maintenance, repair and rework facilities for the fleets of transport aircraft that would begin the regular shuttle service over the 'Hump'. Contracts were placed with Hindustan for such work and due to the pressure from Army work, production of the Hawk was dropped after only a further four examples had been completed.

IRAN (PERSIA) The vital oil-producing country of Iran had definite pro-Nazi ties before the start of World War Two. To prevent possible German occupation, Allied forces occupied the country on 25 August 1941. The Iranian military was primitive in the extreme but they had ordered ten H–75A9 Cyclone 9 fighters (apparently Seversky was not the only American aeronautical company who would eagerly sell warplanes to countries with questionable political leanings). The British expeditionary forces discovered the ten Hawks still in Curtiss factory packing crates – the reason for the lack of Iranian interest in assembling and flying the aircraft has been lost to time – and the aircraft on close inspection,

proved to be in good condition. The Hawks were brought up to more or less RAF standards and transferred to No 5 Squadron, which is mentioned in the notes on RAF Mohawk operation.

NORWAY When the Germans moved against Norway on 9 April 1940, the small air arm of Norway was able to field only a few fighters to attempt to stem the might of the *Luftwaffe*. Re-equipment of the air force had just begun as Norway had ordered 12 H–75A6 fighters with Twin Wasp engines and four .30 caliber machine guns. At the same time the initial order was placed, a licensing agreement was reached which called for the production of 24 more Hawks in Norway. The order was placed in the autumn of 1939 and, realizing that they had waited too long, Norway placed another frantic order for a further 12 A6s but, due to the lack of time and the speed of the Germans, the Norwegian Hawks were never to see service in that country.

While assembly of the first Hawks had begun at the factory at Kjeller, another order was placed for 36 Hawk H–75A8s that had the Cyclone 9 engine and two .50 caliber guns in the nose and four .30 caliber weapons in the wing. The Germans attacked Norway and Denmark with Operation *Weserubung* on 9

With pilots and ground crews standing at attention, these Curtiss H75–A7s are seen on display at Bandoeng, Java, Netherlands East Indies. Twenty A7s were ordered, equipped with Cyclone engines, by the Netherlands but the aircraft were all diverted to the East Indies after the German invasion of Holland. (Curtiss Wright)

Opposite top and bottom
H75–A8s being flown by Free Norwegian pilots training in Canada. Norway had ordered 36 A8s with R-1820–G205A Cyclone engines of 1,200 hp but the Germans invaded the country before deliveries could be made. Six of the aircraft were allocated to the training program in Canada while the remainder were taken on by the US Army and designated as P–36Gs.

April 1940 and an initial bombing attack on the air force factory at Kjeller demolished the first four 75A6 fighters. German forces found eight other A6s in their factory crates at Oslo harbor and these were the aircraft that were later sold to Finland.

PERU The 36 Hawk H–75A8 fighters that had been ordered by Norway were undelivered when that country fell. The aircraft were transferred to Canada where they served as trainers for the Free Norwegians who were learning to fly at Canadian bases. The aircraft were eventually purchased by the American government, overhauled, and sent to Peru as P–36Gs to reinforce that country's small air arm. Thirty aircraft were supplied (USAAF serials 42–36305 through 36322, and 42–108995 through 109006) and their civil designated Wright Cyclone engines were re-designated with the military terminology of R–1820–95. At least one of these aircraft is currently preserved in Peru.

PORTUGAL The rather impoverished country of Portugal was extremely anxious to maintain some form of neutrality to keep out the Germans during the early days of World War Two. Its military forces were basically just a token and the aerial defenses were sadly lacking. Having had fairly close relations with the British, who had supplied Gloster Gladiator biplanes during 1938, the Portuguese sought further aid via the ancient Alliance Treaty of 1373 and the British responded with a dozen Mohawk Mk IVs which they were more than happy to get rid of. The *Arma da Portugal* was probably hoping for something with a bit more performance than the Mohawk but the fighters were gladly accepted (RAF serials were AR642, AR643, AR652, AR664, AR666, AR668, AR671, AR673, AR679, AR680, AX882 and AX886). Unfortunately one of the Mohawks was destroyed immediately upon arrival and the surviving fighters were coded 480 to 490. The Mohawks served at various bases in Portugal and were transferred to the Azores in 1944 to protect those vital islands. The Mohawks proved to be faithful mounts in Portuguese service and actively participated in the defense of the Azores until 1945 when the aircraft were withdrawn and scrapped.

SOUTH AFRICA After the threat of invasion by the Germans had passed, the British were eager to get rid of the Mohawks that they had held in reserve. A willing customer was South Africa which needed more modern aircraft for its air force. An eventual total of 72 Mohawk

Mk IVs was received in South Africa. The first unit to operate the type was No 4 Squadron which equipped with Mohawks during May 1941. The Mohawks were used as operational trainers. Only one unit, No 6 Squadron, was operational with the Mohawk, for home defense duties, but they were phased out when the threat of aerial invasion passed.

THAILAND (SIAM) Twenty-five H–75N fixed gear Hawks were ordered by Thailand with deliveries starting during November 1938. Originally only fitted with the standard twin nose guns, provision was made to carry a podded .30 caliber gun under each wing panel. Some aircraft were later modified to carry the Danish 23 mm Madsen cannon under the wing. Curtiss records show only 12 construction numbers – c/n 12756 through 12767 – assigned to the Thai order. The Thai Hawks saw action, initially in the Thai invasion of French Indochina during early 1941 and some victories over French aircraft were claimed but the French denied these claims. When Japan invaded Thailand on 7 December 1941, the Hawks were again in action but, being no match for the Japanese, one-third were soon lost before the cease-fire. The Japanese tested some of the captured Thai Hawks. One H–75N is currently preserved in Bangkok.

CURTISS P-36 VARIANTS, SERIAL NUMBERS AND SPECIFICATIONS

Curtiss Variants

Model 75 Prototype for series. First flew during May 1935 carrying civil license NX17Y. Modified several times, including 75A with 900 hp XR-1670-5 and 75B with 850 hp XR-1820-39. One .50 and one .30 caliber machine gun in nose. Painted yellow and blue.

Y1P-36 Three test examples ordered during July 1936 and delivered in February 1937. Differed from Model 75 by having modified cockpit and canopy, and retractable tail wheel. Powered by 950 hp R-1830-13. Designated Model 75E. Designated P-36 after completion of testing. Delivered in natural metal finish.

P-36A Curtiss Model 75L. Similar to the Y1P-36 but with 1,050 hp R-1830-13 and three-blade constant speed propeller, and cowl flaps. Armed with one .50 and one .30 caliber machine gun in upper engine and accessory compartment. Order for 210 aircraft at $4,113,550 was largest fighter order since World War One. Delivery of P-36As started during April 1938 and, after 177 were completed, the remainder were finished as P-36Cs. USAAF s/n 38-1 and 38-85 were converted to prototype P-36Cs while 38-20 temporarily became the sole P-36B. S/n 38-10 was converted to the prototype XP-40 while 38-4 became the XP-42. P-36As were delivered in natural metal finish.

P-36B During November 1938, 38-20 was converted to P-36B standard by the installation of an 1,100 hp R-1830-25. Aircraft reverted back to to P-36A standard after testing completed. Natural metal finish.

P-36C Similar to P-36A. Equipped with 1,200 hp R-1830-17 with additional armament of two .30 caliber machine guns mounted in the wing. Other small improvements. Delivered in natural metal finish.

XP-36D P-36A 38-174 converted to carry four .30 caliber wing guns and two .50 caliber nose guns.

XP-36E P-36A 38-147 modified with eight .30 caliber wing guns and one .50 caliber nose gun.

XP-36F P-36A 38-172 equipped with two Masden 23 mm cannon mounted under the wing, but retained standard P-36A nose armament.

P-36G-CU Aircraft originally ordered for Norway but sent to Canada to train free Norwegian pilots after Norway had fallen to the Germans. Later designated RP-36G-CU and entered USAAF service. A number were later supplied to Peru.

Model 75A-1 Similar to P-36A but with four 7.5 mm guns (two in nose, two in wing). Powered by 1,050 hp R-1830-SC3-G engine. One hundred to France. Some escaped after French surrender to UK and were designated Mohawk Mk I in RAF service.

Model 75A-2 Similar to A-1 but with four wing guns and two nose guns. One hundred to France. Escaping aircraft to UK became Mohawk Mk II.

Model 75A-3 Similar to A-2 but with 1,200 hp R-1830-S1C3-G engine. France ordered 135 but only about 60 were delivered. Others diverted to French Morocco; 20 to UK as Mohawk Mk III.

Model 75A-4 Similar to 75A-2 but with a 1,200 hp GR-1820-G205A. Only 284 built out of French order for 795. Majority of order taken over by RAF as Mohawk MK IV.

Model 75A-5 Export version for China. Prototype and several sets of components supplied to China for license manufacture. Powered by Wright GR-1820-G205A and armed with six .30 caliber machine guns. Only a few were built in China before the factory was badly damaged by a Japanese bombing attack. Surviving jigs and tooling went to the Hindustan Aircraft Factory at Bangalore, India. Production began in late 1941 but only five aircraft were built before new projects were undertaken. These aircraft were taken over by RAF as Mohawk Mk IV.

Model 75A-6 Similar to Hawk 75A-2. Armament consisted of four .303 machine guns. Norway ordered 12. License-manufacturing was requested from Curtiss for building a further 24 A-6s by the Army Aircraft Factory. It quickly became apparent that these aircraft could not be manufactured in a short period of time, so a further 12 were purchased from Curtiss. However, due to the war, these 12 aircraft were not delivered to Norway but sent to France and then, after the fall of France, to England. Original group captured by Germans and eight sold to Finland.

Model 75A-7 Twenty aircraft ordered by the Dutch for the Royal Netherlands Army's Air Division, after political squabbling had reduced the original order for 36 aircraft. Powered by the GR-1820-G205A and was armed with one .50 and one .30 caliber weapon in the nose and one .30 caliber gun in each wing panel. When the German invasion began, the aircraft were sent to the Netherlands East Indies. While in the East Indies the .50 caliber gun was replaced with a .30 caliber weapon because of the shortage of ammunition.

Model 75A-8 Order placed by Norway during January 1940 for 36 A-8s powered by GR-1820-G205A Cyclones, and armed with two .50 caliber guns in the nose and four .30 caliber weapons in the wing. After the fall of Norway, the newly completed aircraft were delivered to the Norwegian training center in Canada. On 5 May 1942, the USAAF purchased 18 of the A-8s, refurbished them as P-36G-CUs and supplied them to Peru. On 29 May 1942, the USAAF purchased 12 more A-8s and supplied ten to Peru, the remaining two aircraft apparently being converted to parts.

Model 75A-9 Ten purchased by the Imperial Iranian Air Force, and delivered during the summer of 1941 but never uncrated. Taken over by the British as Mohawk Mk IVs. Powered by R-1820-G205A, and armed with six .30 caliber guns.

Model 75H Model 75B rebuilt and fitted with an 875 hp GR-1820-G3 and a fixed and spatted landing gear to simplify maintenance in primitive countries. Registered NR1276, aircraft went to China. Second prototype 75H (similarly equipped to the Y1P-36) had underwing racks. Registered NR1277, the aircraft was sold to Argentina.

Model 75M Production version of the 75H with modified landing gear fairings and four .30 caliber guns. China ordered 112.

Model 75N Similar to the 75M but purchased by Thailand, which ordered 25. They differed from the 75M by having the landing gear fairings redesigned. Two .30 caliber guns in the nose with two 23 mm Masden cannon in fairings under the wing.

Model 75O Thirty aircraft purchased. Similar to the 75N but with electric cooling gills at the rear of the cowling and a redesigned exhaust system and armed with four .30 caliber Masden machine guns. License construction begun by *Fabrica Militar* and 20 Hawks were built in Argentina.

Serial Numbers

Model 75	NX17Y
YP–36	37–68 through 37–70
P–36A	38–1 through 38–180
P–36B	38–20
P–36C	38–1, 38–85;
	38–181 through 38–210
XP–36D	38–174
XP–36E	38–147
XP–37F	38–172
P–36G–CU	42–38305 through
	42–38322; 42–108995
	through 42–109006

Specifications

Model 75B

Span	37 ft 4 in
Length	28 ft 1 in
Height	9 ft
Wing area	236 sq ft
Empty weight	4,049 lb
Loaded weight	5,075 lb
Max. speed	285 mph
Cruise speed	260 mph
Ceiling	32,500 ft
Rate of climb	2,500 fpm (initial)
Range	730 miles
Powerplant	Wright
	XR–1820–39 of 850 hp

Y1P–36

Span	37 ft 4 in
Length	28 ft 2 in
Height	9 ft
Wing area	236 sq ft
Empty weight	4,389 lb
Loaded weight	5,437 lb
Max. speed	294.5 mph
Cruise speed	256 mph
Ceiling	35,100 ft
Rate of climb	3,145 fpm
Range	752 miles
Powerplant	Pratt & Whitney
	R–1830–13 of 1,050 hp

P–36A

Span	37 ft 4 in
Length	28 ft 6 in
Height	12 ft 2 in
Wing area	236 sq ft
Empty weight	4,567 lb
Loaded weight	5,650 lb
Max. speed	300 mph
Cruise speed	270 mph
Ceiling	34,000 ft
Rate of climb	3,400 fpm
Range	825 miles
Powerplant	Pratt & Whitney
	R–1830–13 of 1,050 hp

P–36C

Span	37 ft 4 in
Length	28 ft 6 in
Height	12 ft 2 in
Wing area	236 sq ft
Empty weight	4,620 lb
Loaded weight	6,150 lb
Max. speed	311 mph
Cruise speed	270 mph
Ceiling	33,700 ft
Rate of climb	3,100 fpm
Range	820 miles
Powerplant	Pratt & Whitney
	R–1830–17 of 1,200 hp

P–36G

Span	37 ft 4 in
Length	28 ft 10 in
Height	9 ft 6 in
Wing area	236 sq ft
Empty weight	4,541 lb
Loaded weight	5,750 lb
Max. speed	323 mph
Cruise speed	262 mph
Ceiling	33,600 ft
Rate of climb	n/a
Range	1,003 miles
Powerplant	Wright
	R–1829–95 of 1,200 hp

Model 75R

Span	37 ft 4 in
Length	28 ft 6 in
Height	12 ft 2 in
Wing area	236 sq ft
Empty weight	5,074 lb
Loaded weight	6,163 lb
Max. speed	330 mph
Cruise speed	302 mph
Ceiling	n/a
Rate of climb	3,000 fpm
Range	600 miles
Powerplant	Pratt & Whitney
	R–1830–SC2–G

Model 75

Span	37 ft 4 in
Length	28 ft 7 in
Height	9 ft 4 in
Wing area	236 sq ft
Empty weight	3,975 lb
Loaded weight	6,418 lb
Max. speed	280 mph
Cruise speed	240 mph
Ceiling	31,800 ft
Rate of climb	2,340 fpm
Range	547 miles
Powerplant	Wright
	GR–1820–G3 of 840 hp

Model 75A–1

Span	37 ft 4 in
Length	28 ft 7 in
Height	9 ft 4 in
Wing area	236 sq ft
Empty weight	4,483 lb
Loaded weight	5,692 lb
Max. speed	303 mph
Cruise speed	260 mph
Ceiling	32,800 ft
Rate of climb	2,340 fpm
Range	677 miles
Powerplant	Wright
	R–1820–G105 of 900 hp

Curtiss XP-37
Variation On A Theme

This design represented a search for a practical formula for high-speed fighters

During the 1930s the odd pastime of air racing was at a fever pitch in America. While air racing was also popular in Europe, it seemed that the American designs were creations of brute horsepower while the British and Continental racers tended towards highly developed small powerplants and extremely refined airframes. In the States the 'barnyard' designers were slapping together machines that were showing their heels to the best pursuits owned by the Army. Such actions were, of course,

embarrassing to the Service who prided itself on the performance of its elite pursuit squadrons. Aircraft such as Wedell-Williams, Lairds, Gee Bees, and a whole crop of other unusual racers were making history by constantly raising the top speed of aircraft. Records did not last more than a couple of months in this mad quest for the goddess of speed. The path towards this goal was paved by broken aircraft and broken pilots but they usually died as heroes, adulated by a public that the popular press claimed was 'air-minded'. Whether this simplistic phrase was true or whether the masses enjoyed the sport of aircraft rushing

The Curtiss XP–37 certainly looked different when it was rolled out of the Curtiss plant during April 1937. The cockpit was placed to the rear of the fuselage because of the space taken up by the Allison engine, three radiators, turbosupercharger, and fuel cell. Visibility was extremely poor and the engine and turbo unit gave many problems. No armament was ever fitted to the prototype and it appears that the YP–37s were to be fitted with two .30 caliber guns in the nose but were never so equipped. Two lessons were learned from the P–37: not to put the cockpit in the rear fuselage, and to position the turbosupercharger in the bottom of the fuselage where it would not interfere with the location of the pilot and other equipment. The XP–37 was retired from flying after only 150 hours. (USAF)

around a pylon course at unheard of speeds with the chance of a gruesome accident always in the cards is a topic that is open to considerable speculation. The point is that these civilian pilots were taking the glory away from the military and the Army did not like that one bit.

Most of the crop of really fast racers were small machines powered by very large radial engines: Placement of engine and fuel were important and the pilot wound up where there was room. The best example of this spacing problem was the barrel-like Gee Bee racer which had an immense radial tied on to the smallest airframe possible. The only room for the pilot was in the extreme rear fuselage where his head was literally touching the vertical fin. The rest of the aircraft was occupied by fuel and engine. Now this was fine (perhaps fine is not the right word since only one pilot that raced a Gee Bee survived and that pilot was none other than Jimmy Doolittle whose skills can safely be classified as above

average) for a racer whose only goal was to break and make records but the Army cast a glance at these glamorous machines and was able to see the future; no longer would the biplane fighter dominate the air, for the monoplanes had too much to offer. The sleek racers were also having their effect on established airframe manufacturers who were quickly, and usually without any credit or compensation, adopting the best features of the racers to aircraft which they were trying to pedal to the military.

Curtiss had lost an important contract to Seversky for building the first modern fighter for the Army. However, all was not lost for the Hawk 75 series as the Army eventually bought the aircraft as the P-36 and Curtiss would go on to reap the benefits of a number of foreign contracts. Curtiss designers decided that something could be done to the basic Hawk 75 airframe to jazz up the design and give the appeal of the civilian racers. Curtiss submitted a quickly prepared outline for the new aircraft to the Army who immediately snapped at the proposal and assigned the designation XP-37 to the new aircraft. On paper the plane looked most impressive and certainly would have looked right painted up in gaudy civilian colors and parked on the ramp at the world-famous Cleveland National Air Races.

Assigned the company designation Hawk 75-I (the I standing for inline engine) the aircraft was to be basically a P-36 airframe with drastic modifications. Power was to come from a turbocharged Allison V-1710-11 that was capable of 1,150 hp. The contract was signed on 1 April 1937 (researching aviation history leads to many fascinating gems of information – one being the number of aircraft that either flew for the first time or had contracts signed on April Fools Day) and the Army was most anxious to test the new plane with its projected top speed of at least 340 mph.

Room for the inline engine, GE turbocharger and fuel cells meant that the pilot would have to be assigned to the rear confines of the fuselage. As mentioned, this was probably all right for a racer with just one function but for a military combat aircraft the choice was less than ideal.

The exhaust was tunnelled back into the fuselage and through the turbocharger while three radiators were supplied with air from scoops in the cowling. The Army, hoping great things from the prototype, also placed an order for 13 YP-37 service test aircraft which would be equipped with V-1710-21 engines and

improved GE B-2 turbochargers, a number of minor airframe changes, and a 25-in extension to the rear fuselage behind the cockpit. The YP-37 was quickly put together, using the airframe of the Model 75 prototype, and was in the air by the end of April.

Problems immediately cropped up and the prototype was plagued with engine and turbo problems while the test pilot complained of the non-existent visibility from the cockpit. The aircraft was transferred to the Army in June and the same problems kept appearing while the top speed was well below the quoted figure. The aircraft was eventually sent to a mechanic's training school after only 150 hours flying time.

The YP-37s did not perform any better and most were rarely flown, the highest time example had only just over 200 flying hours. The aircraft were quickly scrapped or sent to mechanic's training schools where they were taken apart and put back together countless times by students who were having the fine art of taking care of aircraft beaten into their heads. One YP-37 was transferred to the National Advisory Committee for Aeronautics (reason unknown) and it survived until 1946 when it was scrapped.

The idea presented by the P-37 series was certainly not unworkable for Curtiss had another aircraft under development that would perform much better and would create aeronautical history and that aircraft was the P-40.

CURTISS YP-37 SERIAL NUMBERS AND SPECIFICATIONS

Serial Numbers

XP-37	37-375
YP-37	38-472 through 38-484

Specifications

YP-37

Span	35 ft 3.5 in
Length	32 ft 11.5 in
Height	11 ft 1 in
Wing area	236 sq ft
Empty weight	5,592 lb
Loaded weight	6,700 lb
Max. speed	325 mph
Cruise speed	293 mph
Ceiling	34,000 ft
Rate of climb	3,000 fpm
Range	n/a
Powerplant	One Allison V-1710-21 of 1,150 hp

Lockheed P-38 Lightning — The Fork-Tailed Devil

Although its development took longer than originally planned, the Lightning became one of the greatest fighters of World War Two.

As Lt Benjamin Kelsey surveyed the crumpled wreckage of the Lockheed XP–38 interceptor, he probably reflected on the radical new aircraft's future with the Army Air Corps as well as his own career. The circumstance of a lieutenant wrecking a brand new fighter was not a happy one – even though Kelsey had held that lowly rank for nearly ten years! This was not because of any incompetence on Kelsey's

part, but rather the opposite, since he was one of the best test pilots in the Army. Kelsey's lack of promotion was due entirely to the slow pace with which the Army Air Corps of the 1930s progressed. There were few aircraft and few positions to fly them, so promotions were more than agonizingly slow – they were almost non-existent, even if individual pilots were rated more than outstanding. That fact did not help Kelsey on 11 February 1939, for the new and glistening aircraft that would have pushed the Army Air Corps into the forefront of military aviation was nothing more than scrap.

During the 1930s, the Army Air Corps was stocked with a curious collection of 'combat' aircraft. A majority were 'O-birds', lightly armed observation craft that performed little in the way of function besides providing a platform for pilots to fly. The pursuits of the day were little more than glorified sport planes, built for a war that would never happen, while strategic bombing rested on the broad fabric wings of aircraft whose design would not have been out of place during the Great War.

The Army was not completely deaf to the appeals by far-sighted officers for new, dy-

...amic aircraft which would inject needed life into the Air Corps and provide America with a realistic defense capability, but the government, still struggling with the disasterous effects of the Great Depression, was almost completely reluctant to supply the Army with money for anything as frivolous as aircraft.

From 1935 to 1937, the growing menace of a Hitler-dominated Germany began to register on even the most isolationist of American politicians and some money began to flow from the depleted government coffers to the military for limited research and development on advanced aircraft projects.

The fact that money was now available meant that the few Army officers who were concerned with aircraft development could now start voicing ideas as to the direction of fighter design. Observations in Europe had led to the idea that American aircraft development was much too conservative and that funds should be allocated to companies which had

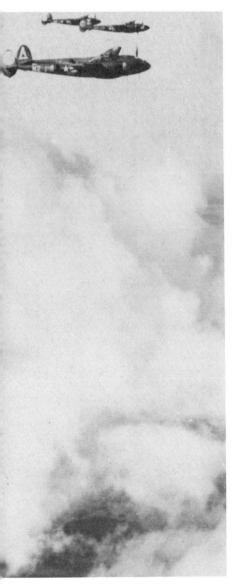

Well-worn Olive Drab and Neutral Gray P–38J of the 383rd Fighter Squadron, 364th Fighter Group, seen on patrol over Britain. The large size of the fighter is evident in this view. The pilot sat high in the cockpit, visibility being generally good. N2 was the squadron coding while K was the individual letter assigned to the aircraft, repeated on the insides of the vertical fins and on each boom. The squadron's identifying symbol was a large white circle painted on the vertical tails and unfortunately obliterating the serial number. (USAF)

designers who could creatively form new concepts and put them into production. One of the developmental projects envisioned was a twin engine interceptor that would be capable of carrying a heavy armament to high altitudes which would be achieved via new turbosuperchargers that were also being developed. The new design would have long range and be able to climb quickly in order to intercept high-flying bombers. Also, a tricycle undercarriage was specified so that ground handling could be simplified. The requirement was given the title of 'Specification X–608' and was circulated among interested aircraft manufacturers, which meant virtually all aircraft builders, since the industry was in a depressed economic condition and military contracts were something to fight over.

One of the companies that was deeply interested in the 1937 specification was Lockheed Aircraft Corporation. The company, located in Burbank, California, had gone through many ups and downs over the past decade as the poor world-wide economy decimated the aviation manufacturing community. Lockheed had developed a reputation for designing and building high-performance aircraft that offered advanced aerodynamics and an ability to grab records and headlines. Pilots of the caliber of Amelia Erhart, Wiley Post and Howard Hughes had flown Lockheed aircraft such as the Vega and Lodestar to garner new speed and distance records. Nevertheless, profits were small and, during a few years, the company quite often went into the red. The Models 10, 12 and 18 airliners were gaining acceptance among the growing air transport system, but lucrative government contracts were needed to assure stability and growth.

Lockheed responded promptly to Specification X–608, which required an aircraft that could climb to 20,000 ft in six minutes and offer a top speed of 360 mph at altitude by assigning its best engineers to come up with a 'paper aircraft' that would satisfy the specification. One of Lockheed's brightest lights in the engineering department was an unassuming young man named Clarence Johnson. Nicknamed 'Kelly', Johnson had been hired as a graduate from the University of Michigan in 1933, after a senior designer had been impressed by a report (a critical one) that Kelly

had written on a Lockheed transport. Johnson would go on to have what reasonably could be described as one of the most impressive careers in American aviation, designing such diverse aircraft as the U–2, F–104 and the always amazing SR–71 'Blackbird'. However, in 1937 Kelly was still proving his stuff and looking forward to bringing some of his radical aeronautical concepts to fruition.

Johnson looked at X–608 with a critical eye and realized that the biggest handicap would come from the lack of a suitable powerplant. Working with experienced Lockheed engineer Hal Hibbard, Kelly immediately began making sketches of proposed aircraft. The interesting common denominator of the drawings was that all the designs had two engines. One engine would simply not provide the performance for the top speed or the rate of climb required by the Army. Kelly was always one to keep aircraft designs as sleek as possible and for a powerplant he chose the V–12 Allison V–1710 since it could develop at least 1,000 horsepower and its low frontal area offered better streamlining. It was also the only high horsepower American inline engine in series production.

Initial sketches showed a wide variety of possible configurations – combined pusher and puller engines, all pushers or all pullers with engines on the wing or buried in the fuselage. Lockheed had been considering a high-performance military aircraft for the past year to be produced as a private venture in hopes of capturing Army orders so useful contacts had already been made with influential Army officers and they were given advanced 'previews' of the new Lockheed designs in order that the company could benefit from their criticism.

The new interceptor was assigned the designation Model 22 by the factory. Attention rapidly settled on one of the paper aircraft that had elegant twin booms with a fuselage pod mounted on the wing between the booms. Power was to come from twin Allison engines (V–1710–C series) that could produce a maximum of 1,150 hp each, and high-altitude performance would come from twin General Electric turbochargers located in the booms and connected to the engines through a complex system of tubing. Tricycle landing gear, the nose gear in the fuselage pod and the main gear in the spacious booms, was provided to help ground handling. Another radical design feature was the armament system. Concentrated in the nose, it comprised a large cannon with a battery of machine guns, giving the interceptor unprecedented fire power. The armament was not immediately finalized since a variety of cannon was under consideration, but, by putting all the armament in the nose, a

The highly polished XP–38 epitomized the Art Deco elegance of the late 1930s – an era when streamlining was applied to even the most mundane of household items. March Field, whose barren terrain can be seen in the background, was selected as the test base for the XP–38 mainly because the Army Air Corps field was fairly close to Burbank and away from prying eyes. Although the entire production run of P–38s looked similar, the XP–38 was almost completely different than the production aircraft. By comparing with other Lightnings illustrated in this chapter, several important differences are evident including the hand-made extremely tight cowlings around the Allisons and the small radiator openings. A small retractable airscoop can be seen immediately below the left cowling. The photograph was taken shortly before the start of Ben Kelsey's ill-fated cross-country speed dash. (Lockheed)

concentrated stream of lead and high explosive could be accurately aimed at an enemy with devastating results.

The Army officer in charge of overseeing the development of the new interceptor was none other than Lt Benjamin Kelsey who, from his Wright Field office, carefully went over proposals entered by Lockheed and other manufacturing concerns. Kelsey was impressed by the sheer power represented by the Model 22 and he recommended, after Lockheed president Robert Gross delivered the Model 22 drawings to Kelsey during February 1937, that the Army issue a prototype contract to the Burbank firm.

After consideration by other Army officials, the government issued Air Corps Contract Number 9974 to Lockheed on 23 June 1937 for the construction of one XP–38 that was to carry the Army serial 37–457. Lockheed was extremely pleased with this bit of work

although they realized that the new XP–38 was radical and one aircraft might not lead to production if the aircraft did not perform correctly. Johnson, ever the optimist, predicted that the XP–38 would fly at 400 mph, some 40 mph faster than the speed that the Army had calculated. The magic figure of 400 mph really appealed to the Army since a very high top speed would help impress Congress when it came to ordering more aircraft.

Lockheed began construction of the XP–38 in a partitioned portion of one of their Burbank hangars. Model 22 was classified as a secret project so access to the area was limited but most employees certainly knew what was going on, a far cry from the company's now famous 'Skunk Works' (started by none other than Kelly Johnson), a branch of Lockheed created to develop extremely classified projects. As with most aircraft of the period, even for those as advanced as the XP–38, construction

progressed rapidly. Actual metal cutting and work began in July 1938 and the fighter was physically complete by the end of the year.

For a fighter, the XP–38 was certainly like nothing else that had flown in America. First of all, it was just plain *huge*. Weighing in at a bit over 15,000 lb and with a wing span of 52 ft, the XP–38 looked more like a stylized bomber than an interceptor. Lockheed had come up with a beautifully sleek installation for the twin Allisons and the cowlings were so snug that they would have looked more at home on the front of a custom-built European racing machine. Every bit of the latest aeronautical technology had been employed in the airframe. The flush riveting was first-rate, the polished metal barely marred by any sort of bump or protrusion that could harm streamlining. Lockheed workers took special care and pride in what they built and, with the XP–38, this dedication really showed.

Large Fowler flaps, employed by Lockheed with great success on their transport aircraft (business for which had picked up considerably – especially since the British were placing large orders for a modified transport that was to gain fame as the Hudson bomber) were added to both of the XP–38's wing sections in order to improve low-speed handling characteristics, while the installation of the large Allison gave the engineers some headaches since a failure of one engine while the aircraft was at low speed could cause lots of trouble. The right engine was modified to turn opposite from the left unit, thus the propeller of the right engine would turn in a clockwise direction to counter the torque forces of the left propeller. The pilot, on takeoff and landing, would not have to put up with the tremendous pulling force created by the torque of two engines turning in the same direction.

The long slim booms that took the place of a

Magnificent aerial photograph of a YP–38 cruising over Pasadena, California. The YPs were basically test machines and in no way represented combat ready aircraft. Armament for the YP was to include a 37 mm cannon, two .50 caliber machine guns and two .30 caliber weapons but these were never fitted. The good visibility from the P–38 cockpit is evident as is the large 'steering wheel' which was unusual since most fighters employed a stick-type control column. The windshield was a curved piece of plexiglass and no armor protection was fitted. Test pilot Milo Burcham is in the cockpit. (Lockheed/X2081)

Tension from the rapidly approaching war was clearly evident when this camouflaged P–38D arrived at the Naval Air Station at Oakland, California, on 16 November 1941. The aircraft had been carrying the pre-war identifier 99–51P on the vertical fins but this had been quickly sanded off in the favor of security. The identifier meant that the aircraft was assigned to the 51st Pursuit Group, 16th Pursuit Squadron, out of March Field. This P–38D was a long way from combat fighting since its guns had not been installed, some form of gun port covering being attached in their place. (W. T. Larkins)

normal fuselage, housed General Electric Type F turbosuperchargers and the main landing gear, and supported the graceful twin tail unit. The pod for the pilot was mounted on the very substantial wing center section between the two engines. The nose landing gear was housed in the forward portion of the pod below the armament. The design crew liked the idea of centering the heavy armament for several reasons: ease of maintenance; a more concentrated cone of firepower could be achieved by a gathered battery of weapons compared to guns spread out over a wing; and the center of gravity could be more accurately maintained. The XP–38's armament had been standardized on one 23 mm Madsen cannon (although a 22.8 mm T1 cannon was considered as a replacement in case the Madsen was not available in sufficient quantity) and four Browning .50 caliber M2 air-cooled machine guns with 200 rounds per gun. However, the XP–38 prototype was never fitted with the proposed armament.

Unlike other fighters either in production or under development, the XP–38 was designed from the outset to have metal-covered control surfaces rather than the more traditional fabric-covered units. Since the new aircraft would be operating at high altitudes and at high speeds, the metal covered surfaces would be more efficient when recovering from high speed dives as well as not being easily prone to damage. The controls were manually operated and were dynamically balanced, but this would be changed much later in the P–38 production line.

Lockheed, Allison and General Electric worked closely together as the prototype was built to insure that the operation of the engines at high altitude would be as efficient as possible. A complex network of tubing connected each engine to its individual turbosupercharger in the tail boom. The turbine wheel was located in a semi-flush housing atop each boom over the trailing edge of the wing. As the aircraft gained altitude, the turbosupercharger would begin to function, taking exhaust gases from the engine to the turbine by means of the tubing system. The turbine would be spinning at tens of thousands of rpm, compressing the exhaust gases and passing them through an intercooler in the leading edge of the wing and then channeling the compressed and cooled gas back down the throat of the engine to maintain manifold pressure and offer greatly improved performance at altitude. Such a complex system has to have problems and the P–38 series would be bothered with developmental bugs in the turbosupercharger system but a more pressing problem was that of adequately cooling the tightly-cowled Allisons.

Hibbard and Johnson knew that the engines would have to be cowled as sleekly as possible to obtain maximum streamlining but the best location for the radiators and oil coolers posed a problem. Openings would have to be as large as possible so that cooling air could do its jobs but, at the same time, the openings would have to be as small as possible so that performance would not be degraded by the additional drag. The XP–38 presented particular difficulties since it had two of everything. The radiators were located in the middle of the boom and were housed in large blisters that had their opening in the front and a controlled shutter at the rear. The oil coolers were immediately behind the spinners. Once again, the cooling fluid (Prestone) had to be pumped from the radiator to the engine via tubing and a series of pumps but this function did not provide completely adequate cooling for the Allisons and overheating was a major problem during much of the P–38's operational career.

When basically completed, the XP–38 was trucked from Burbank to the Army's March Field in Riverside. The lengthy journey was accomplished with a great deal of secrecy and the XP–38 was carefully wrapped in canvas to prevent prying eyes from getting a close view of the new aircraft. March, an Army bomber base, offered long runways and, in those days, it was remote from major population centers. After the aircraft arrived, several days were spent reassembling the fighter and then several more were required to service it and make sure that the engines and systems were functioning correctly. Lt Kelsey carefully supervised the assembly of the fighter and made sure that he learned how the aircraft functioned so that, hopefully, nothing would come as a surprise during the first flight.

The first step in finding out whether a new aircraft is ready for flight is a taxi test. During these tests, the aircraft is trundled down the runway at various speeds and the pilot and crew hope that any possible flaw will be discovered at this time. Kelsey quickly found that the XP–38 had a number of disturbing problems, one of which almost resulted in the loss of the prototype even before it had flown. As the speed of the taxi tests increased it became apparent that the XP–38 did not have sufficient braking power. One high speed taxi test resulted in the brakes becoming extremely hot and losing all function. Kelsey was sitting atop an out of control 15,000 lb monster that was rapidly eating up the remaining portion of March's runway. The XP–38 shot off the end of the paved area and bounced through the grass and dirt, hit a ditch and stopped. By the time that Kelsey had unstrapped and clambered from the cockpit, Lockheed engineers had already arrived in speeding cars. The frightened team inspected their creation, running hands over the sleek skin to feel for any deformation of structure. After a quick walk around they were surprised and delighted to find no damage. Now, something had to be done about those brakes.

March Field was home to a number of different types of Army bombers so, after the XP–38 was moved to one of the hangars, Lockheed engineers did some quick scavenging through the Army's spares bin and found some items that they could put to use. Using a cylinder from a Northrop dive bomber and an extra small tank to contain additional hydraulic fluid, the engineers and mechanics attached the pump and tank inside the XP–38 so that the pilot, when the brakes began to fail, could pump additional fluid into the brake reservoir thus providing increased braking pressure and cooling. This was an emergency lash-up, Kelsey and Lockheed both realizing that the brakes would be good for only one or two landings. Kelsey decided that the best way of getting the XP–38 safely back to its parking spot would be to bring the big fighter in over the fence at the slowest possible speed – right on the edge of the stall – so that the fighter could use the long runway to stop with absolutely minimal braking. Kelsey and the Army, both entering a new phase of high performance aerodynamics, learned that dragging an aircraft in over the runway threshold at a very low speed was both unwise and unsafe.

Work and maintenance was finally completed on 27 January 1939 and on a clear California morning, the XP–38 was pulled from its hangar and a series of final checks began. The fighter looked truly beautiful in its polished natural aluminium finish, the only markings being the colorful pre-war Army red, white and blue rudder stripes and the blue cocarde, white star and red center painted on the outer wing panels. Even the three-bladed Curtiss propellers had been carefully polished. The attention to detail on the XP–38 was very evident, the hand-made cowlings were wrapped as tightly as possible around the Allisons while every item that stuck into the slipstream had been made as small as possible and this included the air scoops for the radiators.

Kelsey, dressed in the standard Army garb of the period, boarded the fighter, went through a brief engine check to keep temperatures in the green and began to taxi towards the runway, using the rudders for directional control and staying off the brakes as much as possible. Slowly but positively advancing the large throttles with his left hand while feeling the speed build up through the big control column, Kelsey made the decision to go after rolling a couple of hundred feet. Speed quickly built up. A tug on the control column lifted the nose wheel into the air and the XP–38 lifted from the runway, the roar of its twin Allisons turned

An interesting comparison that illustrates the relative size of the Lightning next to a Supermarine Spitfire Mk V W3119. The Lightning could usually be spotted at some distance by enemy pilots who often took the opportunity to give the fighter a wide berth. The Spitfire was probably in Burbank to do comparison testing with the American fighters that were being produced in the Southern California area. (Lockheed/Y6787)

into a muted rumble as the exhaust gases passed through the turbosuperchargers. However, it was not to be a smooth flight and only Kelsey's skill would save the new fighter from destruction. Just after the main wheels lifted from the March Field concrete a dreadful flutter set in, causing the instrument panel to disappear in a violent blur. Fighting to maintain control with the vibrating wheel that was trying to shake itself out of his hands, a quick glance out of the cockpit nearly caused Kelsey's heart to stop – the wingtips were shaking so violently that they were travelling three feet up and down!

Kelsey grabbed the flap handle and pulled the flaps up – the Fowler flaps had been half down, a procedure for take-off that had been recommended by Lockheed engineers. As the flaps came up into the wing, the intense flutter stopped – only Kelsey was still shaking.

Reducing speed and keeping the nose high, Kelsey flew the XP–38 near March Field for 34 minutes – making the gentlest of maneuvers and trying to figure out what caused the fighter to nearly shake itself to pieces. During the intense flutter, Kelsey had noticed a portion of flap shaking particularly violently. The fact that the flutter had disappeared when the flaps were retracted led the Army pilot to attempt a landing with the flaps in the full up position. Since the flaps had to stay up, Kelsey was forced to keep the fighter's nose at about an eighteen degree up angle during the approach, and the fins of the twin rudders contacted the runway before the main wheels.

Once back on the ground, the XP–38 wa closely examined and the cause of the flutte was immediately discovered. Three of four so aluminium control rods for the flaps ha broken due to the intense flutter which in tur had come about from lack of gap sealing an poor flap installation. This matter was quickl rectified by adding steel control rods, cuttin away some parts of the wing skin and provid ing adequate gap sealing for the flaps. Damag to the fins was also repaired. Still, the fla arrangement was far from ideal, but Kell Johnson modified the flaps sufficiently on th YP–38 to rid the aircraft of the problem.

It was urgent that the testing progran continued as quickly as possible, so by 1(February the XP–38 had completed five ad ditional flights, accruing nearly five hours o flying time. With the flutter gone, Kelsey foune that the XP–38 was a dynamic aircraft whicl handled really well for all its size. Develop mental problems occurred with the engine and turbosuperchargers but this was expecte(and both Lockheed and the Army felt like the) had a winner on their hands.

Official Army testing of new aircraft wa: carried out at historic Wright Field near Day ton, Ohio, so the XP–38 would have to be transported to that location. Lockheed felt tha too much time would be involved by taking the prototype apart and shipping it by rail. Kelsey then decided the easiest way to get it to Daytor would be by air. To gain some publicity at the same time, the Army decided that Kelsey should attempt to set a speed record between

os Angeles and Dayton. A stop at Amarillo, exas, was planned.

Fully fueled, the XP–38 departed March ield on 11 February and Kelsey was going to ly on its cruise performance and not push the ngines or the airframe in order to set a record. uickly into the flight profile, Kelsey realized at the XP–38 was really moving. He was at marillo in just two hours and 48 minutes. apidly refueling, it was on to Dayton in two ours and 45 minutes. Chief of the Army Air orps, General Hap Arnold, was on hand to reet Lt Kelsey and discuss the flight. General rnold had been under pressure to get the rmy Air Corps in the news with positive ems. The European air forces were setting ecords constantly and the Army needed a orale boost that would also help in obtaining ontracts for new aircraft. The cross-country peed record was, at that time, held by Howard ughes. Since a cross-country speed dash was ot considered from the start of the XP–38 light, the time spent on the ground at Amarillo neant that Hughes' overall record could not e beaten but his total hours in the air record ould be taken if the Army acted rapidly. After brief discussion, Arnold said 'Take it' and the leek silver fighter was on its way to Mitchel ield Long Island, New York, as soon as fuel nd oil supplies could be replenished. The visdom of sending such a new and basically ntested prototype would probably be questoned by today's strict aeronautical testing tandards but procedures were much more lax n 1939.

Averaging 360 mph, a tired Kelsey began his descent into Mitchel Field when the carburetors began, apparently, to pick up ice. Carb ice comes about in certain weather conditions when, with the engines at reduced idle, ice begins to form in the throat of the carburetor and, if the ice builds up enough, the fuel supply to the engine can be choked off. Most aircraft are equipped with carburetor heaters, a system that supplies heat to the carbs when the engines are at low power, virtually eliminating the chance of ice forming. The P–38 had such a system. Kelsey had the carb heat turned on during his descent but, unknown to him, the deadly ice had started to form in the carb throats. Kelsey carefully brought the flaps down, reduced power even further and raised the nose in order to bring the XP–38 in as slow as possible since the braking system was still less than adequate.

As he approached the runway's threshold, Kelsey saw that he was a bit low so he eased the throttles forward and was faced with the shocking realization that there was no power. The forward movement of the throttles produced absolutely no response from the engines and the XP–38 slammed into the ground short of the runway's threshold, destroying the gleaming prototype. Kelsey escaped with minor scrapes.

Lockheed and the Army were now faced with the problem of having an interesting concept but no hardware to back up the program. The Army reconsidered the Lockheed aircraft and, on 27 April 1939, instigated a contract with Lockheed for thirteen service test YP–38 aircraft. Hap Arnold had been one of the supporters of the program and he campaigned with the government for the new aircraft. The fact that the contract was issued so quickly really was due to how persuasive Arnold's argument was. The XP–38 had never really established any performance or combat specifications that the Army could study and consider, and they were basically taking the word of one man, relying on his uncanny judgement that Lockheed could produce what the Army needed.

Contract 12523 spelled out the terms for the production of the YPs but the YP was to be a much different aircraft than the XP and problems were to develop. Lockheed gave the YP a new company designation, Model 122, and the engineering team went to work on refining and developing the basic design which would need extended development to make into a combat ready fighter.

Improved Allisons were used in the YPs.

Pre-war long-distance pilot Jimmie Mattern shows how the Lightning handles with one engine out to a young Army pilot uncomfortably crammed behind Mattern in the space previously occupied by the bulky radios. The Lightning could be quite a handful on one engine, especially if the engine was lost during landing or takeoff. Many fatal accidents resulted when the stricken P–38 began a roll that could not be corrected before slamming into the ground. Mattern attempted to illustrate that the Lightning was not a killer on one engine but he advised that a critical engine loss during landing or takeoff was best handled by immediately pulling power off the remaining engine and crash-landing straight ahead. Serial number 42–67079 is a P–38H–5–LO. (Lockheed)

These were the new F series powerplants, – V–1710–27 (F2R) and V–1710–29 (F2L) engines, which had both propellers turning outboard in an effort to reduce airflow turbulence over the tail surfaces. The fact that both propellers were turning outboard meant that the effect of torque, if both engines were operating correctly, was counteracted as in the earlier XP configuration. British contracts for Hudsons had brought new prosperity to Lockheed and the company management had enough sense to see that aviation's dark age was at an end and massive orders for military aircraft were in the very near future. The company made plans to expand rapidly its Burbank facilities and work force.

As design work continued on the YPs, a decision was made to change the cannon armament to the Colt Browning 37 mm weapon with fifteen rounds. The machine guns were changed to two .50 calibers with 200 rpg and two .30 caliber weapons with 500 rpg. Since the XP–38 had been virtually handbuilt from engineering drawings, the YPs had to be designed with large scale production in mind. Other detail changes included modifications to the turbosupercharging system,

radiators and cockpit, and the addition of mass balances on the horizontal stabilizer. Fillets between the fuselage pod and the wing center section were also eventually added. The cowlings were gradually expanded to allow for better cooling and the radiator wells were also enlarged. The Army was concerned about overall weight and specified that the YPs weigh 1,500 lb less than the XP, imposing further design problems since weight tends to rise as aircraft become closer to being produced to military standards.

The new aircraft did not go without notice in Europe. French and British Purchasing Commissions were soon at Burbank to be briefed on the P–38 and to visit the new production line and view the technical staff at work. Both commissions liked what they saw and orders, huge for the time, were placed. The French wanted 417 to be designated Model 322–F, while the British opted for 250 Model 322–B during May 1940. The Army was not far behind the two Europeans, and an order for 66 Model 222 fighters, to be designated P–38, was entered in July.

As engineers struggled to make an aircraft that could be mass-produced, the production

*S*ergeant pilots relax on the desert sand of Muroc Air Base (now the site of Edwards AFB) as they watch four of their peers return from a training flight on 12 March 1942. Aircraft are P–38Fs of the 95th Fighter Squadron. (Lockheed)

P–38Fs of the 95th Fighter Squadron are seen on a patrol along the Southern California coast. Stationed at Mines Field, the 95th would go on to compile a distinguished combat record. It is interesting to note that the 95th was originally composed of enlisted pilots although many of the pilots would rise to high rank as the war progressed. This formation photo was taken from a Lockheed Hudson bomber. (Lockheed)

For all its size and bulk, the P–38 was an exceptionally clean aircraft – especially when viewed from head-on. Carrying twin drop tanks this factory-fresh P–38 is seen on a test flight from Burbank but the meaning of the rather unusual nose marking, an 'M' and an arrow, is unknown. Of interest are the polished alumimum 'mirrors' attached to the inside of each nacelle, one of which can be seen on the right nacelle. These were added to enable the pilot to watch the main gear, letting him make sure they were either up or down since the gear was not visible from the cockpit. (Lockheed)

line for the thirteen YPs got underway as frantic building at the Burbank airport rapidly began to expand Lockheed's facilities. Though XP–38 construction had proceeded at very fast speed, the YPs were dragging their feet as change after change had to be done to the technical drawings as well as to the partially completed airframes. During this critical period in history, time was something that was just not available in surplus quantities. France fell to the German *Blitzkreig* shortly after negotiations for the Model 322–F had been completed and suddenly Britain was left alone, looking across a small channel of water at a hostile Europe and licking its wounds from the pounding that the British Expeditionary Force

had taken at Dunkirk. Aircraft were being built by the hundreds and pilots were being trained as fast as possible, but the Royal Air Force was not in an ideal position to meet the *Luftwaffe* in aerial combat.

The Army Air Corps watched the unfolding events in Europe with horror and attempted to spur Lockheed and the production of the new fighter. The first YP did not fly until 16 September 1940 when test pilot Marshall Handle took the fighter up from Burbank for a short proving flight. Although the YP looked a great deal like the XP, the YP was basically a new aircraft and the Army knew that testing would have to be intensive to prove the new design ready for military service. However, the flow of YPs from the factory was not especially fast but the Army wanted more and increased its order to 673 machines. The thirteenth YP was not delivered until May 1941 but flying hours were being built up as quickly as possible by Lockheed's test pilots and new problems soon developed.

The weight of the YP–38 came in at 11,171 lb empty and 13,500 with a normal load so the design team had been able to knock

the weight down a bit but not as much as the Army desired. Weight was not to be the main problem once the flight test program for the YPs had started, rather a new and frightening aerodynamic force called compressibility came into focus. Defined, compressibility means that, as an aircraft travels faster through the atmosphere, air molecules begin to compress around certain points of the airframe. If the compression occurs around vital control surfaces, then the flying quality of the aircraft can drastically be affected and this is exactly what happened to the YPs.

Lockheed test pilots such as Jimmy Mattern (holder of the impressive 1930's long-distance flight records in a Lockheed Vega) had been test hopping the YPs and then turning them over to the Army for extensive test flying. One of the Army's favorite test maneuvers of the period was called, by a popular name, the power dive. The test pilot would take the aircraft up to altitude and then push the nose down and get going as fast as possible to see how it would handle and how it would recover. It was not uncommon for prototype aircraft *not* to recover or to break up from the

great pressures exerted in pulling up from a power dive, so the test pilots were more than earning their modest salaries.

During one of these testing flights, Major Signa Gilkie had taken a YP up to altitude and then nosed the aircraft into a screaming power dive with the throttles of the Allisons pushed all the way forward. The sleek YP picked up speed like a rocket and the altimeter unwound like an elevator with its cables cut. The pilot felt the control column becoming nose heavy as the air speed passed 500 mph and Gilkie began to pull back on the column to ease out of the dive. He quickly discovered that the column would not move, no matter what strength he exerted, and that the nose was tucking under even further causing the YP to head straight down at an ever increasing speed. Jumping out and relying on a parachute was a distinct option but the pilot realized that the chance of surviving such a high speed jump was not good and the fact that the large tail surfaces were just waiting to squash the unwary pilot who did not carefully exit the cockpit.

Trying to move the control column back and forth did no good since the column reacted like

it had been set in cement. Desperate to do something which would stop the dive, Gilkie grabbed the elevator trim mechanism and added nose-up trim. The trim tab, located on the horizontal stabilizer, is usually utilized for making small adjustments during flight to trim the aircraft and reduce pressure on the control column. It was a combination of using the trim and the fact that the YP was rapidly entering the thicker air of the lower atmosphere that caused the nose to begin to rise. The test pilot was able to regain control and easily pulled the fighter back into level flight, at which time he headed back to Burbank to have a very close talk with the design team and to examine the airframe for signs of overstress.

A close examination of the YP did not reveal any signs of airframe fatigue but reports from other pilots began to tell a strange story of the tail surfaces buffeting and vibrating at certain power settings and speed ranges. Lockheed test pilots began experimenting with a couple of the YPs and found that the vibration was indeed present – looking over their shoulder they could see the tail moving in a blur. As mentioned previously, this type of flutter or

White spinners contrasting brilliantly with dull camouflage, this P–38H–5–LO was assigned to a training unit in Orlando, Florida. The large numbers in the oval on the side of the engine nacelle denote the training role. Barely seen in the deep shadows under the wing center section are two 1,000 lb bombs. Orlando was the site of the Army Air Force's Tactical Training Center where pilots were given training in the fighter-bomber role. (USAAF)

vibration was regarded as extremely serious since it could possibly separate the tail from the booms. Hibbard and Johnson quickly went to work on this problem and found that fitting pod/wing fillets cured the problem which turned out not to be flutter but rather a vibration in the tail caused by an airflow disturbance at the pod/wing juncture. Testing at the Cal Tech wind tunnel helped cure the problem and fillets were soon fitted to all the YPs and became a standard item for production aircraft.

Testing of the compressibility problem continued and one YP was fitted with boosted trim tabs which would give the pilot an easier way of pulling the aircraft out of the dive. However, the new tabs did not cause the problem to go away and Lockheed test pilot Ralph Virden

The real failure of the Lightning production run was the Royal Air Force's Model 322, or Lightning Mk I. Originally, 243 Mark Is were ordered but the type proved to be so dismal that the British refused to accept the aircraft. Delivered without turbosuperchargers and with propellers that rotated the same way (causing extreme torque), the Mark I could not even come close to its projected performance specifications. Most were taken on charge by the Army who assigned the planes to unfortunate training units where they were universally hated by instructor and student alike, both realizing the aircraft's deadly characteristics. Still carrying its RAF serial of AE992, the Mark I also still has its RAF day-fighter camouflage with USAAF insignia painted over the British roundels.

Lightning Mk I AE979 seen on a test flight from the Burbank factory. This high-angle view illustrates the lack of turbosuperchargers, normally located in the top portion of the tail boom, which made the Mk I a slug that could not fight its own shadow. (Lockheed)

was killed when the tail of the number one YP came off on 4 November 1941 during the recovery from a power dive. The compressibility problem would not easily be solved and would affect production aircraft, as we shall see later in this chapter.

As testing of the YPs continued, the first of the 66 P–38s began to take form. These aircraft were identical to the YPs except for some minor changes. Lessons in Europe saw the addition of armor plate protection for the pilot and the elimination of the small .30 caliber weapons in favor of more .50 caliber

machine guns. The XP and YPs had all been left in their beautiful polished natural aluminium finish but there could be no doubt that the new P–38s were machines of war for they left the production line in a coat of Olive Drab and Neutral Gray, giving them a singularly purposeful look. The production run of P–38s did not proceed smoothly; one aircraft was pulled out for modifications and designated XP–38A for testing with a pressurized cockpit, while 36 were completed as P–38Ds. The P–38D saw the deletion of some items that the Army figured were not necessary, such as the

high pressure oxygen system (a safer low-pressure system was added), while more armor and self-sealing fuel tanks were fitted in an attempt to make the design combat worthy. Armor glass was installed over the instrument panel along with fluorescent instrument lights for night flying. A retractable landing light was put in the wing. The maximum internal fuel capacity was reduced to 300 US gallons from 410 US gallons in an effort to keep weight down. Some of the P–38s and P–38Ds were set aside for research and development use and some of the modifications were strange, such

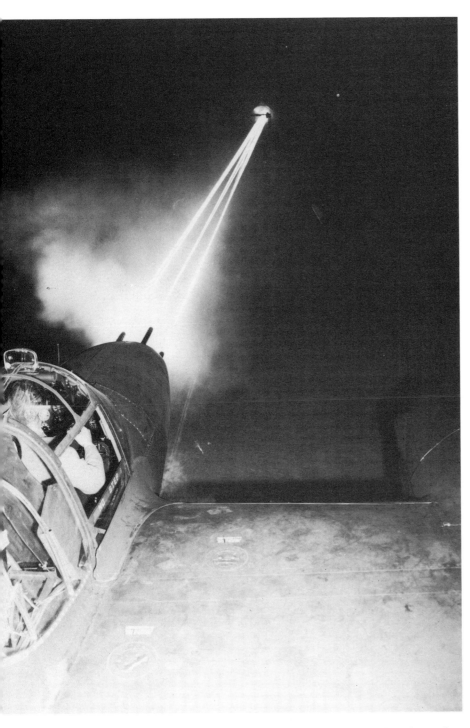

received their fighters in the spring of 1941, the nose cannons had not been fitted and the aircraft were really not combat ready. However, the 1st was ready to test their new fighters in a realistic combat environment and the twin-tailed P–38s went to Louisiana and the Carolinas for the extensive war games which were carried on through September to November. The pilots of the 1st were able to test their aircraft against other Army fighters such as the P–35, P–36 and P–40, finding the P–38 generally superior in all categories.

While the 1st PG was trying out its new aircraft, Lockheed decided that the P–38 needed a name and came up with the appellation of 'Atlanta'. Such a name conjures up a nightmare of an entire generation of American fighting aircraft named after second-line cities. The mind boggles at such fearsome aircraft as the Cincinnati, the Detroit or even the Milwaukee. Fortunately, the British were also in the market for the P–38 and they had much more experience naming aircraft (even though, British names ran the gamut from the ridiculous – the Tomtit – to the sublime – the Fury), whereas the Army and American manufacturers simply settled for numbers. The British liked the name Lightning and, after consideration, so did Lockheed. The new fighter received a name that would prove to be most appropriate.

When France fell during June 1940, the French order for Model 322s was added to the British order. The French and British aircraft had several major differences when compared to their American counterparts, differences which negated the Lightning's main virtues. First, the Model 322s had V–1710–C15 engines *without* turbosuperchargers which had less horsepower (1,090 hp at 14,000 ft) than the American variants and were geared to have the propellers rotate in the *same* direction. Apparently, the thought behind this disastrous combination was that the engine and propeller combination would be the same as the Allisons used in the Royal Air Force's Curtiss Kittyhawks, and therefore interchangeable. However, the deletion of General Electric turbosuperchargers was not solely due to a requirement of the British specification; rather, it was the fact that production at GE could not even keep up with the US Army's demands. The British were faced with accept-

as those to P–38 s/n 40–744 which had a cockpit installed in the left boom to test the effects of an asymmetrical layout on the pilot whose sense of balance could have been disturbed by the placing of his seat away from the aircraft's centerline. [This aircraft, along with other Lightning modifications, can be found in the sub-chapter titled 'Lightning Oddities'.]

Lockheed was having a bit of a problem getting P–38 production on a schedule which would make the Army happy; the rapid expansion and the hiring of thousands of new

workers was causing expected confusion, but management felt the situation would soon be sorted out and the production rate for the new fighter would rapidly rise. With P–38s and P–38Ds being added to the inventory, the Army made the decision to send the fighters to the 1st Pursuit Group, Selfridge Field, Michigan. Many of the 1st's pilots had test flown YP–38s and the Army felt that the experience gained in the type would help to introduce the P–38 more quickly to operational service.

The fact that P–38s were now in unit service did not mean all that much. When the 1st PG

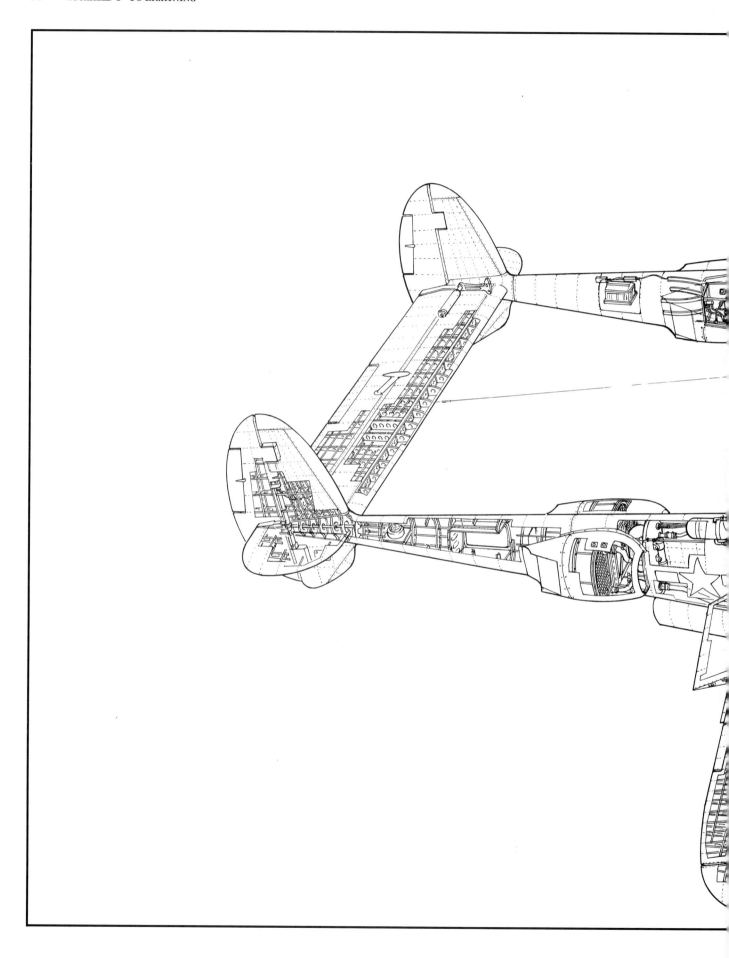

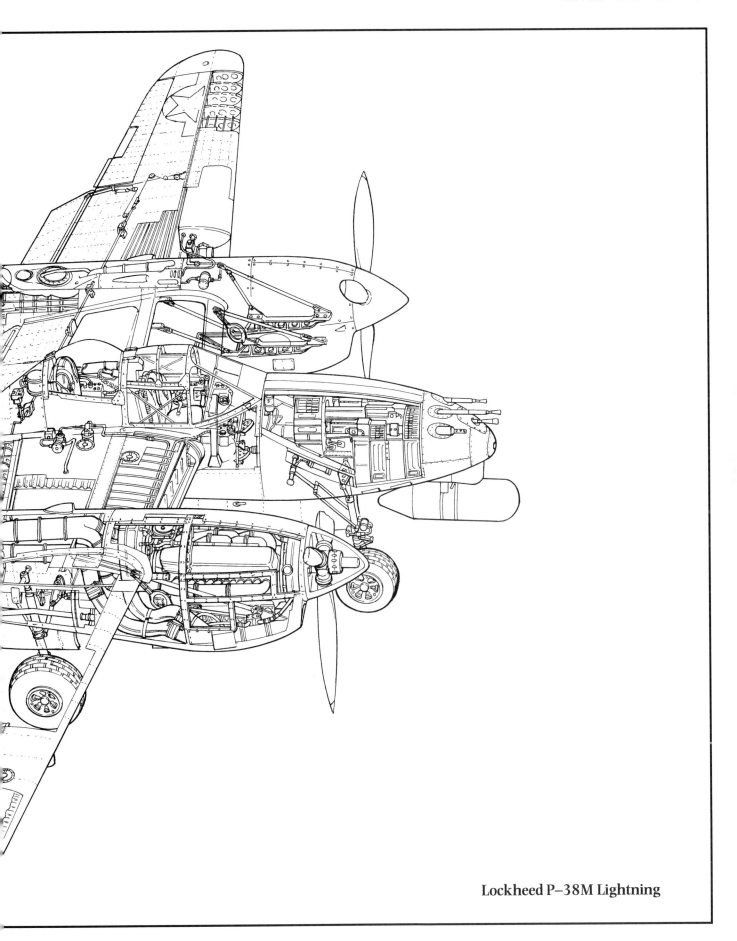

Lockheed P–38M Lightning

ing the aircraft without the units or having the fighters stored in the open until the turbosupercharges became available.

Given the designation of Lightning Mk I, the first aircraft flew from Burbank in Royal Air Force colors during August 1941 but the second did not get airborne until October. British pilots stationed in America went to Burbank to fly the new fighter and they were unanimous in their dislike of the British variant. Performance was considerably below specifications and above 12,000 ft the Lightning Mk I was virtually useless.

So rapid was the British condemnation of

These four pilots have a reason to be happy: they have just completed a successful ferry flight from America to Britain. From the left to the right are Colonels Ben S. Kelsey, Cass S. Hough, James E. Briggs and John K. Kerheart. These long-range ferry flights proved that the Lightning could avoid the U-boat menace and fly directly to the battlefronts. (Lockheed)

the Model 322 that only one example, with RAF serial AF106, was even shipped to Britain. There it was tested, again with negative results. It was reported to have good handling characteristics but the restrictions on performance made the fighter of little use for combat over Europe. The British were quick to cancel their large orders with Lockheed but the Army was equally quick to pick them up. A Lightning Mk II had also been planned but only one example was finished in British markings before that order was also dropped. The Mk II had more powerful Allisons, turbosuperchargers and other uprated equipment. These aircraft were also taken over by the Army. Comprising 524 machines the Army divided the batch into P-38Fs (150 Mk IIs), the P-38G (374 Mk IIs) and the P-322 (140 Mk Is). Most of the P-322s, a very unusual designation for an Army aircraft, were sent through a re-engineering depot to receive

more powerful Allison F series engines and then scattered around the country to various training bases. Few student pilots remember the P-322 with any fondness since, even with the new engines, it was still underpowered with vicious engine cut-out characteristics. Quite a few P-322s were operated by the USAAF in RAF camouflage and serials.

As the end of 1941 loomed closer, more variants of the Lightning came from the Burbank production line but it was not until the P-38E and the P-38G that the Lightning became combat ready. The P-38E (Model 222-62-09) was the first major production version of the Lightning and it was considered as an interim step to the combat-ready P-38G. On the P-38E, the 37 mm cannon was replaced by a license-built Hispano 20 mm weapon with 150 rounds of ammunition. Once again, most of the P-38Es were scattered to training units, but the Army and Lockheed

A P-38H-5-LO displays the short-lived red border around the national insignia (used only from July to August of 1943). The P-38H was equipped with Allison V-1710-89/-91 engines that gave improved altitude performance. The H model also introduced automatic engine controls, larger oil coolers and improved turbosuperchargers. Maximum take-off weight increased to over 20,000 lb. (Lockheed/V7823)

With production increasing, Lightnings found themselves on every warfront. This well-worn P-38, named Golden Eagle, is receiving another bomb mission marker on the side of the nacelle. Pilot Captain Billy Beardsly and crew chief TSgt V. DeVito are seen adding to the tally. Operating in the China-Burma Theatre, the P-38 has its own Chinese guard. When the photograph was taken in 1945, Golden Eagle was billed as one of the oldest fighter planes in the inventory of the 14th Air Force. (USAF/54130)

ferried long distances overwater. Fortunately, this plan never got beyond the tail modification stage. Others were used to tow gliders while 41-2048 was converted to dual controls and used to test various airfoil sections.

Along with 377 Army ordered machines, the P-38F series incorporated 150 Lightning Mk IIs originally intended for the RAF. Retaining the same armament as the P-38E, the Fs were powered with 1,325 hp Allison V-1710-49/-53 engines. These machines were produced in five different batches, each with its own set of updates and modifications. The F series included the first Lightnings to carry drop tanks (P-38F-5-LO): two 155/165 US gallon tanks could be carried on pylons located between the engines and the fuselage pod; two 1,000 lb bombs could also be fitted to the pylons in place of the drop tanks.

Built with 1,325 hp Allison V-1710-51/-55 engines, 708 P-38Gs (Model 222-68-12) were ordered in six blocks by the Army. The P-38G was generally similar to the F but with some detail refinements including an updated radio package, a new oxygen system, strengthened pylons that could carry 1,600 lb bombs, and winterization equipment. The P-38G-13-LO and P-38G-15-LO (a total of 374 aircraft designated Model 322-68-19) came from the British order for Lightning Mk IIs.

While Lightning production was rapidly building up, the Japanese struck American military installations at Pearl Harbor, Hawaii, on 7 December 1941 with a devastating blow. A panic immediately swept America concerning a possible invasion of the West Coast. Intelligence was limited and rumors were rife, reports of Japanese submarines off Los Angeles and of paratroopers landing in the desert caused a wave of anti-Japanese sentiment resulting in the interning of all West Coast Japanese – even if they were American citizens.

It must be remembered that the threat of a Japanese invasion was a very real possibility and to counter the threat the 1st Pursuit Group with its testing and training P-38s and P-38Ds was rushed to California to provide a modicum of air defense capability. The 1st was one of America's most historic air units and it is fitting that the unit was quickly moved to counter a possible threat. The 1st PG had been formed in France on 5 May 1918 and immedi-

did retain some of the aircraft for modification and testing purposes. Those assigned to training units carried the 'R' prefix, indicating that the aircraft was for a non-combat role. Thus, the Army operated RP-38s, RP-38Ds, and RP-322s as of 1942 when the designation change came into effect.

As detailed in our 'Lightning Oddities' section, many RP-38Es were put to extremely strange uses. Several had a cramped second seat installed directly behind the pilot where an unwilling student could be crammed for a demonstration of the Lightning's handling. Another was fitted with a massive, upswept tail in the anticipation of adding floats to the airframe, creating an aircraft that could be

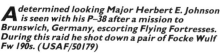

A determined looking Major Herbert E. Johnson is seen with his P–38 after a mission to Brunswich, Germany, escorting Flying Fortresses. During this raid he shot down a pair of Focke Wulf Fw 190s. (USAF/50179)

ately went into action using a variety of foreign-built equipment that included the Nieuport 28, SPAD and Sopwith Camel. Two of the 1st's most distinguished pilots would go down in the history books: Captain Edward V. Rickenbacker became America's leading ace, while 2nd Lt Frank Luke, Jr, became known as the unit's maverick. In 1939, the 1st was reconstituted and consolidated into the 1st PG (Interceptor) in December 1939 and the 1st PG (Fighter) in March 1941.

The P–38s of the 1st arrived at the Naval Air Station in San Diego amid a flurry of activity and military preparations. Although the ground crews, spare parts and supplies did not arrive until a few days later, by train, and some of the early P–38s were completely unarmed, the Lightnings were immediately ordered into the air on combat patrols, and the pilots headed aloft – not really knowing what to look for since they could be opposing anything from high flying recon aircraft to an entire Japanese battlegroup.

The 1st soon moved to sprawling March Field near Riverside, California, to join the 14th Pursuit Group (the term fighter would replace pursuit early in 1942) which was in

the process of equipping with Lightnings to form the only really modern high altitude defense available on the entire West Coast. Launching from March, the P–38s patrolled up and down the coast, usually heading up to Santa Barbara and then turning back towards San Diego before returning to March. Since Los Angeles was the main center for aircraft production, it was a prime target for a possible Japanese attack. However, as the weeks slid by it became obvious that the Japanese were not coming and it was time to send the Lightnings to confront the enemy directly.

Early in 1942, the United States Army Air Forces felt that combat ready Lightnings should be sent to Britain to reinforce America's growing presence in that island nation. Getting the P–38s to Britain was another problem. U-boats were taking a heavy toll of supply ships but flights across the Atlantic were still in the pioneering stage and considered very hazardous. With the P–38F and the development of reliable drop tanks, an island-hopping route would get the Lightnings to Britain safely and in record time. With drop tanks the P–38F had a maximum ferry range of 3,100 miles, demonstrated by Lockheed test pilot Milo Burcham; this was an exceptional range but probably could not be achieved by the average service fighter or average service pilot.

The Army notified the 1st and 14th Fighter Groups that they would be the first Lightning

units to deploy to Britain, so both units pulled up stakes in California and headed for the East Coast for final training and modification of the P–38s for the long overwater flight. Starting in June 1942, groups of P–38s headed for Britain by flying via Goose Bay in Labrador, Bluie West One in Greenland, and Reykjavik on Iceland, landing at Prestwick, Scotland. Usually using a B–17 'mother ship', these flights were quite successful and the time gain over surface transportation was obvious.

By August, the Army Air Force had eight-one P–38Fs in Britain and preparation was underway to deploy the fighters in combat.

Half a world away, other P–38s were being readied for combat to fight in one of earth's most inhospitable climates: the Aleutians. Japan had been quick to realize the significance of the chain of islands that led directly into the American possession of Alaska. They knew that, by occupying the islands, a dagger could be aimed directly at Alaska – drawing America's limited military might away from the war in the Pacific. Accordingly, the Japanese landed in battalion strength on the Aleutian's Attu and Kiska islands. The occupation of these two islands became a thorn in America's side and a major effort was undertaken to dislodge the Japanese.

American military presence in Alaska had always been a rather token effort, but with the

P–38J–25–LO 44–23654 drops a 1,000 lb bomb during a training flight. Part of the P–38's great versatility was the fact that it could easily be converted to a 'B–38', a long range bomber carrying more bomb load than a B–25 Mitchell. During these bomber raids, the 'B–38s' were led by 'Droop Snoot' Lightnings with a lead bombardier who would give the entire B–38 formation the signal when to release their bombs. The bomber Lightnings would usually be protected by an equal number of P–38s although, once their bombs were released, the bombers would immediately revert to their fighter status. (Lockheed/E. Miller)

Dramatically illustrating the change-over from Olive Drab and Neutral Gray camouflage to natural metal finish, is Lockheed P–38J–10–LO 42–68040 seen taxiing down a row of camouflaged fighters at Burbank. The Army dropped camouflage to speed production, gain a couple of miles per hour, and reduce overall costs. The small opening in the extreme forward portion of the nose cone is for a gun camera although this installation was less than ideal since the guns made the camera vibrate, quite often making the film illegible for intelligence officers. The gun camera was moved to the wing with the P–38L. (Lockheed/T1262)

Japanese invasion a force of P–38s was gathered and sent on the long flight north. The 11th and 18th Fighter Squadrons of the 28th Composite Group were equipped with tired P–40s and P–39s so the new squadron of P–38s was most welcome. The islands of the Aleutians are spread over a 1,200-mile strip of ocean so incredibly hostile that a pilot would die after just a few minutes of exposure to the frigid water. The Kittyhawks and Airacobras were limited in range and their single powerplants offered no margin of safety. The Japanese were expanding efforts in digging in and fortifying the two islands against American attack. A few limited air clashes had taken place before the arrival of the P–38s and several Japanese aircraft had been destroyed by the P–40s.

The P–38s were soon put into action, their range stretched to the maximum, and an attack was launched on the enemy base at Kiska. Some ships in the harbor were bombed and shot up while the ground installations and airfield were given a good working over, much to the surprise of the enemy who probably thought that such an attack was impossible. American engineers began to construct airships on the islands nearer the enemy and some of the problems associated with the long-

range missions began to disappear, but it is a sobering fact that only ten of the original 31 Lightning pilots survived their Aleutian tour. Most were victims of the foul weather and freezing sea. Parts for the fighters were non-existent and wrecks had to be scavenged by the mechanics for every useable piece. Some of the damaged aircraft which were still flyable were flown all the way back to Texas for repairs but this was not an easy flight and several pilots were lost.

Engineers had established bases on Adak and Amchitka, putting strike forces much closer to the enemy and attacks were launched whenever weather permitted. Pilots of the 54th FS were regularly hitting the Japanese in company with the P–40s and P–39s, and the B–24 Liberator heavy bombers and during September 1942, the 54th, 11th and 18th Fighter Squadrons were amalgamated into the 343rd Fighter Group, 11th Air Force. The enemy was always ready to oppose the attacking Americans but the fight slowly began to tilt in favor of the Americans. P–38s went up for mission after mission, usually carrying a 500 lb or 1000 lb bomb under one wing and a fuel tank under the other. The Japanese always put up a fairly stiff resistance and the Zeros were tough opponents. Aerial slaughters that

Allison V–1710 is lowered into position on a P–38J as it moves down the Burbank production line. Known as QEC (Quick Engine Change) unit, the engine and auxiliary systems were contained in a power 'egg' that could quickly be removed and replaced with a new unit, thus greatly reducing the number of manhours needed for an engine change. (Lockheed)

soon became common over the South Pacific were not unknown in the Aleutians. On 24 May 1943, a group of 25 Betty bombers was intercepted and all but three were destroyed.

On 11 May 1943, the Navy landed an invasion force on Attu and, after three weeks of fighting, the Japanese force of 2,300 was overwhelmed. In July, Kiska was invaded but the Americans were suprised to find that the Japanese had left in their ships during a heavy fog, leaving piles of abandoned military equip-

ment. P–38s were to be stationed in the area for the rest of the war, but the heavy fighting at the top of the world was over.

Back over the North Atlantic, the ferry flights to supply the USAAF effort in Britain were continuing and Lightnings were regularly crossing but losses were incurred. Six P–38s and their two B–17 mother ships went down in Greenland on 27 June 1942 after bad weather prevented them from landing at their assigned base. The aircraft all safely crash-landed on the ice cap and none of the pilots were injured but it was a few days before they could be removed. The aircraft were left where they went down. In 1983, with a growing interest in the history of World War Two and its artifacts, an expedition was launched from

America to find and recover the fighters and bombers. The featureless terrain of the ice cap proved to be a major problem but, by using sophisticated sonar gear, large metal targets were found buried under *seventy-five feet* of solid ice! The expedition had to abandon its base camp with the onset of winter and there has been some discussion of going back and melting the ice with a jet engine but such an undertaking would entail a vast expenditure.

Other Lightnings went down on the ferry route but their pilots were not so lucky – they simply disappeared. The Germans did not like the idea of the aerial supply line but there was little they could do about disrupting the flow, not like the U-boat's slaughter of Allied transports. However, the Germans did develop several clever means of damaging the supply line. Powerful radio beams were used to misdirect Allied aircraft and Germans speaking perfect English were employed to give incorrect orders over the air. Far ranging Focke Wulf Fw 200 Condors went out over the Atlantic to observe the flights and attack any possible stragglers. The hunter became victim on 15 August when a Condor was jumped by a P–38 from the 27th FS and a P–40 from the 33rd FS, both out of Greenland. The Condor was sent down on fire into the ocean for the honor of being the first German aircraft destroyed by the USAAF during World War Two in the European Theatre of Operations. The 27th FS had been on its way to England when orders directed them to remain in Greenland to bolster the island's P–40 defense. The long-range Lightning proved to be a great threat to the prowling Focke Wulfs and the Germans were much more careful about sending out the lumbering four engine aircraft. The 27th only stayed in Greenland for two months before departing to Britain but they had helped dilute the German threat.

The Olive Drab and Neutral Gray Lightnings of the 14th Fighter Group arrived in Britain at the end of August, their unique configuration capturing the fancy of every British schoolboy. The Lightnings were not immediately ready for combat and practice flying, tactics and local familiarization flights had to be undertaken, but the deployment of the P–38 in a combat situation was not to have as much to do with the Lightning's battle readiness as with international politics.

President Roosevelt and Prime Minister Churchill felt that the opening of a front on enemy territory was a political and military necessity. Several influential generals were pushing for a major landing in France but the politicians were against the projected invasion, feeling that the situation was not right for such a major military move. Stalin was also against a direct invasion of France, but he did avor heavy intervention on some other front o take the immense German pressure off Russia. A major attack, Operation TORCH, was planned against North Africa but there was considerable military opposition to this move and it took almost ten days of heavy arguing before Roosevelt won out and the invasion was planned. Currently, some historians feel that this major delay of landing forces in France gave the Soviets a distinct advantage in later claiming all of Eastern Europe.

Operation TORCH needed a vast amount of planning and material to ensure its success – failure at that point in the war would have spelled disaster. Due to the pressing needs for effective airpower in the invasion, a new air force was created – the USAAF 12th Air Force. Aircraft were urgently needed to fill the new air force, but were not yet coming from America's increased production lines to fill the needs of the Allies' far-flung military operations. Accordingly, the USAAF looked to the 8th AF in Britain to see what could be taken without decreasing the effective strength of the 8th. The P–38s of the 14th FG were an obvious

answer since the unit had not been fully committed to combat; in fact, the unit had only flown a few combat bomber escort missions during October 1942.

In October, orders were received to move the 14th, its pilots, aircraft and other ranks to a new secret location. Spare parts and ground personnel were loaded aboard cargo ships – the men having absolutely no idea of where they were going – while the P–38s launched to Gibraltar, timed to arrive on 8 November, the day planned for the invasion. Once again, the pilots had little idea of what was going on but some of the more politically astute must have figured that a strike at Vichy-occupied North Africa was in hand.

The strike at North Africa was indeed an attempt to open a new 'front' on basically what would be the easiest military target. The invasion would give the Allies a needed emotional boost while attempting, for the moment, to pacify the Russian demand for the opening of a major offensive on the German military machine in the west. Trouble would be encountered because the Allies were attacking

not only the enemy but also the French who inhabited the area. Many French had escaped during the initial German invasion but many more had stayed, more or less leading the everyday existence that they had before the start of the war. The French government and military forces in the area had been quickly reorganized by the Germans with Vichy figureheads who obeyed the orders given by their masters.

Overall military commander for TORCH was General Dwight Eisenhower. Air Marshal Tedder's command included the newly formed Desert Air Force which, in itself, included the equally new USAAF 9th AF. Jimmy Doolittle commanded the 12th AF. Field Marshal Erwin Rommel commanded the elite *Afrika Korps*. Historians would later write that such a gathering of capable leaders had the makings

Inverted 'Christmas tree' rocket launchers, standard installation on P–38Ls, could also be attached to other variants of Lightnings by simple modifications at forward bases. An improvement over the earlier bazooka style launchers, the rocket trees carried a total of ten 5-in high velocity rockets. (Lockheed/P9906)

of one of the war's most epic fights. In Egypt, General Bernard Montgomery's British 8th Army was taking advantage of the victory at El Alamein in Egypt in October 1942, and was applying considerable harassing pressure on Rommel that would be very useful for TORCH.

The logistics for such an invasion, while not approaching the scope of the later Normandy landings, were immense. The Allies poured ashore on 8 November 1942 at Casablanca, Safi, Fedhala, Port Lyautey and Oran, catching the enemy, if not entirely by surprise, at least in a state of confusion. The French *Armée de l'Air* put up its Curtiss Hawk 75s and a few brief but bloody air battles ensued with US Navy Wildcats and Dauntlesses and British Seafires, during which both sides suffered losses.

The French did not really have much of fight in them and a surrender was worked out on 11 November, the day which the Gibraltar-based Lightnings flew their first missions. The Lightnings had departed Gibraltar on the day of the invasion and landed on the airfield at

Carrying two 500 lb bombs, Lightnings taxi for takeoff on a dive bombing mission against von Runstedt's forces during December 1944 which, at this time, was within fifteen miles of this P–38 base in Belgium. These Lightnings were from the 485th Fighter Squadron, 370th Fighter Group, and carry the identifying code 7F. It is interesting to note the colorful checkered nose on the P–38J in the right background. Some P–38s, such as the one in the foreground, had the extreme tip of their nose cone highly polished with a white band added behind the polished area. This was done with the hope of confusing the German pilots into thinking that the fighter was an unarmed 'Droop Snoot' Lightning. (USAF/58856)

Tafaraoui on the 11th. The 14th FG pilots were basically on hostile soil by themselves since the supply train with their ground crews and spare parts had not yet arrived. As the days passed, more P–38s arrived along with the missing ground crews and operations were undertaken on a limited basis.

The Germans were by no means hiding and when the 48th FS moved to the famous Maison Blanche airfield during the middle of the month, the *Luftwaffe* caught them by surprise in a strafing and bombing attack that knocked out airfield facilities and crippled seven of the Lightnings. This was just the first of several visits that the Germans paid to the field – a raid on 20 November destroyed over 20 Allied aircraft.

Besides the use of fast-moving bombers and Stukas during the *Blitzkrieg*, the Germans never took full advantage of developing an efficient ground attack force that could directly and repeatedly hit Allied airfields, destroying aircraft and equipment on the ground. The slim Allied airpower force in North Africa is an ideal example of the *Luftwaffe*'s blundering since the few ground attack missions against the Allies did a tremendous amount of damage to already limited resources, but they were never pressed to full advantage.

The Lightning pilots, besides putting up with the German hit-and-run raids, had to cope with the harsh realities of living 'in the field'. Living conditions were, at best, primitive and pilots found themselves living in tents, in structures made of discarded fuel barrels or,

quite often, just in the open where they had to put up with dust when it was hot and an incredibly tenacious mud when it rained. The ground crews maintained the Lightnings as best they could in these harsh conditions, but mechanical and engine failures were not uncommon. Along with the growing score of *Luftwaffe* and Italian aircraft destroyed, the P–38 pilots were also beginning to take heavy losses; when the 14th Fighter Group was withdrawn from combat at the end of January 1943, 32 of the original 54 pilots had been lost in combat or in accidents while the Group claimed 62 enemy aircraft destroyed.

As Operation TORCH progressed, the P–38 forces consolidated and gradually began to increase their firepower as new aircraft and pilots arrived. Rommel began moving his famed *Panzer* units against the Allies in a series of daring attacks that usually resulted in heavy losses on both sides, but the sharp conflicts mainly resulted in German defeats or stalemates. The Germans were receiving a great deal of their supplies by air and Allied intelligence felt that if the aerial supply train could be broken, then there was a good chance of the entire German military machine in North Africa grinding to a halt. The P–38s of the 1st and 82nd FGs became part of Operation FLAX, a massive Allied effort aimed at attacking and destroying German supply lines.

The German transport fleet consisted mainly of slow, ungainly Junkers Ju 52 trimotors that were efficient cargo haulers but easy aerial targets for fighters. The other main *Luftwaffe*

This was just the beginning of the slaughter of the *Luftwaffe* transports.

For the next several days, Lightnings, P–40s and Spitfires attacked huge formations of German aircraft and, although Allied aircraft were always lost in these swirling battles, the Germans really came out on the losing end, hundreds of transports falling to the Allied fighters. The *Luftwaffe* became unable to protect the transport flights and supply missions became virtual suicide trips. By destroying the German transports, the Allies took a major step in gaining control of the airspace over North Africa. The German/Italian armies began to crumble, with a massive surrender of men coming in mid-May. Field Marshal Rommel and most of his staff managed to escape the final defeat. Rommel continued to fight the Allies on different portions of the battlefront until after the Normandy Invasion when he was forced by Hitler to commit suicide.

The Lightning had proven itself in a wide variety of missions: the high-altitude fighter sweeps, bomber escort, medium altitude dogfights, ground attack missions and recon flights. The harsh conditions of North Africa had taken a heavy toll of Lightnings and USAAF pilots but the aircraft had established itself as a valuable military tool and new combat areas were rapidly opening.

Back in Burbank, Lockheed was paying attention to reports from their field representatives and the USAAF. Hundreds of modifications were incorporated into the Lightning production line while the design department came up with new variants. Reports from the combat areas had told of power falling off above 25,000 ft. Automatic oil radiator flaps were fitted to the new P–38H (226 P–38H–1–LO variants constructed) that not only enabled the Allison V–1710–89/91 powerplants, with a take-off rating of 1,425 hp, to run cooler but let the pilot keep military power on the engines above 25,000 ft where 1,240 hp per engine could be achieved. The P–38H–5–LO (375 built) had the more powerful B–33 turbosuperchargers installed in the booms.

Major improvements were introduced with the P–38J. One of the key identifying features of the earlier Lightnings was the elegant swept-back 'shark' air intake behind and below the spinner which gave the Allison engine installation an extremely streamlined appearance. Although the installation was streamlined, cooling became a problem as demands on the Lightning increased. A P–38E (s/n 41–1983) had been modified at the factory to

transport was the even more ungainly Messerschmitt Me 323, a variant of Germany's massive glider transport powered by six engines. Slow, unmaneuverable and not very well armed, these transports were usually protected by hordes of fighters that would slowly weave back and forth over the transport flights. However, the transports were so slow that the fighters would have to reduce speed drastically and then gently maneuver in S turns to keep their own speed even further down. High-performance engines were often victims of fouled plugs as the fighters flew for

extended periods at the reduced power settings.

Operation FLAX proposed to blast through the enemy fighter defense and decimate the aerial supply line. The first major encounter happened on 5 April 1943 when Lightnings of the 1st and 82nd FG flew their usual bomber escort mission and ran into 65 Ju 52s which they bounced from high altitude, roaring directly through the defending fighter formation and hitting the transports. Eleven of the Junkers fell into the ocean near Cape Bone along with several of the escorting fighters.

These Lightnings serve as a symbol of the overwhelming American airpower that blasted the Axis into rubble. Beautiful formation of D-Day striped Lightnings practice in England before a mission over the Continent. This formation was developed for the 'B–38' bombing raids. A 'Droop Snoot' Lightning would lead the formation on a bombing attack at altitudes over 20,000 ft. (USAF/51937)

incorporate larger radiators and much larger scoops under the engine. This did detract from streamlining but, at the same time, offered an impressive increase in power. With the larger radiator area and new Prestone coolant scoops mounted on the booms, the Allisons could operate more efficiently. Testing with the P–38E had proven the installation more than satisfactory and the modification was incorporated into the new P–38H production run. The P–38J (Model 422–81–14) kept the same engine installation as the P–38H but the

increased cooling meant that power at 27,000 ft would go from 1,240 to 1,425 hp. War emergency power selection at that altitude would take engine power to 1,600 hp for a few minutes. The Model 422–81–14 was built in large numbers: ten P–38J–1–LOs, 210 P–38J–5s and 790 P–38J–20s. Each block variant had improvements that included the addition of two 55 US gallon fuel cells in the space previously occupied by the intercoolers (J–5) which increased internal fuel to 410 US gallons. Flat armored windshields were added to the J–10 along with other minor improvements.

The Model 422–81–22 production was divided into two main batches; the P–38J–15–LO (1,400 built) had an updated electrical system while the J–20 (350 built) had new turbosupercharger regulators. The Model 422–81–23 block consisted of 210 P–38J–25s that had

dive flaps located under the wing that wer electrically powered and they were also fitte with ailerons that had power boost system These new variants would soon be on thei way to all corners of the globe, replacin earlier Lightnings and giving the USAAF fighter that was greatly feared by the enem *Luftwaffe* pilots calling the P–38 'the Fork tailed Devil'.

After the Allied victory in North Africa USAAF units re-equipped and built up strength before entering combat over the Mediter ranean in preparation for the invasions o Sicily and Italy. One of the first targets was th fortress island of Pantelleria, the site of heav enemy concentrations and location for one o the Allies' more ambitious experiments: t destroy completely, an enemy target from th air. Every aircraft that could carry a bomb wa thrown into the attack on Pantelleria and fo days on end the island was repeatedly blaste until final victory was achieved. Lightnings o the 1st and 82nd FGs carried out hundreds o strafing and dive bombing missions against th stronghold. USAAF pilots had to be particu larly careful when taking the '38 out for a div bombing run since the problem of compress ibility was still plaguing the design. Pilots ha to monitor carefully their speed since it built u so quickly and to allow for loss of contro which could quite often be followed by air frame disintegration.

Lightnings had joined other Allied air unit in hitting targets in Sicily during July 1943 i preparation for Operation HUSKY – the invasio of Sicily and the first probe into the 'so underbelly' of the Axis. Battling in the Mediter ranean proved to be anything but soft and th enemy was not only well-equipped but als tenacious. Sicily was invaded on 10 July 194 but did not fall until 17 August.

After the capture of Sicily, the three Light ning groups (the 1st, 14th and 82nd) bega concentrated attacks against the Italian main land – bombing, escorting and intercepting On 1 November, a change in paperwor assigned the three P–38 groups to the Fif teenth Air Force, giving the Lightning pilot the main assignment of escorting heavy bom bers to enemy targets in Austria and other Axi locations such as Greece, the Balkans, Franc and Italy. These missions were hazardou since they were over enemy territory for a goo portion of the flight time and opposition fron the *Luftwaffe* and flak batteries was intense.

Proponents of the Lightning maintaine that the P–38 would make a good pin-poin bomber since it had twin-engine reliability an could easily carry a 1,000 lb bomb for a lon distance. Usually, another aircraft or a modi fied Lightning provided the role of pathfinde for the Lightning force and, after some prac ice, the first of these pioneering missions was flown on 10 June 1944. Nearly 50 82nd FG P–38s dropped their 1,000 lb high explosive bombs on an oil refinery in Rumania. These refineries had been subject to constant American attention and, while never being able to knock them out completely, enough damage was done to hinder the German's war effort. The targets were very heavily defended and the Lightnings paid dearly on this first mission. The 'bombers' were escorted by an equal number of P–38s that kept a look-out for enemy fighters. Near the target area, a massive dogfight developed and 22 Lightnings fell in the fight, devastating losses that were not really equal to the results obtained.

The Fifteenth Air Force kept hammering German and Axis targets thus drawing valuable supplies, men and material away from the Western and Eastern fronts and sending them south to fight the American advances. For aviators of the Fifteenth, their zone of combat was extremely dangerous if they were shot down and it was not uncommon for pilots and crews to be badly beaten or killed by hostile civilians – rescue, oddly enough, coming only

when the Germans intervened to haul the downed fliers to a prison camp.

Raids on German and Italian airfields proved to be an effective but dangerous way of reducing the enemy's air force. The P–38's heavy, concentrated armament was particularly useful in this role although liquid-cooled engines could easily be damaged by small arms fire. One epic raid on 25 August 1943 sent 65 Lightnings from the 1st FG and a near equal number from the 82nd FG out to demolish the enemy airfields that surrounded Foggia, Italy. In order to achieve total surprise, the Lightning pilots flew on the deck and the raid hit the enemy so quickly and so hard that very little anti-aircraft fire was received. The raid was a total success and about 200 German and Italian aircraft were destroyed or damaged in exchange for two P–38s being lost. Such massive losses did not stem the enemy's will to fight and huge dogfights were still the rule of the day, neither side giving quarter.

General Montgomery made his landing in southern Italy on 3 September 1943 to be followed by General Mark Clark and the American 5th Army on 9 September near Salerno.

The 'soft underbelly' was not living up to its name and the Germans fought back so fiercely that the Allied high command suddenly became fearful of the final result of the invasion.

Once again, every available P–38 was thrown into the battle but the heavy aerial fighting had reduced the number of Lightnings available for combat. Prime targets were German troop and supply concentrations along with the enemy airfields. The three weary Lightning groups could muster a bit less than 250 of the twin-tailed fighters and quite a few of these machines would be destroyed or damaged during the September fighting. Airfields felt the bite of the Lightning and on 18 September, nearly 300 more hostile aircraft were destroyed or damaged when the airfields around Foggia were once again raided. Foggia was denied to the enemy on 27 September when it was overrun by units of the American

Ninth Air Force Lightning pilots, their briefing for the day's mission completed, pile into trucks for a ride to the hardstands where their fighters were parked 'somewhere in England'. Note the diversity of uniform dress. (USAF/A55543)

A fully modified 'Droop Snoot' Lightning seen in Britain. The forward section of the P–38J's fuselage pod containing the guns and ammunition was removed and a new nose section was built housing a bombardier, bomb sight and associated navigation equipment. (Lockheed/P8486)

8th Army. Lightnings began to use the airfields and the pilots were amazed to see the stacks of destroyed Axis aircraft – the fields looked like massive scrap yards. The devastating attacks and the slowly advancing infantry were finally taking an irreparable toll on the Germans. With Italy's surrender, many of the former enemy airfields were occupied by Lightnings and the bomber force, each step closer to the heart of Germany, but the Germans in Italy fought on, hard.

By February 1944, the newer P–38Js were arriving in Italy and the Lightning groups began to venture further into enemy territory. Plans for co-ordinated raids into Germany and

Austria were undertaken by the Eighth and Fifteenth, putting the enemy in a pincher and reducing his forces even more. Using their increased range, the Lightnings participated in some of the epic air battles over Austria and Germany. At this stage of the war, the *Luftwaffe*, although reeling could be counted on when bomber raids hit strategic targets. The Germans would throw everything into these aerial battles but aircraft such as the Bf 110 and Me 210 were easy prey for the Lightnings. Experienced *Luftwaffe* pilots in Bf 109s and Fw 190s were more than a handful and the pilots of such caliber had to be respected. Still, it was a war of attrition and, bit by bit, the Germans were able to put fewer aircraft into the air while the Allies were able to get more and more over the target areas.

As the war progressed into mid-1944, ground attacks had virtually stopped all rail traffic in the portion of Italy still held by the

Germans. Lightnings and Thunderbolts attacked anything that moved and it was not safe for the enemy to use roads or rails in the daylight. With the Normandy invasion, Lightnings of the 1st and 14th FGs staged through Corsica to support the Allied landings. These missions were less than easy and in a few days 23 P–38s were knocked down. German air opposition began to fall off drastically over Italy during August and September and the bombers were able to pound targets more effectively. Photo recce Lightnings ranged far into enemy territory, bringing back damage reports and finding new targets. The war, for the Fifteenth, from late 1944 on was to be one hard and long advance. The enemy remained dangerous and Lightning losses, although decreasing in number, continued until the final victory. As aerial targets became harder to find, the Lightnings intensified their ground attack efforts even though these misions were very dangerous. For example, on 14 April 1944, 15 Lightnings were shot down during strafing and bombing attacks on enemy positions. When, on 2 May, more than one million Germans surrendered, the war in Italy was finally over.

Since the Fifteenth Air Force had absorbed virtually all of the Lightnings in Britain, it is interesting to note that the Eighth Air Force did not begin to re–equip with the P–38 until September 1943 when the 55th FG and its P–38Hs arrived at Nuthampstead. By mid-October, the unit was ready for combat and began to fly missions over France and other occupied countries. Re-equipping with P–38Js during December 1943, the 55th now had the range to escort bombers all the way to Berlin and back – a distance of 1,300 miles, thus becoming the first Lightning unit capable of

protecting the hard-pressed bombers through an entire mission; the first mission of this type taking place on 3 March 1944.

The 55th FG was to be joined by other Lightning units: the 20th FG in December 1943, the 364th FG in March 1944, and the 479th FG in May 1944. The 55th was originally equipped with P–38Hs which were not really suited for high altitude operations. Pilots complained of bitter cold at altitude and cases of frostbite were recorded. Even though the aviators were encased in leather and lamb's wool, the cold of the high European skies was like a prolonged torture and pilot efficiency rapidly dropped. The P–38Hs were also prone to windshield icing and fogging of the cockpit plexiglass – certainly not a safe situation in a fighter aircraft where visibility often meant the difference between life and death. At altitude, there was also a problem with overboosting

the Allison engines, much the same problem as suffered by P–47 pilots with their turbosupercharged P&W R–2800s. Blown engines were not uncommon among the more inexperienced pilots and the Allison, in the ETO, began to get a reputation as a 'boat anchor'.

Since the Army and manufacturers had so many field modification kits to update or modify their combat aircraft, it does not seem unreasonable that some form of efficient heater and windshield de-icer could have been devised and quickly added to the P–38Hs. As it

Kicking up a trail of dust, a P–38J lands on a newly made airstrip near the Omaha beachhead, Vierville sur Mer, France. Photographed on 10 June 1944, the Lightning was the first aircraft (besides light observation types such as the L–4 Cub) to land on the strip. These airfields made safe havens for damaged Allied aircraft that were unable to get back across the Channel. (US Army/190118–S)

was, many Lightnings that went out on the early ETO missions simply never came back – whether from enemy action, engine failure or other reasons – and pilot morale began to take a distinct downward turn which was unusual for American fighter groups.

Increased instruction on the correct operating of the Allisons at altitude began to cure some of the overboosting problems but it was obvious that high altitude brought out many problems with the P–38H and there was relief when the more advanced P–38Js began arriving in the United Kingdom, although the supply of the J was not as fast as the fighter

On 11 March 1943, these four 9th Fighter Squadron P–38 pilots accounted for five Japanese aircraft during a raid on Dobodura airstrip. From left to right: Lt T. R. Fowler (1 victory); Capt Sidney Woods (1); Lt J. C. Mankin (1); and Lt Dick Bong (2). Bong would go on to become America's ace of aces with forty victories. The heat and humidity of New Guinea meant that the pilots wore only the lightest of khaki uniforms. (US Army/168528)

groups wished. The J, along with its increased range, featured improved cockpit heating and windshield de-icing systems while the new radiator system helped a bit with the overboosting problem and engine failures decreased. The more reliable cooling and improved superchargers meant that more power could be obtained from the Allisons at higher altitude but it was not uncommon to have mixed formations of Hs and Js until the supply of Js greatly increased towards the middle of 1944.

The 55th FG was basically fully equipped with pilots and aircraft but the other groups were only partially operational at first and took a while to build up to combat readiness. Beacause of this, FGs would usually send their limited number of aircraft out with the 55th on bomber escort missions. By combining forces, two FGs could usually get around 90 Lightnings airborne for the bomber escort missions. Since the Lightnings were larger than their

fellow escorting Thunderbolts, German pilots could usually spot the P–38 sooner and they would stay away from the twin-boomed fighter. The trips deep into Germany were no piece of cake, even in the improved P–38Js, and losses were common due to mechanical failure, flak and fighters. Many P–38s did make it back to base with one engine out, thus proving the feasibility of the twin-engine concept.

The Lightning did not serve solely in its role as high-altitude escort. A major modification was undertaken on some of the fighters that led to the new name of 'Droop Snoot' along with a rather ungainly profile. The nose section and armament of the Lightning were removed and a new nose was installed that included a plexiglass dome in the extreme forward nose with a seat and associated equipment for a bombardier. Although the new position certainly could not have been too comfortable for the unfortunate in the nose, the modification did give the Lightning new

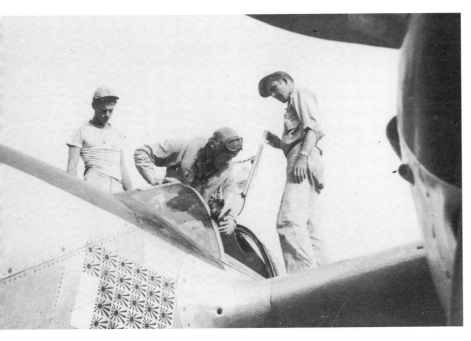

versatility and the 'Droop Snoots', modified at Lockheed's major overhaul center at Langford Lodge, Ireland, were spread around the combat units.

The idea behind the 'Droop Snoot' was simple and effective: the bombardier-equipped Lightning would lead the fighter P–38s that had been fitted with a 1,000 lb bomb on one of the underwing pylons (a fuel tank would be on the other) and the 'Droop Snoot' would do all the navigating to the target. When approaching the target, the bombardier would take over the formation and all the bombs would be dropped on his order. This method of delivering high explosives to the enemy was effective and bombing altitudes were usually 20,000 ft and above. After bomb release the P–38s could defend themselves against fighter opposition. While in the bomber configuration, other 'regular' P–38s would circle the 'B–38' formation for protection on the run-in to the target area.

As Mustangs and Thunderbolts took the bombers to Germany, the Eighth decided to employ the P–38s in ground attack as well as escort missions. From 6 June 1944, the P–38s were in the air all day, escorting and attacking targets of opportunity although, from this point on, German fighter forces rapidly began to decrease in number and quality so ground attack missions became more and more common for the USAAF fighters.

When General James H. Doolittle took command of the Eighth AF in the middle of 1944, he made a sweeping decision that would drastically affect the role of the P–38 in the ETO. His decision was that the P–38 and P–47 groups should be equipped with the P–51 Mustang. Doolittle felt that the Mustang was a more efficient and more cost effective aircraft than either the Thunderbolt or the Lightning and that it could perform the high-altitude escort and ground attack role more effectively. The decision was not overly popular with the P–47 commanders since they had grown to love their big fighters and had learned to take advantage of the Thunderbolt's great diving speed, massive firepower and strong airframe. P–38 group commanders seemed to take the decision a little bit more philosophically since they realized that the P–38J was only just becoming a fully combat effective aircraft and, besides, many of them had the chance to fly Mustangs and realized the potential of North America's sleek fighter.

The Ninth Air Force, whose mission was primarily tactical, sent its first combat Lightning patrol out on 25 April 1944 with its 474th FG but the Ninth was to be also effected by Doolittle's orders. Although the Ninth had gotten two other Lightning groups (the 367th and 370th) operational, the units found themselves quickly converting to the Mustang and the Thunderbolt.

The Lightning's role in the ETO was not particularly long nor particularly covered in glory but every British schoolboy that saw the Lightning's distinctive shape was fascinated by the 'Yank' warplane and probably carries the memory with him today. Although the Lightning had given distinguished service in North Africa and Italy, had taken the bombers to Berlin from Britain and had performed invaluable recon work, its true fame was yet to come: the Lightning would achieve immortality over the vast Pacific, fighting the Japanese.

The Lightning met the Japanese for the first time in an unlikely location which was also one of the most hostile places on the face of the earth: the Aleutians. The Japanese, wishing to secure as many fronts against the weakened Americans after Pearl Harbor, invaded the island of Kiska in the Aleutian chain off the northwest tip of Alaska during June 1942. The enemy quickly set up fortifications, an airfield and a crude port that could receive both warships and floatplanes. As mentioned earlier in this chapter, the Aleutians proved to be such a hostile environment that more aircraft were lost to the terrible weather than to the enemy. However, the early P–38s used in the fighting gave good service and scored the first Lightning victories over the powerful Japanese.

The enemy moved quickly after Pearl Harbor, capturing one Allied stronghold after another until it seemed the Japanese tidal wave could not be stopped. Australia was a particular plum which the Japanese had been eyeing for quite some time, as the huge island continent would serve as an ideal base for future conquests. The rag-tag US Fifth Air Force which was headquartered in Australia had a motley collection of fighting machines, some of them survivors of earlier, disastrous battles with the Japanese.

The first Lightnings in Australia were not desperately needed fighters but four F–4 photo recon birds that arrived on 7 April 1942 under the command of Major Karl Polifka and designated as the 8th Photographic Squadron. They were needed just as badly as combat aircraft since Allied commanders had little idea what the Japanese were doing. Reports from the coast watchers were often out of date because of the time that it took them to reach headquarters, but a fast-moving aircraft equipped

*By all accounts, Thomas B. McGuire was an
unpleasant man with a large ego but he was
also a top-notch fighter pilot. Caught up in the ace
'race' with Dick Bong, McGuire was always a step
or two behind Bong. McGuire had started out his
military career flying Airacobras in the Aleutians
and he took the 'race' very seriously. When Bong
was sent back to the States after breaking
Rickenbacker's WWI record, McGuire thought that
he had the field to himself and was not pleased
when Bong returned for a second tour. Bong raised
his score to forty and was sent home for good so
McGuire tried frantically to break the forty mark.
When McGuire got his score up to thirty-eight,
General George Kenney (who favored the easy-
going Bong) grounded McGuire until Bong could be
fully honored upon his return home. Airborne
again after a few days on the ground, McGuire went
after a Japanese fighter at very low altitude and, in
the rush for a victory, committed one of the most
basic errors: stalling the P–38. The fighter slammed
into the ocean and he was killed.*

with reliable cameras could carry out recon missions over vast stretches of territory, relying on speed advantage to stay out of the reach of enemy fighters. Quickly moving to the famous Port Moresby airstrip, the 8th began operating from New Guinea searching out enemy airfields, shipping and troop concentrations, and bringing back hundreds of high quality photographs that could be interpreted carefully to gain valuable knowledge upon which future raids could be based. These four F–4s provided virtually the entire intelligence on which the early battle strategy against the Japanese empire would be based.

The first fighter Lightnings to arrive in

Australia consisted of 25 P–38Fs that were assigned to the 35th Fighter Group as the 39th Fighter Squadron, which converted from very tired Bell Airacobras. The Lightnings' first combat base was Jackson Field, Port Moresby. The P–38Fs had been plagued with mechanical problems during training in Australia and some of these problems continued in New Guinea when the squadron was taken into combat under the command of Captain George Prentice. Entering combat in October, it was not until 27 December 1942 that the 39th scored its first success when eleven Japanese aircraft were knocked down in exchange for the loss of one F model. One of the pilots achieving two victories was Lt Richard Bong who would go on to become America's ace of aces.

Major General George Kenney was in charge of the Fifth and he was a proponent of the P–38 from the start. Lobbying hard and long, Kenney was not successful in getting the numbers of Lightnings that he required. P–38s dribbled into the Fifth's inventory and many of the missions had to be flown with a mixed gaggle of very tired P–40s and P–39s. The Lightning was very fast, heavily armed and, while not as maneuverable as the Japanese fighters, could still tackle the enemy if they did not attempt to engage in a dogfight at low or medium altitudes. An extra bonus was the two engines which gave pilots an extra chance of survival when operating over the uncharter ed Pacific. Kenney's demands did produce a limited flow of Lightnings and the second unit to form with the new fighter was the 8th FG with the 49th FG following shortly. However, the fighters were in such short supply that each Fighter Group could only form one Lightning squadron apiece. The Thirteenth Air Force, operating out of the Solomons, also wanted P–38s because of their range and twin engines and the 339th FS, 347th FG was equipped with Lightnings and began operating out of Henderson Field, Guadalcanal, with its first combat occurring on 18 November 1942 when the Lightnings flew a bomber escort mission.

Late 1942 and early 1943 saw the small numbers of Lightnings combined with Bell P–39s, P–400s and Curtiss P–40s and sent out on endless missions to combat the Japanese. Even though the Bells and Curtisses were outmoded they did an excellent job attacking Japanese ground and shipping targets while performing creditably in aerial combat. The P–38s also participated in the ground attack missions and quite often they were called upon for long range escort missions with the Mitchells, Fortresses and Liberators. With the American high command deciding that new fighters must first be supplied to USAAF units

U.S. ARMY P-38J-20-LO
AIR FORCES SER.44234GI
CREW WEIGHT 200 LBS
SERVICE THIS AIRPLANE
WITH 100 OCTANE FUEL
SUITABLE FOR AROMATICS
IF NOT AVAILABLE CONSULT
T.O. 00-2-1 FOR EMERGENCY

in Britain, the pilots and commanders in the Pacific knew that they had a long, hard war in front of them with only the barest minimum of warplanes to put up against the enemy.

Adversity often breeds success, and the pilots and mechanics of the Fifth and Thirteenth Air Forces literally performed miracles by keeping the Lightnings operational and by beating, over and over, the Japanese – an enemy that probably thought their secure island bases would never be challenged, much less defeated. One of the greatest of all Lightning missions was flown on 18 April 1943 when pilots from the Thirteenth's 18th and 347th FGs literally assassinated one of Japan's greatest commanders.

American cryptographers had scored a major coup when they broke the Japanese secret code which was used to transmit important messages across the Pacific. The code breakers discovered that Admiral Isoroku Yamamoto (one of the main planners of the

Pearl Harbor attack) would be flying to Ballale airfield on Shortland Island in a Betty bomber. Several other Bettys would be in the flight, also carrying high-ranking Japanese. The flight would be protected by Zeroes but the Japanese thought that the vast stretches of Pacific airspace would make an American interception of the flight unlikely, which was probably true if the code had not been broken.

With only a short time to prepare, P–38Fs and Gs were equipped for the long range flight and a mix of 165 and 310 US gallon drop tanks were added to the underwing pylons. The pilots were briefed on the mission and its importance – both in propaganda and in the denying to the Japanese one of their greatest military minds. Timing was absolutely essential since range was a prime consideration and a mistake in timing could cause the P–38 flight to miss the enemy formation completely. Sixteen P–38s launched from Henderson Field, Guadalcanal, on the 18 April and headed out

Major Richard Bong, America's ace of aces with forty confirmed victories, stands by P–38J–20–LO 44–233461, one of several Lightnings that he flew in combat. Bong, regarded by the military as a 'boy next door' type (and heavily promoted as such), survived his combat tours without a scratch only to die after returning to Burbank to fly a new P–80 jet fighter. The engine quit shortly after takeoff and crashed into a parking lot on 6 August 1945.

on the 500-mile flight to Shortland Island. The enemy was intercepted on schedule and the P–38s immediately attacked the Betty bombers. The Betty carrying Yamamoto was hit repeatedly by shells from Captain Thomas Lanphier Jr's guns and it rolled over and plummeted into the jungle, killing all aboard. [The wreckage of the Betty was recently discovered, covered by jungle growth, and the special seat in which Yamamoto sat was recovered.] Another Betty and five fighters were dispatched before the Lightnings turned and headed home, leaving the Japanese naval command stunned over their loss.

General Kenney's requests for more Lightnings kept falling on deaf ears. Although the 475th FG was able to equip completely with Lightnings during August 1943, this was not a signal of improved conditions. The 475th was able to keep operational with hard work and creative repair of damaged aircraft since replacement parts and engines were in very short supply. On the debit side, the 35th and 49th FG had to *drop* their only P–38 squadrons because of insufficient numbers and convert to Thunderbolts. The long and costly fight towards the end of 1943 saw heavy casualties for both sides as fierce air battles raged over contested islands. Giant dogfights regularly took place, but, when the final results were analyzed, the Japanese kept coming out on the losing end. The vast loss of aircraft and experienced pilots, many whose service dated back to the Manchurian campaign, was to be an irreplaceable blow to the Empire. The Japanese scheme for training new pilots was not sufficient to supply needs and, rather than

revise and form a more sensible training program, a new training program was instigated that produced hurriedly trained aviators that were not really fit for combat. The Japanese were also having the same problem with their aircraft. The Zero was a superb dogfighter, perhaps the best ever built, but once the Americans learned the rules of the game, the Zero was an easy mark with its fragile construction, lack of armor protection and non-sealing fuel tanks. American pilots, particularly P–38 pilots, began building rapid scores over the enemy.

The American P–38 aces were a mixed bunch, ranging from rather unpleasant career builders to quiet introverts. One of the quieter ones was Daniel T. 'Preacher' Roberts. Roberts had intended to become a minister, hence the nickname, but the coming war convinced him to join the Army and take up flying – winning his wings just a few weeks before Pearl Harbor. Roberts did not drink, did not use profanity and was not a hell-raiser – making him a bit

P–38s were often very colorfully marked as is the case with Pappy's Birr-die, the P–38 flown by Major Pappy Kline shortly after he took over the 431st Fighter Squadron following the death of Tom McGuire. (N. Krane)

different from his fellow fighter pilots. Sent to combat with the 80th FS, 8th FG, Fifth Air Force, Roberts was shipped to Darwin, Australia, to fly P–39s and P–400s and it was in these obsolescent fighters that he gained his first two victories. After the unit had been operating in New Guinea and seeing heavy action, it was pulled back to Australia for re-equipping. Roberts, now a captain, was pleased to see the new fighters were P–38s, and the squadron returned to Port Moresby in March 1943, beginning combat missions soon after.

Roberts found the P–38 to his liking. On one of the first combat patrols, the squadron ran into a huge formation of enemy aircraft, estimated at 20 Val dive bombers and an equal number of escorting Zeros, that was on its way to attack Allied shipping in Oro Bay. The P–38s screamed into the enemy, catching the Japanese by surprise. Roberts sent a burst into a Val and saw pieces of it fly off but he was then attacked by three fighters. Yanking the '38 around, Roberts got beneath one of the Zeros and blew off a wing with a burst of machine gun and cannon fire. The rest of the squadron was doing equally as well and, when the combat ended, eleven Zeros and three Vals had been knocked down – Roberts being credited with two.

When the 475th FG became an all-Lightning unit in May 1943, experienced officers were sought out to join the group. Accordingly, Roberts was transferred to the 475th's 433rd FS in order to instruct younger pilots on the virtues of the P–38. Roberts' talent was sufficiently appreciated that he was made squadron commander on 4 October 1943. His main tactic was to have the squadron stick together and hunt like a wolf pack rather than to rely on individual action.

Roberts' score continued to grow when he destroyed three Zeros over Rabaul on 23 October. The Zeros were attempting to intercept a flight of Liberators that the 433rd was protecting and the resulting battle decimated the determined enemy. The last two months of 1943 merged into a blur of constant missions as the P–38s flew several times a day. The least liked target was Rabaul, very heavily defended by anti-aircraft guns, but it was frequently visited by American bombers that were attempting to knock out the airfields in the area. The P–38s had to fly at reduced speed when protecting the bombers and were quite often subjected to intense flak. One memorable mission on 9 November saw 20 enemy fighters attack Roberts' 433rd Squadron and the group of B–25 Mitchells that they were defending. His P–38s had to stay near the bombers and were subjected to repeated attacks but the P–38s of the 431st and 432nd Squadrons were providing high cover and their diving passes eventually broke the enemy's will, but not before three Lightnings fell in flames. The bombers got through and blasted their targets.

Flying fighter aircraft in the heat of combat calls for immense skill and judgement and the slightest error can be fatal. On 9 November, Roberts' squadron was once again on a bomber escort mission to Rabaul and, once again, were met by a determined enemy. Roberts got a long burst into a Hamp which smashed into the ocean and exploded. By this time the dogfight had descended to virtually sea level and wingtips were almost hitting the water as the fighters maneuvered into firing positions. A single Zero was spotted racing low, heading for its home airfield. Roberts, his wingman and another Lightning pilot spotted the Zero and took off in pursuit. The Zero pilot saw his pursuers, kicked in right rudder in an attempt to make a very tight turn which the P–38s would not be able to follow. Roberts rolled his Lightning hard right but his wingman, acting a split-second too slowly, smashed into the tail booms of his leader's aircraft. Both fighters exploded and fell into the ocean. Preacher Danny Roberts was dead. He had shot down 15 aircraft and the 433rd, during his 37 days of command, had destroyed 55 Japanese aircraft with a loss of only three Lightnings. His story was not atypical.

The American war machine in the Pacific began to pick up speed and compile victory after victory over what was thought to be an invincible enemy. The American public, most only dimly aware of the exotic battle locales mentioned on the radio news reports, began to idolize the young pilots and their distinctive twin-boomed fighters that would not give way to the enemy. War correspondents did their part, sending long stories back home on how the Lightning pilots were enduring hardship on the ground as well as in the air to defeat the enemy. It was a deadly battleground over the vast jungles or over the brilliant blue Pacific where no quarter was given. Back home, a popular song was written about the P–38 while women wore P–38 silhouettes as jewelry – made out of the new 'miracle' material lucite.

General Kenney's long argument to get more Lightnings to the battlefront was finally paying off and aircraft directly off the production line were shipped to the Pacific. The newer variants of the Lightning were much better suited to Pacific operations and, with their improved range and increased horsepower, began to take an even bigger toll on the Japanese. By the middle of 1944, the Fifth and Thirteenth Air Forces were consolidated into the Far East Air Forces (FEAF) under Kenney's capable command. Kenney was now able to field five P–38 groups (8th, 18th, 49th, 347th and 475th) and among these groups were many aces whose scores were rapidly on the rise. Over 40 pilots were to become aces in the Pacific by flying Lightnings exclusively. In the summer of 1944, the enemy was in retreat – giving up each island in a bloody and costly battle which usually left most of the Japanese defenders dead – and the Lightnings were ranging far and wide on a variety of missions including dive bombing, fighter sweep, escort and recon.

The press had developed a contest between two P–38 pilots, Dick Bong and Tom McGuire, whose scores were rising. In actuality, it *was* a contest since McGuire was determined to become the top scoring American pilot. McGuire, by reports from the people who served with him, was an unpleasant individual with an immense ego but, at the same time, he was also a very good fighter pilot. Bong, on the other hand, projected an image of the 'All-American Boy'. By late 1943, it was clearly apparent that the race was on. However, when Neel E. Kearby and his 348th FG equipped with Thunderbolts entered the area, it became a three-way race. Kearby, an aggressive commander and pilot, rapidly pushed up his score with the powerful P–47D. On one mission, on 11 October 1943, he blasted seven enemy fighters but was only credited with six because his gun camera ran out of film! Kearby's race was ended on 9 March 1944 when he was shot down and killed. His official score stood at 22.

Using Captain Edward Rickenbacker's WWI score of 28 German aircraft destroyed as a watershed mark, the press gleefully reported on the exploits of the two pilots. Bong, 49th FG, was the first to reach the 'magic' score, but he was soon sent home on leave to give War Bond lectures. Thomas McGuire, 475th FG, took advantage of Bong's leave to raise his score to 28 and was irritated to discover that Bong was to be sent back to the Pacific for a second combat tour. Bong tackled the enemy with his usual skill and daring, running up his score to 40 destroyed by 17 December. Having been awarded the Medal of Honor earlier, Bong returned to the United States a hero and was sent on an extensive press and patriotic tour around the country. McGuire, once again taking advantage of Bong's absence, made a determined effort to raise his score as high as possible but, on 7 January 1945, he committed a basic error that ended the race. McGuire and three other P–38s were dogfighting with a single Japanese fighter when he racked his P–38 in a tight turn, entered a high speed stall and spun into the ocean. McGuire's final score was 38 destroyed and he was awarded a posthumous Medal of Honor. Bong did not enjoy his title for long. During August, he was killed when the new P–80 jet fighter he was flying crashed shortly after take-off from Burbank.

One reason that so many pilots were successful with the P–38 in the Pacific is the fact that the later versions of the fighter were superb fighting machines. The factory had been working constantly on improving the aircraft, and one of the major improvements was the addition of dive brakes which would fight the compressibility problem in a steep dive. The flaps were attached to the main spar outside each engine nacelle. The flaps could be activated instantly via a button on the control wheel, enabling the pilot to recover from a dive bombing run or after building up speed to escape an enemy fighter. A Lightning was fitted with the brakes during February 1943

*The colorful nose art on **Windy City Ruthie** illustrates ten kills along with various crew names. Since the P–38 had so much room for names and personal markings, it was not uncommon for the crew chiefs to decorate the engine nacelles with their own art, leaving the fuselage pod for the pilot.*

and was flown by none other than Colonel Ben Kelsey who felt that the device should immediately be incorporated into the P–38 production line. However, due to politics and other bureaucratic considerations, the dive brake was not incorporated until 14 months later! This damning bit of negligence certainly cost many P–38 pilots their lives while restricting the fighter from becoming a very efficient warplane. The modification was not incorporated until the P–38J–25–LO.

As the island-hopping war drew near to the Home Islands, P–38s were regularly overflying areas such as Formosa and Korea. Bases in the Philippines and Ie Shima provided the staging points needed for the long-legged Lightnings. Saved from a costly final combat by the

dropping of two nuclear bombs on Japan, the Lightning had the honor of being the first Allied fighter to land in Japan after the unconditional surrender of that country on 15 August 1945.

Unfortunately, there was no career for the Lightning after the end of World War Two. Many aircraft were not even brought back to the United States for disposal. Instead, a demolition man would throw a grenade into the cockpit and the mangled fighter would be pushed into a pit by a bulldozer – an inglorious end for the Army fighter that had defeated the Japanese. The military decided to standardize on the P–51 as the main propeller-driven fighter back in the States. Besides, all those new jets were coming into service and the Army did not want 'obsolescent' propeller-driven fighters. The final indignity was that the Army did not even bother to save a Lightning for Hap Arnold's proposed air museum.

Some mention should be made of the brief foreign use of the P–38. During World War

Two, the Lightning was operated by the Free French in some numbers in the *Forces Aeriennes Françaises Libres.* Operating photo recon variants, the French performed useful work in North Africa. One of the most famous French Lightning pilots was the author Commandant Antoine de Saint-Exupery who simply disappeared off southern France on 31 July 1944. The Australians received three F–4s whose entire service life amounted to less than three months. China received an unspecified number of fighter and photo recon Lightnings. Some Lightnings that had force-landed in Portugal during 1942 were retained and operated by the Portuguese Air Force. After the war, Italy received 50 Lightnings to help re-equip its new air force while a handful went to Honduras in Central America. Today, the Lightning is an extremely rare type with only a few in museums. However, about six are still flown by civilian collectors and serve as a reminder of the greatest twin-engine propeller-driven fighter.

BLACK BIRDS

The war ended before the P–38M night-fighter had a chance to prove itself in combat.

The young pilots who reported for duty as night-fighting trainees were more than a bit disappointed when they saw the sort of aircraft that lined the hot ramp at Williams Field in Arizona. It was early 1943 and the hopes of a rapid entry into service by the advanced Northrop P–61 Black Widow were becoming dim because of developmental problems with the big twin-engine fighters. The aircraft which awaited the trainee pilots were a mixed and motley bag of RP–322 Lightnings and Douglass P–70s.

The RP–322 had come about through a strange gestation. The British, during their massive aircraft orders of 1939 and 1940, contracted with Lockheed for 667 P–38 figh-

ters. However, the British apparently wanted to keep the big fighters as simple as possible so they specified in the contract that the counter-rotating propellers and turbosuperchargers (this particular item being in short supply) be removed in the Lightning Mk I. Without this equipment, the twin-tailed fighter was limited to low altitudes and engine-out flight became a real difficulty. After testing the first few of these machines, the British decided to cancel their order and around 138 completed aircraft were transferred to the Army with the designation RP–322.

The Army did not quite know what to do with their new mount so they were assigned as restricted twin-engine trainers and sent to various training fields in the American Southwest. These were the aircraft with which the new pilots were burdened. (The Douglas P–70s are another story and their lack of success is described in a separate chapter.)

In the Army's quest to build an effective night fighter force, most hopes were pinned on the massive Black Widow but, with delayed deliveries, some sort of make-shift night fighter force had to be concocted. These trainee pilots who were gathered at Williams were to become the central core for the 418th and 419th Night Fighter Squadrons but there was a long way to go before they became an effective unit. Training in the RP–322 and P–70 gave valuable twin-engine experience but both aircraft were so slow that they stood little chance of catching the more advanced enemy aircraft. Various tactics were experi-

Posing for the Lockheed photographer during a test flight from the company's Burbank, California, facility is P–38M 44–27234. During test operations in warm Southern California the radar operator must have baked in his tight fitting bubble. All Ms were conversions of P–38L aircraft. Note the unpainted stainless steel panels that surround the turbosuperchargers on top of the twin booms. (Lockheed)

*F*uture P–38 night fighter pilots were horrified to find that part of their training would be undertaken with obsolete and dangerous RP–322 fighters abandoned by the British. Originally designated Lightning Mk Is by the RAF, the British fighters were a far cry from the American operated P–38s. The British wanted nothing to do with contra-rotating propellers and turbosuperchargers – against Lockheed's strenuous advice – and the resulting aircraft was a poor performer with dangerous engine-out flying characteristics. The USAAF assumed the bulk of the order and made the aircraft restricted pursuit trainers with the designation RP–322. The fledgling night fighter trainees flew these machines and equally obsolete P–70s. A well-worn RP–322, still retaining its RAF serial AF101, is seen undergoing engine tests at Newark, New Jersey, on 16 April 1946.

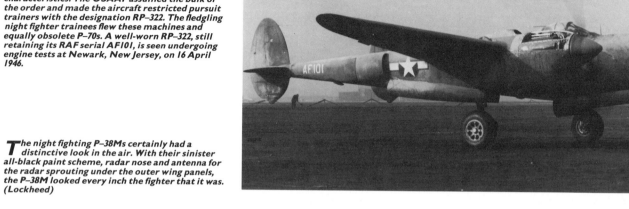

*T*he night fighting P–38Ms certainly had a distinctive look in the air. With their sinister all-black paint scheme, radar nose and antenna for the radar sprouting under the outer wing panels, the P–38M looked every inch the fighter that it was. (Lockheed)

mented with in the clear night skies over Arizona but an effective method of dealing with enemy aircraft at night did not evolve. They key to the whole operation lay with an effective radar system and the speed to intercept and destroy the night intruders.

By the end of their training period as night fighter pilots, the group of students realized that the Black Widow would not be forthcoming and resigned themselves to the fact that they would be going overseas with P–70s. At least the Douglas twin-engine fighters were superior to the RP–322s – but then, just about anything was superior to the RP–322!

The night fighter pilots were sent by ship to Guadalcanal where they arrived near the end of 1943. The 418th Night Fighter Squadron had been activated on 17 March 1943 and its first overseas base was Milne Bay, New Guinea, which was occupied on 2 November 1943. The 418th NFS pilots had high hopes of taking

care of any Japanese night intruders and devised a colorful emblem to be carried by their aircraft. Official records describe the insignia as:

Over and through a blue-green disc, a king bee black and golden orange, wearing a red crown, holding aloft a lighted lantern proper with the right foreleg, and grasping a gray machine gun in the left foreleg, tip-toeing across a white cloud formation in base, and peering over the edge with a look of ferocity on his face; a crescent moon and two stars of yellow in the background.

In operation, the P–70 proved to be a failure in most respects and some of the enemy bombers could actually outrun the modified Douglas light bomber. The 419th NFS arrived at Guadalcanal on 15 November 1943 and immediately began experiencing the same problems as the 418th. Supplies of P–70s were not sufficient to bring the units up to full strength so each squadron was assigned a

small number of P–38H Lightnings which was a great improvement over the RP–322.

With mixed bags of Lightnings and P–70s prowling the skies, pilots began working on tactics to intercept enemy bombers. The P–38s were stock day fighters with absolutely no radar or any other equipment for finding the enemy at night. The Lightning pilots would wait until the enemy aircraft were over target and, hopefully, illuminated by the defender's searchlights. They would then try to pick out the outline of the enemy aircraft and intercept. This was a dangerous method of operation because the P–38 was subjecting itself to anti-aircraft fire from the defenders as well as to being spotted by the bomber's gunners.

419th pilot Lt Donald Dessert checked out in the first P–38H assigned to the unit and flew the first of the searchlight patrols between 1945 and 2145 hrs on 10 December 1943. This patrol did not have any result and other pilots were equally baffled in trying to find the enemy by searchlight. The method had been used in Britain during the early days of World War Two with some success but it was a still far from ideal method. Ground Control Intercept (GCI) radar was installed later to help vector the P–38H pilots towards the enemy but

this did little good. A fast, powerfully armed fighter with its own radar was needed and the Black Widow was still months away.

With almost 400 night missions being flown by the end of 1944, the 419th pilots only claimed three enemy aircraft. One pilot, Henry Meigs, nailed two Mitsubishi G4M Betty bombers over Guadalcanal and was awarded the Distinguished Flying Cross by Admiral 'Bull' Halsey who was probably happy to see something finally happening with the night fighter unit.

The American talent for improvising in the face of adversity came to the fore during the quest for an efficient night fighter. Pilots and mechanics of the 6th Fighter Squadron (whose ancestry goes directly back to the 6th Aero Squadron of World War One) fitted out at least two P–38G Lightnings with a second seat and a radar unit mounted in a drop tank. The

SCR–540 gave the two man crew the 'night eyes' they needed but the New Guinea detachment of the 6th was disbanded before the ingenious 'Rube Goldberg' invention could be put to combat use. Other modifications by other units were also apparently carried out and the 547th NFS in the Philippines modified at least two single-seat P–38J fighters with APS–4 radar but the results of most of these field modifications are lost to time.

As with most ideas, it seems that the thought of converting the Lightning into a real night fighter came to a number of men at roughly the same time. The Lightning was a good choice for the mission: it had excellent visibility, long range, heavy armament and the added reliability of a second engine. Stateside, at least one P–38J had been reworked to carry AN/APS–4 radar in a large fiber pod. During initial tests, the pod was carried under the rear

The pilot's position in the P–38M was basically the same as on the P–38L. (Lockheed)

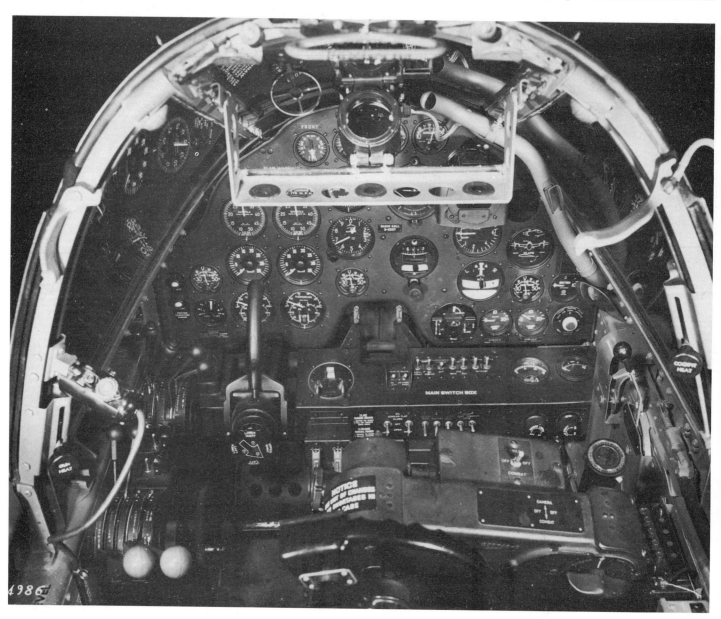

On the P–38M, the scope for the radar unit projected directly into the R/O's face. If the war had continued there was some discussion of using the basic two-seat P–38M concept as a dual control trainer. Note how the black paint quickly scuffed and chipped away. (Lockheed/AD–6541)

Working accommodations for the P–38M crew were far from ideal. R/Os were probably ideally of small stature for, with a back pack parachute, the R/O's head was firmly jammed against the top of the bubble canopy. (Lockheed/AD–6540)

AD-6791

*D*etail view illustrating the fiber dome for the radar unit and its mounting to the standard fighter nose on P–38M–5–LO 44–26865. This shot also shows to advantage the blast muzzles on the four .50 caliber machine guns and one 20 mm cannon. Pylons on the wing center section could carry bombs or extra gas tanks. Lockheed/AD–6791)

*A*fter the war, the P–38Ms were quickly disposed of, most having only a few flying hours. P–38M–1–LO 44–53085A, still with factory stencilling applied, is seen 'out to pasture' in company with at least two other Ms. At least one M was supplied to the air force of Honduras but it was probably operated as a day fighter.

fuselage but it was quickly damaged by the rain of expended cartridges when the machine guns and cannon were fired. The pod was later moved to an outboard wing panel and the installation worked fairly well. A number of Lightnings had been converted in the field to two-seat configuration. These aircraft were often used as squadron hacks and to give the ground-bound mechanics a taste of what flying was like (or to carry the mechanic after an engine overhaul – a method which was sure to result in excellent workmanship during the engine rebuild). Other two-seat modifications were used to carry high-ranking officers on fast – and heavily escorted – trips over battlefields to see what the situation looked like from the air. The P–38 was fully capable of carrying a second seat but the installation – usually in the space directly behind the pilot – gave little room.

All these factors were eventually combined and, during the last months of 1944, the Army contracted with Lockheed for the conversion of a P–38L into the new role of night fighter. While all this was happening, deliveries of P–61 fighters to combat units had started and the Black Widow, while it had a number of problems, was infinitely better than any other Army attempt at a night fighter. The 418th NFS quickly dumped all but two of their P–38s, but these two aircraft continued night operations and, on 22 February 1944, Lt Dorval Brown made the first nocturnal bombing drop on Rabaul in company with Captain Emerson Baker in the other Lightning. These non-radar P–38s still had no success in tracking enemy fighters but they did participate in night-time harassment missions against the Japanese.

Serial number 44–26865 became the first P–38M (there were no XP or YP M models, the series just assuming immediate production). Modifications included the installation of the radar in a large fiber pod under the forward nose, blast muzzles on the weapons to prevent the pilot's night vision from being ruined and a second seat for the radar operator behind the pilot. The radar operator (r/o) sat perched higher than the pilot with the viewing port for the radar set projecting directly into his face. To give the r/o some headroom, his position was fitted with a blown bubble canopy but, even so, it was a very tight fit and the r/os would have to be chosen with a regard to their height or lack of it. The first flight for the night fighting Lightning took place on 5 February 1945, by which time the P–61 was firmly established in service and setting an impressive record against rapidly dwindling enemy air forces. The USAAF ordered 75 M models but this seemed almost a token gesture since the war was obviously winding to a conclusion.

Flight testing of the P–38M started in July 1945 at Hammer Field, the large night fighter base just east of Fresno, California. Testing revealed that the M had a better performance envelope than the P–61 but that the P–61 was better suited as a night fighter. Records on the deployment of the P–38M are not entirely clear but it does appear that only four made it to the Philippines before the war ended. However, P–38Ms were stationed in Japan with occupation forces, but the majority of completed aircraft were either scrapped or put for sales as surplus. A couple of P–38Ms appeared at the post-war Cleveland Air Races and at least one was sold to the air force of Honduras as a day fighter. This aircraft survived a long period of service, although gathering only a few hours of flying time, before being returned to America. Today, this P–38M is beautifully restored and displayed at the Champlin Fighter Museum, Mesa, Arizona, as the sole surviving example of the Lightning night fighter.

LIGHTNING ODDITIES

Like any other World War Two production fighter, the P–38 was subjected to a wide variety of modifications – some successful, some not . . .

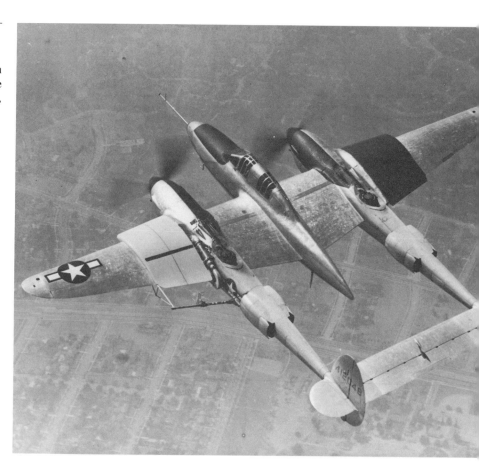

*C*ertainly one of the worst looking modifications ever performed on a P–38, this one-off Lightning was a drastic conversion of P–38E 41–2048 and was used for a wide variety of tests. In this photograph the aircraft, dubbed 'Swordfish', is testing airfoils. Note what appears to be a spray boom behind the airfoil addition on the left and the extra and complex ducting near the wing root. Thirty inches were added to the front portion of the center fuselage pod and forty-eight inches to the rear, and two cockpits were installed. This creation first took to the air on 2 June 1943 and Tony Le Vier found that the aircraft dived at a faster speed than any other Lightning. The Swordfish survived the war and was used by Lockheed to test concepts for other aircraft (as it is doing in the photograph), but was eventually surplused and turned up as a civilian aircraft with at least four seats! The Swordfish finally met its doom in the early 1960s when it was destroyed in a crash. (Lockheed)

Attractively decked out in bare metal finish, a red fuselage stripe, red, white and blue tail stripes, and the name Piggie Back on the boom intake, P–38F–1–LO 41–7485 was retained by Lockheed for use as a development airframe. In this role the P–38 was modified to have a second seat directly behind the pilot. From this extremely uncomfortable position, pilot trainees were to be introduced to the wonder of Lightning operations. The use of such a trainer was limited but it would be of value to illustrate some of the P–38's more dangerous flight characteristics such as engine out operation. Flown by famed 1930's record flight pilot Jimmy Mattern, the P–38 was used briefly in this role before the idea was dropped. Note the ADF 'bullet' under the nose. This aircraft did not carry any armament. (Lockheed)

Another bizarre P–38E conversion was this aircraft which featured drastically upswept tail booms in an attempt to cure the early Lightnings' problems of compressibility in a dive. The idea behind the upswept tail was to raise the unit above the disturbed airflow from the wing and thus aid in control during high speed dives. Serial number 41–1986 was flown by Lockheed test pilot Ralph Virden but he was killed when the aircraft failed to pull out of a high speed dive. Engineers eventually found the answer by installing new wing fillets, a modification that would not slow down the production line because of drastic airframe modifications. (Lockheed)

Opposite

One of the many weapon configuration experiments carried out by Lockheed with the Lightning was this modification of a P–38F to carry two torpedoes. Fitted with sway braces, the torpedoes were dropped without any problem but the concept was not put into operation. This aircraft also has its nose armament removed. (Lockheed/Z3561)

Right

Yet another P–38 weapon configuration experiment, the P–38F in the photograph is equipped with four bazooka-style rocket launchers that each carried three 4.5 in rockets. (Lockheed/Z5600)

Opposite below

Well-worn RP–38 40–744 Jollie was subject of an interesting modification. Army scientists were studying the effects on the human body of flying in a different position other than the center line of the aircraft. The Germans were also experimenting with this concept and the Army found that the easiest test bed for conversion was, of course, the P–38 with its twin booms. 744 was accordingly modified to carry an extra cockpit in the left boom in place of the turbosupercharger and testing was carried out at Wright AAFB in Ohio. (Lockheed/F1361)

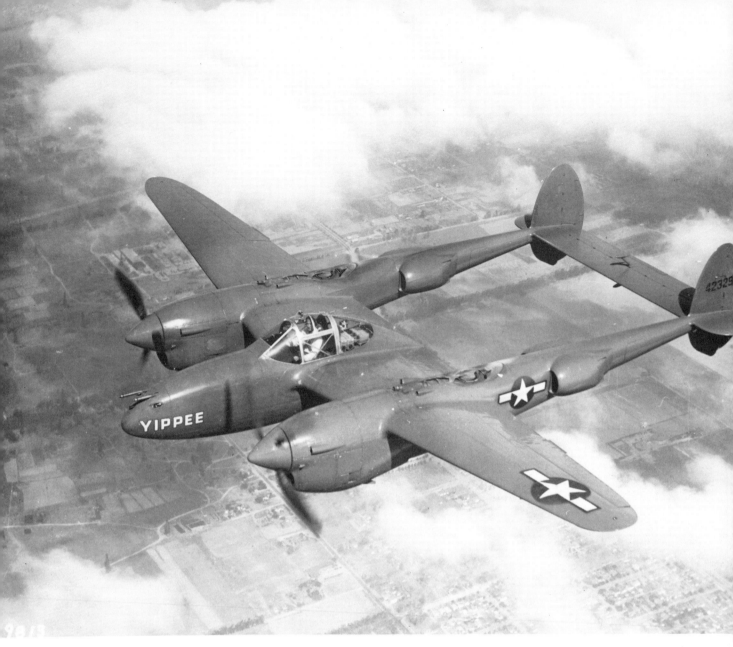

*C*ertainly the most colorful Lightning ever
built, P–38J–20–LO 44–23296 was painted a
glorious bright red overall with the name Yippee
painted on the nose and under the wing in white
with a black outline. The unusual paint scheme was
applied to celebrate the 5,000th Lightning built.
The aircraft was used for publicity and war bond
drives before going into regular military service.
(Lockheed/T9813)

*A*mong the armament experiments with the
Lightning was this P–38L–1–LO with 14 rockets
mounted on zero length launchers under the wing.
Rocket mounting was eventually standardized on
the 'Christmas Tree' arrangement that had the
rockets mounted in clusters of five.
(Lockheed/S5858)

*O*ne of the more interesting modifications to
be forced on the P–38 airframe was the
addition of tow harnesses to the rear of the tail
booms that enabled the Lightning to test its
capabilities in hauling Waco CG–4A combat
gliders. Seen during an initial test, the P–38 is still
on the ground as the CG–4 begins to rise in the air.
Plans were under way to enable the P–38 to carry as
many as three CG–4s into combat but the idea was
dropped when the decision was made to delegate
the transport of gliders to cargo aircraft such as
the C–46 and C–47. (Lockheed)

S-5858

'*D*roop Snoot' Lightnings (about 25 had been so modified) were replaced by the more sophisticated P–38L Pathfinder aircraft. The Pathfinder had a greatly extended nose that carried AN/APS–15 radar (Bomb Through Overcast) which was called 'Mickey'. The operator sat behind the radar and had two windows from which he could contemplate the outside world. This prototype aircraft was photographed at Lockheed on 6 June 1944 and the XP–58 can be seen parked in the background. (Lockheed/S527)

PHOTO FIGHTERS

Although totally unarmed, these Lightnings made an invaluable contribution to the war effort by being able to photograph enemy territory in considerable detail.

An F–5B–1–LO 42–67332, is seen in company with P–38J–5–LO 42–67183 during a photo flight over the San Gabriel Mountains near the Lockheed plant in Burbank, California. The F–5B–1–LO was the reconnaissance version of the P–38J–10–LO and 200 were built, four being transferred to the Navy as FO–1s. Most of the early photographic Lightnings were painted in a strange color scheme with what was known as Haze Paint. The original Haze Paint was found to actually make the aircraft more visible at altitude so there was a fairly rapid shuffle to find a replacement. Sherwin-Williams Paint Company and Army officials came up with what was known as 'Synthetic Haze Paint'. This color scheme consisted of Sky Base Blue and a synthetic haze enamel called Flight Blue. The Lightning test aircraft was painted overall Sky Base Blue and then Flight Blue was sprayed over the shadow areas of the aircraft and in light coats on the side of the fuselage pod and booms. The new combination seemed to work fairly well and was adopted by March 1943 as the official paint scheme for the F–5s coming off the Lockheed line. However, the interpretation of this scheme was open to question and, depending if the aircraft was painted at the factory or in the field or modification depot, there was a wide difference of application style. The F–5B in the photograph also carries the short-lived red surround to the national insignia. (Lockheed)

From D–Day minus seven until D–Day plus fourteen, F–5s took 3,000,000 aerial photographs of the Normandy coast and General Eisenhower credited the F–5s with furnishing him with the most valuable information on invasion progress during the period. General Hap Arnold once commented: 'Our photo-reconnaissance pilots are instructed to fly on the theory that fighter planes win battles while camera planes win wars.' The warmly dressed pilot of this Lockheed F–5A watches while camera gear is installed in the spacious nose compartment that held guns and ammunition for the P–38s. This particular Lightning is painted with Haze Paint. The original application of Haze Paint was a bit complex: the Lightning was supposed to be painted overall black, a thin coat of haze being applied over the top of the aircraft and down the sides which resulted in a very dark blue color. Heavy haze was then sprayed on the undersurfaces and the remainder of the aircraft, producing a very light blue color. The point between the heavy and light coats of haze was sprayed with a medium coat of the paint and the resulting color was a sort of a medium blue. Needless to say, this process was time consuming and it took a full working day just to let the paint dry and extreme quality control and good lighting were necessary to have the paint applied according to specification. The finish itself quickly changed color and weathered in the sun and, as previously mentioned, the Haze Paint became very visible above 20,000 ft when, due to changes in lighting, the colors intensified. During October 1942, Lockheed was told to drop the Haze Paint and replace the color scheme with the ordinary Olive Drab/ Neutral Gray scheme. However, the Army was still not convinced that Haze Paint was all that bad – anything that gave the unarmed photo planes an extra chance of survival was seriously considered – and development proceeded to Synthetic Haze Paint. (H. W. Kulick)

Opposite
*S*ince many of the photo Lightnings were painted at British depots where they were prepared for service with combat units, it was not uncommon that some of the aircraft were finished with the paints that were at hand. This F–5B appears to be finished in an overall single color, the most likely shade being British Photo Reconnaissance (PRU) Blue. (Lockheed)

Right
F–5A–10–LO 42–13291 during a test flight from the Burbank factory. The color scheme on this aircraft is extremely dark, indicating that the aircraft was finished in an overall dark blue color or, perhaps, the black base coat prior to the application of Haze Paint. The F–5A was the reconnaissance version of the P–38G and 181 aircraft were built. (Lockheed)

*V*ery well-worn F–4A (based on the P–38F) shows off its Haze Paint to good avantage. The theory behind the haze scheme was that the application of colors would 'break up' the lines of the Lightning and cause the reconnaissance aircraft to blend with the sky. Lockheed records indicated that all twenty F–4As built were painted in the haze scheme before they left the factory. Primitive field conditions and extreme weather quickly took a toll on the carefully applied paint. This aircraft carries the yellow surround to the national insignia and the wheel covers have been given an individual touch by being painted white with a red star. The use of the yellow surround on the insignia was a common practice in the 12th Air Force during 1942 as an identification feature.

*A*n F–5B beats up its British base prior to landing. A large nude has been added to the side of the fuselage pod. This aircraft appears to be painted RAF Photo Reconnaissance (PRU) Blue rather than in a Synthetic Haze camouflage. The high altitude capabilities of the Lightning helped the unarmed aircraft evade enemy fighters. (USAF/52750)

Opposite above
F–5E–2–LO 44–23226A seen on 7 November 1944 at the large aircraft ferrying depot in Newark, New Jersey. A total of 705 P–38J and P–38L fighters were converted to F–5E configuration. Note the patches over the gun ports and the bulged camera window located in the access hatch. One hundred P–38J–15–LO fighters were built into F–5E–2–LOs. As the war progressed, F–5s were delivered from the factory in bare metal finish and they were painted, if at all, at the base air depots prior to being delivered to combat units. The '172' stencilled on the nose and tail is the last three digits of the construction number.

Opposite below
A dramatic view showing off the graceful lines of the photo Lightning to excellent advantage. The Lockheed F–5 featured an extended and rounded nose that could house a variety of cameras. Ports for the cameras can be seen in the most forward portion of the nose cone and under the nose, directly in front of the nose gear door. The ADF loop can be seen to the rear of the underside of the fuselage pod, in front of the three standard identification lights. The two stub pylons under the wing center section could carry droppable fuel tanks and the extension on the left stub housed a gun camera (presumably eliminated on the reconnaissance versions). (Lockheed)

The F–5G's extended nose gave the aircraft a rather awkward look while on the ground. F–5G–6–LO 44–26592A was converted from a P–38L–5–LO and the long nose carried several cameras in a variety of locations. 6592A is seen at Newark, New Jersey, on 10 July 1945.

LOCKHEED P–38 LIGHTNING VARIANTS, SERIAL NUMBERS AND SPECIFICATIONS

P–38 Variants

XP–38   A highly advanced long-range fighter with two Allison V–12 engines, propellers rotating towards fuselage pod and with provision for four .50 caliber guns and one 23 mm weapon in the nose, but these were not installed. The aircraft quickly set records when first flown during January 1939 but the single prototype was destroyed in a crash on 11 February. Highly-polished metal finish. Lockheed Model number 022–64–01.

YP–38–LO   Thirteen pre-production service test examples (Lockheed Model 122–62–02). Most were delivered in natural metal and sprayed aluminum finish. The Allison engines were equipped with outward rotating propellers. Armament consisted of two .50 caliber, two .30 caliber and one 37 mm weapons.

P–38–LO   The first production version (222–62–02), with 30 built. Limited armor protection and four .50 caliber guns and one 37 mm cannon. Most, if not all were delivered in Olive Drab and Neutral Gray camouflage. Most were used for training.

XP–38A–LO   Experimental conversion of P–38–LO 40–762 to test a pressurized cockpit (622–62–10).

P–38D–LO   Model 222–62–08. Basically the same as P–38–LO but with more military equipment added including self-sealing tanks and extra armor. Flares were also added along with a low-pressure oxygen system. Thirty-six were built, all delivered in Olive Drab and Neutral Gray finish.

P–38E–LO   Basically the same as the P–38D but the hydraulic system had been reworked. The 37 mm cannon was replaced with a more reliable 20 mm Hispano weapon. Some aircraft had Curtiss Electric propellers and most had the SCR274N radio. A total of 210 was built, some converted as F–4–1–LO.

P–38F–LO   Lockheed Model 222–60–09. Variants of the F received new model numbers: the F–1 became Model 222–60–15, F–5 Model 222–60–12; other models became 322–60–19. It had pylons inboard of the engines for the carriage of 2,000 lb of bombs or external fuel tanks. The F–15 saw the introduction of a modified Fowler flap.

P–38G–LO   Basically the same as the F except for new engines (V–1710–51/55) and revised internal radio gear. The G received Lockheed Model number 222–68–12. (G–13 and G–15 were Model 322–68–19; these machines were RAF Lightning Mk IIs that were not delivered).

P–38H–LO   Lockheed Model 422–81–20. Powered by two Allison V–1710–89/91 engines equipped with automatic oil radiator gills for improved cooling. The underwing carriage of weapons or fuel was increased to 3,200 lb. 601 built and 128 were finished or converted as photo recon F–5C–LO.

P–38J–LO   Model 422–81–14 covered the J–1 and J–5; 422–81–22, the J–10; 522–81–22, the J–15 and 20; and 522–87–23, the J–25. The J introduced the most distinctive physical change in the Lightning series, the large chin radiators for improved cooling. All J variants, except the J–1, had more fuel capacity. With the J–10, a flat, optically perfect bullet-proof windshield was finally introduced. The J–25 had the new dive brakes and power assisted ailerons. The majority of these aircraft were delivered in natural metal finish. A total of 2,970 was built, including F–5E/F–5F photo recon variants.

F–38K–LO   One aircraft only, Model 422–85–22. Basically the same as the P–38J, but the Allison V–1710–75/77 engines were equipped with paddle-blade propellers. The earlier XP–38K–LO was a P–38E conversion.

P–38L–LO/VN   Model 422–87–23. Basically the same as the P–38J but with V–1710–111/113 engines, and the landing light now in port wing. 3,810 J–LOs were built, and 113 L–VNs were constructed at the Vultee plant. Connections for ten 5 in rockets under the wing.

P–38M–LO   The Model 522–87–23 was a conversion of the basic P–38L airframe into a two-seat night fighter (75 built), with radar mounted under nose in pod. Solid black finish.

Other Variants

XFO–1   Five F–5B–LOs assigned to the US Navy in North Africa and given Bureau Numbers 01209 through 01212.

F–4–1–LO   An unarmed photo recon version of the P–38E, equipped with four K17 cameras and autopilot. F–4–1–LO, Model 222–62–13, numbered ninety-nine aircraft with serials 41–2098/2099, 2121–2156, 2158/2171, 2173/2218, 2220. The F–4A–1–LO used the P–38F as the basic airframe and twenty were built (41–2362/2381). Most were delivered in special blue/gray 'haze' camouflage.

F–5–A   F–5A–LO was a version of the P–38G modified for photo recon (Model 222–68–16, s/n 42–12667/12686). F–5A was Model 222–62–16 (s/n 41–2157); F–5A–3 Model 222–68–16 (s/n 42–12767/12789); F–5A–10 was Model 222–68–16 (s/n 42–12967/12986, 42–13067/13126, 42–13267/13326). Most were delivered in 'haze' camouflage schemes.

F–5B   Adaptation of P–38J–10–LO airframe to photo recon standards. Designated Model 422–81–21, 200 were built (s/n 42–76312/67401, 42–68192/68301).

F–5C   Model 222–68–16, a modification of the P–38H to a photo recon aircraft with 123 built.

XF–5D   Model 222–68–16. A rebuild of the F–5A–10–LO, modified with a plexiglass nose cone and prone observer's position. Two .50 caliber guns and a vertical camera were fitted.

F5E   A photo recon modification of the P–38J. F–5E–2–LO was Model 422–81–22 (P–38J–15–LO) with 100 built; F–5E–3–LO Model 522–87–23 was a conversion of 105 J–25–LO airframes; F–5E–4–LO Model 422–87–23 was a conversion of 500 L–1–LO fighters.

F–5F–3–LO   Model 422–87–23 recon modification of the P–38L–5–LO.

F–5G–6–LO   Model 422–87–23. Basically the same as the F–5F–3–LO but different cameras.

Model 322   Lightning for the RAF. 243 Mk Is were ordered (AE978/999, AF100/220), but just one was delivered, the rest being taken over by the USAAF as P–322 and flown in a training role. An order for 524 Mk IIs was cancelled. The Mk IIs had serials AF221/744 assigned.

Serial Numbers

XP–38–LO	37–457
YP–38–LO	39–689 through 39–701
P–38–LO	40–744 through 40–773
XP–38A–LO	40–762
P–38D–LO	40–774 through 40–809
P–38E–LO	41–1983 through 41–2097, 41–2100 through 41–2120; 41–2172; 41–2219; 41–2221 through 41–2292
P–38F–LO	41–2293 through 41–2321
P–38F–1–LO	41–2322
P–38F–LO	41–2323 through 41–2358
P–38F–1–LO	41–2359 through 41–2361
P–38F–LO	41–2382 through 41–2386
P–38F–1–LO	41–2387
P–38F–LO	41–2388 through 41–2392
P–38F–1–LO	41–7484 through 41–7485
P–38F–LO	41–7486 through 41–7496
P–38F–1–LO	41–7497
P–38F–LO	41–7498 through 41–7513
P–38F–1–LO	41–7514 through 41–7515
P–38F–LO	41–7516 through 41–7524
P–38F–1–LO	41–7525
P–38F–LO	41–7526 through 41–7530
P–38F–1–LO	41–7531
P–38F–LO	41–7532 through 41–7534
P–38F–1–LO	41–7535
P–38F–LO	41–7536 through 41–7538
P–38F–1–LO	41–7539 through 7541
P–38F–LO	41–7542 through 41–7543
P–38F–1–LO	41–7544
P–38F–LO	41–7545 through 41–7547
P–38F–1–LO	41–7548 through 41–7550
P–38F–LO	41–7551
P–38F–1–LO	41–7552 through 41–7680
P–38F–5–LO	42–12567 through 42–12666
P–38F–13–LO	43–2035 through 43–2063
P–38F–15–LO	43–2064 through 43–2184
P–38G–1–LO	42–12687 through 42–12766
P–38G–3–LO	42–12787 through 42–12798
P–38G–5–LO	42–12799 through 42–12866
P–38G–10–LO	42–12870 through 42–12966; 42–12987 through 42–13066; 42–13127 through 42–13266; 42–13327 through 42–13557
P–38G–13–LO	43–2185 through 43–2358
P–38G–15–LO	43–2359 through 43–2558
P–38H–1–LO	42–13559; 42–66502 through 42–66726
P–38H–5–LO	42–66727 through 42–67101
P–38J–1–LO	42–12867 through 42–12869; 42–13560 through 42–13566
P–38J–5–LO	42–67102 through 42–67311
P–38J–10–LO	42–67402 through 42–68191

P–38J–15–LO	42–103979 through 42–104428; 43–28248 through 44–29047; 44–23059 through 44–23208
P–38J–20–LO	44–23209 through 44–23558
P–38J–25–LO	44–23559 through 44–23768
XP–38K–LO	41–1983
P–38K–1–LO	42–13558
P–38L–1–LO	44–23769 through 44–25058
P–38L–5–LO	44–25059 through 44–27258; 44–53008 through 44–53327
P–38L–5–VN	43–50226 through 43–30338
P–38M–LO	44–25237 (converted from P–38L–5–LO for prototype; other serials random)

Specifications

XP–38

Span	52 ft
Length	37 ft 10 in
Height	12 ft 10 in
Wing area	327.5 sq ft
Empty weight	11,507 lb
Loaded weight	15,416 lb
Max. speed	413 mph
Cruise speed	n/a
Ceiling	38,000 ft
Rate of climb	20,000 ft in 6.5 min
Range	n/a
Powerplant	Two Allison V–1710–11 of 1,150 hp each

YP–38

Span	52 ft
Length	37 ft 10 in
Height	9 ft 10 in
Wing area	327.5 sq ft
Empty weight	11,171 lb
Loaded weight	14,348 lb
Max. speed	405 mph
Cruise speed	330 mph
Ceiling	38,000 ft
Rate of climb	3,330 fpm
Range	650 miles
Powerplant	Two Allison V–1710–27/29 of 1,150 hp each

P–38

Overall dimensions	as YP–38
Empty weight	11,670 lb
Loaded weight	15,340 lb
Max. speed	390 mph
Cruise speed	310 mph
Ceiling	n/a
Rate of climb	3,200 fpm
Range	825 to 1,500 miles
Powerplant	Two Allison V–1710–27/29 of 1,150 hp each

P–38D

Overall dimensions	as YP–38
Empty weight	11,780 lb
Loaded weight	15,500 lb
Max. speed	390 mph
Cruise speed	300 mph
Ceiling	39,000 ft
Rate of Climb	20,000 ft in 8 min
Range	400 to 975 miles
Powerplant	Two Allison V–1710–27/29 of 1,150 hp each

P–38E

Overall dimensions	as YP–38
Empty weight	11,880 lb
Loaded weight	15,482 lb
Max. speed	395 mph
Cruise speed	n/a
Rate of climb	n/a
Range	500 miles
Powerplant	Two Allison V–1710–27/29 of 1,150 hp each

P–38F

Overall dimensions	as YP–38
Empty weight	12,265 lb
Loaded weight	18,000 lb
Max. speed	395 mph
Cruise speed	305 mph
Rate of climb	20,000 ft in 8.8 min
Range	350 to 1,900 miles
Powerplant	Two Allison V–1710–49/53 of 1,325 hp each

P–38G

Overall dimensions	as YP–38
Empty weight	12,200 lb
Loaded weight	19,800 lb
Max. speed	400 mph
Cruise speed	340 mph
Rate of climb	20,000 ft in 8.5 min
Range	275 to 2,400 miles
Powerplant	Two Allison V–1710–51/55 of 1,325 hp each

P–38H

Overall dimensions	as YP–38
Empty weight	12,380 lb
Loaded weight	20,300 lb
Max. speed	402 mph
Cruise speed	300 mph
Rate of climb	2,600 fpm
Range	300 to 2,400 miles
Powerplant	Two Allison V–1710–89/91 of 1,425 hp each

P–38J

Overall dimensions	as YP–38
Empty weight	12,780 lb
Loaded weight	21,600 lb
Max. speed	414 mph
Cruise speed	290 mph
Rate of climb	20,000 ft in 7 min
Range	450 to 2,600 miles
Powerplant	Two Allison V–1710–89/91 of 1,425 hp each

P–38L

Overall dimensions	as YP–38
Empty weight	12,800 lb
Loaded weight	21,600 lb
Max. speed	414 mph
Cruise speed	n/a
Rate of Climb	20,000 ft in 7 min
Range	450 to 2,625 miles
Powerplant	Two Allison V–1710–111/173 of 1,425 hp each

Bell P-39
Airacobra — The Art Deco Failure

The Bell Airacobra did not live up to its initial concept as a fast-climbing interceptor, but distinguished itself in the low-level ground support role.

If life were more simple and only one word could be used to describe the design trend of an entire decade, then the word *streamline* could be used to cover the ten years of the 1930s. The 1920s are fondly remembered as the 'Roaring Twenties'; a term that came about by the rebelling of the younger generation away from the horrors of the First World War and towards a new openness and frankness that was working its way on what had been a staid and upright society. The 1920s were a period of wild pranks, stunts, and fun. The bubbling gaiety of the period collapsed with the spectre of world-wide Depression which covered the globe during the last two years of the decade. A gray drabness encircled America and the European nations while food and steady employment became the paramount objective in nearly every mind.

The 1930s began with the Depression but slowly began to work their way towards a different view on the world. The non-stop quest of entertainment and thrills of the Roaring Twenties was gone and, in its place, was a concerted effort toward goals. Many of these goals were involved with the new technologies that had sprung up with the century: the automobile, the high-speed train and, perhaps most importantly, the aircraft.

National pride began to manifest itself in record setting events; the longest distance covered, the fastest speed, the most people carried. Perhaps it was the concept of speed that most captured the mind of the general public during the 1930s. Speed, once a limited commodity reserved just for the very rich, had become a national stimulant which made the middle-class realize that perhaps, just perhaps, the magic carpet of world travel was unfolding

each time the daily newspaper was opened and the news of yet another daring speed or distance record leapt off the pages.

The clumsy wire-braced cloth and wood biplanes that had characterized the early days of aviation quickly fell by the side of the runway as manufacturers began to build aircraft which could cash in on the sudden mania for high speed. The concept and execution of aeronautical design was still suffering birth pangs as engineers sat down at their drafting boards and began to puzzle over the many ingredients needed in the elusive search

for speed. The engineers realized that the most essential item would be a slick, smooth airframe that could pass through the air with the least amount of resistance or drag. The design of such a clean airframe presented problems with structural strength. Before speed became a paramount consideration aircraft had been built a bit like sea-going sailing ships. Strength was built in with judicious use of plenty of wood, metal fittings, nails, and miles of bracing wire. This combination of materials was just not conducive to the slim shape that was needed to smoothly penetrate the ocean of air.

One of the first service test YP–39s seen during a test flight from the Bell factory. The highly-polished natural metal aircraft shows the streamlined concept so popular with designers of the 1930s. This particular aircraft has no armament. (Bell)

While being drag inducing, the wire braced structures were also strong and aeronautical companies had a devil of a time combining the needed strength with the required streamlining. Many early attempts ended in disaster, often with fatal results, as new designs suddenly converted themselves to junk when a wing or tail surface failed under pressure of the high speed that was being sought.

In the aeronautical industry lessons were quickly learned since mistakes, as well as being fatal, could put fledgling companies out of business overnight. The lust for speed began to

work, and as the miles per hour edged up the scale, the public's imagination was hooked. Records began to tumble. Wiley Post, a black patch over one eye, flew the beautiful Lockheed Vega *Winnie Mae* around the world in seven days, 18 hours and 49 minutes during July 1933. The sleek Vega and its colorful pilot were overnight heroes and the tempo of the worship of speed increased at a fever pitch. Pilots transversed the globe in new creations, each hoping to cut hours off the previous record. Flashing propellers carved the skies as a variety of innovative aircraft and daring

pilots, many of them female, quested for fame and money. The names of the aircraft and pilots became household words even though most people did not understand the technical workings behind these feats; they could, however, feel the heady rush of speed as the skies were split asunder by the roar of aero engines.

The feeling of speed and the allure of streamlining began to make itself felt in the everyday, non-technical, world. Designs for the home began to take on a sleek, smooth look. The lines of automobiles began to look less boxy and more "aeronautical", a term that the auto

*B*ell's first and only aircraft before the Airacobra was the FM–1 Airacuda. Certainly one of the most radical American aircraft of the time, the XFM–I first flew on 1 September 1937 and was intended as a bomber destroyer. The five-man crew had a heavy armament at their disposal including the unique installation of a gunner and a 37 mm cannon in the front of each nacelle which housed a pusher Allison engine. Problems with weight and performance eventually killed the Airacuda concept but it did establish Bell as a manufacturer with different ideas. (Bell)

manufacturers were only too quick to pro-mote. The streamline look touched virtually every facet of 1930s life: passenger trains became streamliners, ocean-going vessels stressed their elegant and fast service; the young air transport industry began to cater for passengers by building aircraft that could reach their destinations almost as quickly as the record setting aircraft. The quest for the ideal form of the fleet-footed god Mercury even took on its own names, 'Art Deco' and 'Mod-ernism' were the terms most heard. They referred to the sleek, modern art forms that were being experimented with in everything from building design to everyday furniture. It was truly a period of daring experimentation with line and shape.

This almost fun-filled quest for speed was not lost on the military minds of the major powers. They viewed the search for speed and great

load carrying ability with something less than the joy of a headline seeker. Germany had taken the genius of their aeronautical design-ers to heart and given them free rein with the development of their 'airliners' and 'mail planes'. The Germans were prevented from designing and building military aircraft and the modern designs from Junkers, Heinkel, and Dornier captured speed and load records as they zipped between European capitals in the service of the national airline, *Lufthansa*. It seems as if the aeronautical press of the period, perhaps caught up in the euphoria of record-setting, failed to notice that the German de-signs, while beautifully efficient, really did not seem to be ideally suited to carrying passen-gers. Did the available room inside the rounded fuselages not seem more likely as a home for high-explosive bombs rather than fare-paying passengers? The questions were on the minds of a few, but their warning voices were lost in the rush of progress and Adolph Hitler quietly went about building his secret *Luftwaffe* while his *Lufthansa* 'airliners' mapped out Europe and proved that certain loads, not necessarily passengers, could be quickly transported over major European airfields, harbors, and cities.

In America and Britain, bomber design had lagged far behind the creative efforts of the Germans. Many of the bombing aircraft still bore a great deal of resemblance to their World War One ancestors. During the early and

middle 1930s, the bi-winged, wire-braced bomber with limited range, limited bomb load, and limited defensive abilities was the order of the day. The role of the bomber was an offensive tool that was to be used to hammer an enemy's strategic targets into rubble. The idea of wanton bombing of civilians and cities had not really been voiced. Some American and British designers saw the streamlined shapes of the German aircraft as the way of the future and realized that the biplane bomber was just as outmoded as the sailing ship. Unfortunately, money for defense orders was in short supply but firms such as Boeing, Martin, and Douglas were able to carry on creative aeronautical design work with a limited amount of money allotted by the government. Aircraft orders of the day were considered good if the requested aircraft num-bered in the dozens.

America also maintained a rather outdated concept with their fighter (then called 'pur-suit') aircraft forces. Once again, military thinking had proven to be stuck in the mud as the accepted doctrine of the day was the 'ascendancy' of the bombardment forces over the pursuit forces. The reason for this doctrine was perhaps explained by the curious Amer-ican policy of isolationism. Americans realized that their country was large and new and that potential enemies were far removed; certainly Mexico and Canada were not threats in the twentieth century although this had not proven true during the early days of the nation. Coupled with this realization of being separated from potential enemies by vast areas of ocean was the feeling that the activities of Europe and Asia were so foreign as not to be related in any way to the American style of life. The vast number of European immigrants that had flooded into the country were viewed with a hostile suspicion by 'native' Americans; a feeling which was not alleviated by the fact that the immigrants usually grouped together by ethnic or religious ties in ghetto communities, allowing for little outside contact. The Depression put so many pressures upon the average working man and his family that very little thought was given to the outside world while the system of news communication to the general public left a lot to be desired. Only the movies and the daring exploits of aviation's record seekers seemed to offer any escape from the harsh realities of daily life.

The pioneer of the American concept of strategic bombing, General Billy Mitchell, had been discredited and court marshalled for his radical views during the 1920s. He must have been a bit rueful as he saw the growing importance with which the American military held the bombing aircraft. It was true that the

American bombing aircraft of the early 1930s were primitive but the policy of placing importance on strategic bombing aircraft would eventually lead to such great combat aircraft as the Boeing Flying Fortress and the Consolidated B–24 Liberator. However, it was the fighter aircraft that was to really suffer from this policy. The most modern pursuit aircraft that the United States Army Air Corps could field during the early 1930s was the Boeing P–26 Peashooter. This curious looking little design was the first monoplane pursuit to enter service with the American military. Although being modern in having one wing instead of two, the aircraft was primitive in the fact that it had an open cockpit, large spatted drag-producing fixed landing gear, wire-braced wings, and an armament of two rifle caliber machine guns which dated back to World War One. The Peashooter would probably have made a fine sport plane for the wealthy pilot but it was not a true fighter or even a pursuit because many of the foreign bombers that it would have to fight if a war broke out during the mid-1930s had a higher top speed!

During the middle of the decade it was becoming increasingly obvious to those concerned with foreign affairs that trouble was rapidly developing in Europe and the areas of

Asia which could be affected by the aggressive new policies of Japan. Military planners were suddenly aware that American defensive and offensive aircraft were woefully outdated and something had to be done to strengthen the Air Corps' striking power. As the decade drew to a close plans were underway which would develop the specifications for a whole new generation of American fighters but these aircraft were still far from the production lines. American aeronautical companies were seeking new designs which would combine the speed and power that had represented many American record flights. New innovations were needed, and needed quickly, and few companies realized the fact more than the Bell Aircraft Corporation and its president, Lawrence D. Bell.

Larry Bell was the model of an American

A turbosupercharged Allison V–1710–17 that developed 1,150 hp powered the XP–39. Weighing in at only 5,500 lb loaded, the XP–39's performance was sparkling. However, Army muddling caused the performance to rapidly drop off when it was decided to order the P–39 without the turbosupercharger and to change the role of the fighter from fast-climbing interceptor to ground support. Note the higher canopy and small fin which were dropped on other versions. Intakes on the fuselage were neatly faired. The aircraft was photographed at Wright Field, Ohio, during February 1939. (USAF)

capitalist who employed his industrious mind to establishing his own corporation and making a profit, hopefully in the shortest time possible. Bell had served as a vice-president with Consolidated Aircraft before that company had decided to pull up roots at its Buffalo, New York, factory and move to sunnier climes in San Diego, California. Bell, apparently liking what New York had to offer, decided to resign and set up his own company in Buffalo. The parting was friendly and the first contract obtained by the new Bell plant was from Consolidated for the manufacture of the retractable wing tip floats for that company's famous PBY Catalina. Bell knew that expansion and large profits could not be realized from sub-contract work and his small staff of 50 employees. Accordingly, Bell decided to under-

take a radical aeronautical project to develop a heavily-armed fighter which would be a completely new concept for Air Corps planners.

Larry Bell and his chief designer, Robert J. Woods, came up with an aircraft that was so startlingly different that even today's aeronautical buffs are puzzled how a new company could have manufactured such an unusual creature. The aircraft was the XFM–1 Airacuda and it embodied a twin-engine pusher configuration with a gunner operating the heavy armament of a single 37 mm cannon in each nacelle! The Airacuda first got into the air on 1 September 1937, and its gleaming polished aluminum airframe appeared to have jumped directly out of one of the countless pulp adventure magazines of the period. It was powered by two turbosupercharged Allison V–1710–13 engines. Their lengthened nacelles overlapped the leading edge of the wing and were equipped with a streamlined canopy and cabin in which a single gunner was installed. These unfortunate individuals were left on their own with the massive 37 mm cannon. The rest of the crew was ensconced under a large green house in the nose of the fuselage while a rear gunner operated a .50 caliber machine gun that was mounted in a large blister, one on each side of the fuselage.

The unusual creation probably had Air Corps officials more boggled than anything

else but the military decided to order, a pre-production batch that would be designated YFM–1. With the turbosuperchargers Bell figured that the YFM–1 could top 300 mph at 20,000 ft. However, in a burst of stupidity that seemed rampant at the time, the Air Corps substituted the turbosupercharged engines with altitude-rated Allisons that limited top speed to 270 mph and dropped the effective ceiling to 12,600 ft. One of the reasons given for the dumping of the turbosupercharger concept was the fact that a turbo had exploded on the YFM–1's first test flight on 28 September 1939. The YFM–1 featured a number of modifications including the placement of the radiator openings in the wings rather than on the top of the nacelle as on the XFM–1. The offensive armament was improved with a .30 caliber Browning being added to each nacelle while the rear defensive position was strengthened with the addition of two .30 caliber guns. The rather bulbous blisters were replaced with a retractable top turret that housed a single .50 caliber while a sliding hatch on the belly revealed another .50. The two .30s were fired

Airacobra Mk I AH621 is seen during flight test trials in North America. Aircraft has various non-standard modifications including 12 exhaust ports with a bulged fairing and modified fin and rudder. RAF pilots and groundcrews both loathed the aircraft. (Bell)

from side windows. Underwing racks could even accommodate a load of small bombs that could have been dropped on enemy bomber formations or on ground installations. The FM–1 was a very interesting concept and one of the most heavily armed fighters ever built but the engine substitution had doomed the project to slower speeds at lower altitudes where many bombers could have outrun the fighter or simply flown above it. Nine of the YFM–1s were built with conventional landing gear but the three YFM–1As that came along in October 1940 incorporated tricycle landing gear, which was to become a Bell landmark in fighter design. The performance of the Air-acuda just did not match up to its exciting looks and most contemporary fighters could have been more than a match for the FM–1.

Even though production orders were not forthcoming, Bell was able to prove that his company could develop startling concepts featuring innovative aeronautical creations. Mr Bell and his design staff were now more than ready for their next project, a project that would garner exactly 9,572 more orders than their first unusual creation!

As previously mentioned, Air Corps think-ing during the 1930s meant that the pursuit aircraft would have to include such interesting and diverse duties as close support for the ground pounders and coastal defense in its repertoire. The item of coastal defense was highly stressed by the military and many concrete forts were built on the east and west coasts which enclosed massive 'disappearing' rifles that could lob shells 20 miles at an approaching enemy fleet and hit them with virtual pin-point accuracy. Of course, the builders of these magnificent weapons did not take into account the fact that the defenses would be immediately obsolete if the invading enemy fleet came in aircraft rather than ships.

A similar lack of reasoning extended to aircraft for there were no real interceptors in the Air Corps inventory nor was there any sort of pursuit that could effectively deal with night attacks by enemy bombers.

Outmoded Curtiss P–36s and Seversky P–35s would have been hard pressed to inter-cept the new Japanese and German bombers of the late 1930s. These fighters were slow, had poor rates of climb, and featured light arma-ment. A new fast climbing machine with a high top speed and heavy armament to blast the bombers were needed and Larry Bell was convinced that his company was going to build the interceptor.

Bell engineers felt that the new interceptor should have a very heavy armament which would spell doom for the bombers that the aircraft was to attack. Most fighter aircraft had stayed with the traditional World War One armament of two rifle caliber machine guns that would be almost ineffective against the new generation of all-metal bombers, many of which carried considerable amounts of armor

*C*amouflage scheme for the RAF's
Airacobra Mk I was an American
interpretation of the British orders and was
changed to conform with British specifications
when the aircraft arrived in England. (Bell)

*T*his technical manual illustration gives
some idea of the length of the drive shaft and
reduction gear for the Allison installed in the
Airacobra Mk I. (Allison)

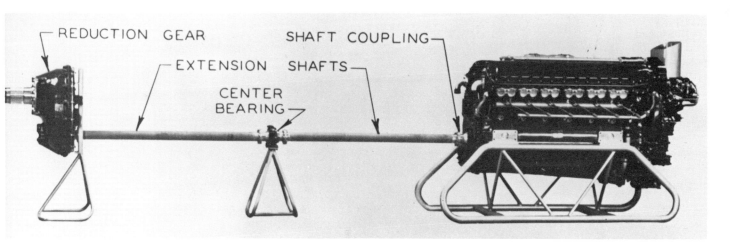

plating. Bell's chief engineers, Bob Woods and Harland Poyer, were in favor of combining a very heavy cannon along with several machine guns. The choice of the cannon was a foregone conclusion, The Oldsmobile T4 37 mm gun. This accurate but slow-firing weapon had been installed in the Airacuda and considerable experience had been obtained with the gun by Bell.

The next problem facing Bell was where to put the heavy gun. A single-engine fighter was extremely limited for placement of such a large weapon and it did not have the convenient nacelles of the FM-1 which easily housed the weapon. Thus the shape of the Bell interceptor was to be dictated by the gun and the aircraft that was to be built would be virtually unique.

The designers felt that an interceptor should have as much weight gathered around its center of gravity as possible. This would make the aircraft less prone to weight changes as ammunition and fuel were expended. It was also felt that the aircraft would be more maneouverable. The initial sketches prepared by Bell placed the engine directly in the middle of the airframe. A long drive shaft would pass through the forward fuselage and attach to the propeller assembly. This drive shaft would also serve as the ideal location for the cannon which would then fire directly down the center line of the fighter, making aiming of the weapon extremely easy. Since the engine was amidships, a great deal of room was left in the

Opposite above
Since the RAF rated the Airacobra as a failure and cancelled their order, the USAAF had to take over 179 examples. These machines were all equipped with 20 mm cannon and many carried their RAF camouflage along with RAF serials while in USAAF service. AP375 has been partially repainted in USAAF Olive Drab. Note the long length of the 20 mm cannon barrel. The name One for the Road has been painted on the nose in white.

Everything ready, the pilots warm up their Airacobra Mk Is for the long flight to Africa. This photograph was taken at the 91st Bomb Group base in Bassingbourne, England, on 10 March 1943. One of the ferry flights to Africa had an inadvertent and unusual side effect. During the flight a number of Airacobras lost their way and were forced to land in neutral Portugal. Eighteen Airacobras were welcomed by the Portuguese when they landed at Portela de Sacavem Airport at Lisbon. The aircraft were quickly grabbed by the

Portuguese and on 23 June 1943 they equipped a new fighter unit, Esquadrilha OK. The aircraft were given serials ranging from 301 to 318 and were flown fairly regularly by the Portuguese pilots who seemed to enjoy the machines. The Airacobras were withdrawn from front-line service during 1946 and scrapped. In this photograph, the second Airacobra from the left is BX249. (USAF/69358AC)

When the RAF rated the Airacobra a total failure in operational service, the USAAF took back 179 of the machines – a fact that made the American pilots assigned to the aircraft distinctly unhappy. Many of the machines were sent to Burtonwood Airdrome where they were fixed up and outfitted for the long trip to Africa where the USAAF felt that the aircraft's ground attack capabilities could be put to good use. The aircraft were left with their original camouflage and RAF serials. BX187 is seen ready for the ferry flight. The camouflage paint has had various comments chalked on by the crew chief relating to the aircraft's mechanical condition. Note the US insignia with a yellow outer ring, and the large ferry tank installed under the fuselage. In the background can be seen the base's 'boneyard' – a collection of wrecked and damaged aircraft that have been gathered for scrapping or salvage of parts. These wrecks include B–17s and B–24s and one solitary Airacobra Mk I. Examining the original print with a high-power magnifier, one can see the wingless Bell fuselage being eagerly stripped of parts by two crew chiefs who were apparently intent on getting a few extra spares for their own aircraft! (USAF/78997AC)

nose, even after installation of the cannon, so Bell was able to apply their famous nose gear which had been developed on the Airacuda. The nose was also able to accommodate two .50 caliber machine guns. Needless to say, the Army was most impressed with the sleek, streamlined plans and, on 7 October 1937, a contract was issued for a single prototype that would carry the designation of XP–39.

The choice of engine was limited to a variant of the Allison since there were no other inline American liquid-cooled powerplants of enough horsepower. Bell decided to go with the V–1710–17 which could develop just over 1,100 hp and was fitted with a turbosupercharger that would be on the port side of the fuselage. In order to keep the design as sleek as possible, Bell located the intakes for cooling air in slim pods on each side of the fuselage. Other intakes were molded into the wing root where they blended with the clean lines of the design. Development of the XP–39 was kept very secret and the public was not aware of the aircraft until it was announced on 9 February 1939 – a comfortable amount of time since the prototype had been placed on flatbeds and sent

by rail to Wright Field where it was flown for the first time on 6 April 1938.

The new fighter appeared to be what the Army had been hoping for – a clean, fast climbing aircraft that could pack a considerable wallop. However, the situation was soon to change. The XP–39 had been flown in a very light condition, armament and a number of other military items not being installed. The National Advisory Committee for Aeronautics (NACA) had studied the XP–39 and recommended changes which would affect the final production aircraft. Even though the prototype was extremely light at well under 6,000 lbs it was felt that a military equipped XP–39 would not weigh in at much more than 6,500 lbs and that the performance the aircraft had demonstrated, including a climb to 20,000 ft in five minutes, would be relatively intact. NACA and Army decisions were to forever adversely affect Bell's slim fighter.

Some of the Army brass, being of the 'old school' which insisted that aircraft should operate subordinate to ground forces, managed to force through a view, aided by NACA data, that the P–39 should be built for a close-

*M*any P–400s were sent to the South Pacific
where they participated in the early heavy
fighting against the Japanese invaders. A number
were retained in the States for the training role,
illustrated by this well-worn example with large
training codes on the nose and still retaining its
RAF camouflage. The aircraft was from the USAAF
Training Command's Central Instructor's School
and was photographed during early December 1943
at Matagorda, Texas, which was an auxiliary field
of Foster Field. (USAF/22504)

*M*echanic checking over the Curtiss
Electric propeller of a service test YP–39.
Service test aircraft were built in batches of 13 and
distributed to various fields for intensive testing.
Note the small fairings over the nose machine
guns. (USAF)

support role which, of course, takes place at
low altitude. Bell was dismayed when the
Army and NACA requested that a number of
changes be made to the P–39, especially since
13 YP–39 service test examples, which had
been ordered on 23 April 1939, were already
on the production line.

The most damaging change insisted on by
the Army was the deletion of the turbosupercharger which would not be needed since the
aircraft would be operating at lower altitudes.
Little thought was apparently given to the fact
that new German and Japanese fighters were
capable of flying and fighting at altitudes
higher than which the non-turbo equipped
P–39 could attain. NACA felt that the high
canopy line should be reduced, making the
aircraft a bit cleaner. The coolant radiator was
moved to the wing center section causing the
carburetor air intake to be moved to a position
atop the fuselage, directly behind the canopy.
Several other small changes such as the addition of landing gear fairings were also incorporated. Power was to be supplied by the
low-altitude rated V–1710–37 Allison which
effectively put the end to the P–39 as an
interceptor, once again leaving the Army

without an effective high-performance fighter.

As these changes were ordered, Bell modified the prototype to conform with the modifications and the aircraft was redesignated
XP–39B. The 13 service test YP–39s began to
enter Army test groups on 13 September 1940
and, one year earlier, Bell had secured an
almost $3 million order for the development
and production of the Airacobra, as the type
had been named.

The YP–39s were fitted with armament but
immediately had two extra .30 caliber guns
mounted in the nose between the two .50
caliber weapons. Testing with the XP–39B
revealed that climb and top speed had decayed
considerably but maneuverability at lower
levels was quite good and the Army was
pleased with the changes that they had
ordered. Maneuverability had also been en-
hanced by the addition of a larger vertical tail
on the YP and XP–39B.

The YP–39s were extensively flown by
service pilots while Bell geared up for the job of
mass-producing fighting aircraft. Up to this
point the only aircraft Bell had produced had
been a few of the unsuccessful Airacudas so
the massive orders for the P–39 which, follow-

Head-on view of a YP–39 illustrates the streamlined shape of the Airacobra. The thick short wing was not suited for dog fighting. The 37 mm cannon was the heaviest weapon to be carried by an American World War Two production fighter. (Bell)

ing a newly established Bell tradition, had taken up the name Airacobra. The Army felt that the many changes which had been app-lied to the original P–39 concept should result in a change of designation with the new fighter being the P–45. However, it was finally deci-ded to let the P–39 designation stay and the original order for 80 aircraft under the P–45 title was changed to read P–39C. The first production Airacobras were very similar to the service test aircraft but, after 20 P–39Cs had been constructed it was decided to change the remaining 60 aircraft on the contract to P–39Ds that would have four .30 machine guns in the wing in place of the two .30 caliber weapons in the nose. With these various modifications, the Airacobra's weight began to creep upwards and, with the low power avail-

able from the non-turbosupercharged Allison, it was obvious that the design was going to be in for trouble.

The Airacobra, for all its radical looks, was a conventionally constructed all-metal aircraft. The airframe was very sturdily built, a con-struction technique that was to become a Bell trademark, and this toughness stood the figh-ter in good stead when it entered the deadly arena of aerial combat. The fuselage of the Airacobra comprised two sections, a forward and an aft unit. The forward section carried the main portion of the entire fuselage – the wing center section, nose wheel bay, nose armament, engine bed, extension shaft and propeller gear reduction assembly mounts, and mountings for all the engine accessories.

The cabin for the pilot, oil and engine cooling systems, and ammunition boxes for the nose guns were all fastened to the forward unit. Needless to say, since all this important equipment was concentrated in one unit then that unit had to be of exceptional strength. To achieve that strength, the unit was built up

from two longitudinal beams which were cradle-shaped in profile. Each beam was manufactured of extruded aluminum angle sections that were tied together with almost solid reinforced aluminum webbing. To this cradle a series of aluminum bulkheads was added to give the fuselage the desired shape. Two of the bulkheads were steel castings and attached to the wing section to create a very substantial unit. A thick aluminum deck plate was riveted to the tops of the bulkheads and went the entire length of the longitudinal beams. Forged angle members were mounted to the rear of the beam to form the bed for the Allison engine.

The forward unit of the fuselage was covered with aluminum sheet skin that was riveted to the bulkheads. The skin on the forward section of this unit and under the pilot's cockpit was .051 sheet while the remainder of the unit was covered in .032 sheet.

The cockpit was an integral unit of the forward section and fume-tight bulkheads were provided between the engine compartment and the cockpit and between the armament in the nose and the cockpit. This unit was very sturdy and saved many an Airacobra pilot's life during a crash landing when, quite often, the only intact portion remaining would be the cockpit area. The fume-tight bulkhead's success was a matter open to speculation for Royal Air Force tests conducted on their Airacobra Mk Is found a lethal concentration of gases in the cockpit after the nose weapons had been fired. The RAF ordered its pilots to wear oxygen masks from the time of engine start until engine shutdown when flying the Airacobra. Many American pilots also wore oxygen masks full time when flying the Airacobra although this was quite often extremely uncomfortable when flying the aircraft on low-level missions in the sweltering South Pacific.

The aft section of the fuselage carried the entire tail section and was of ordinary semi-monocoque construction. The unit was covered with .032 sheet aluminum.

The cockpit had been arranged for maximum visibility and the canopy was the closest thing to a full bubble unit when the Airacobra entered service, being built up from six plexiglass panels while the windshield was formed of $\frac{1}{4}$ in laminated bullet-proof glass. An unusual feature of the Airacobra was the entry method for the pilot. Most fighter aircraft are extremely awkward to enter but the Airacobra offered all the comfort of a family sedan with two full-size doors which afforded easy access (and escape) to the aircraft. The doors even had $\frac{21}{64}$ in laminated glass windows that could be rolled up and down via automobile-like handles. Both doors could be jettisoned in case

of an emergency and the pilot could then either roll out of his seat or, if speed was low enough, get out on the wing before jumping. Indicating how people have grown in the past forty years, the Airacobra cockpit was designed for a 5 ft 8 in pilot that would weigh in at 200 lbs with parachute and survival gear attached. The pilot was protected by a sturdy roll-over structure directly behind his seat that was capable of supporting a weight greater than the aircraft. This unit was built out of two main beams of very heavy gauge aluminum that were joined together by bulkhead sections and heavy-gauge skin that was riveted to the beams and bulkheads. This unit was further strengthened by the use of wire bracing that was tightened by turnbuckles.

The Airacobra's wing had a NACA airfoil that started with an 00015 section at the root of the wing and traveled to a 230099 section at the tip. The wing was of all-metal construction with stamped and pressed ribs and flush riveted aluminum skin which gave a very smooth surface. The wing was equipped with Frise-type ailerons, which were fabric covered (as were the moveable surfaces on the tail). Split trailing edge flaps were also installed.

The armament of the Airacobra was, at that time, the heaviest ever carried by an American production fighter. Replacing the concept of pursuit aircraft having just two rifle-caliber machine guns, the sting of the P–39 made a lasting impression on the Army Air Force whose fighter aircraft would, from that point, be substantially armed. When the armament of the P–39C was revised producing the P–39D, the Army had a fighter that could

carry a 37 mm cannon, two .50 caliber and four .30 caliber guns. The 37 mm cannon was mounted on the fuselage center line just above the extension drive shaft from the Allison. The barrel of the cannon passed through the reduction gearbox and the propeller hub. The two nose mounted Browning M2 machine guns were installed just in front of the pilot's position and synchronized to fire through the arc of the propeller while the four .30 caliber weapons were installed in pairs in each outer wing panel.

All weapons were manually charged and electrically fired by solenoid units that were activated by the two firing switches located on the pilot's control column. One button was for the operation of the cannon while the other button operated the machine guns. In the P–39D the .50 caliber weapons were equipped with blast tubes to minimize flash. Each nose machine gun had its own ammunition holder that accommodated 200 rounds. Spent cases and their connecting links were disposed of via ejection chutes. The .30 caliber weapons were divided with two guns in each outer wing panel and each pair shared a 1,000 round ammunition box.

The real punch from the Airacobra was, of course, the 37 mm cannon. Although slow

The two fighters that typified the Army's airpower during the late 1930s. The P–40 and P–39 were photographed at Indianapolis, Indiana. Maj James H. Doolittle, who became famous during the war for his daring bombing attack on Japan, was flying the P–40 and was visiting Allison in Indianapolis in his position as inspector of engines for the Air Corps. The P–39C was flown by First World War Ace Lt Col H. Weir Cook, a resident of Indianapolis, on duty with the procurement director at Wright Field.

firing, a hit from the cannon would usually destroy an aircraft or a ground vehicle. The cannon was fed by a circular endless-belt holder that was wrapped around the nose machine guns. This holder carried 30 rounds for the cannon and the spent shells were also ejected from under the nose.

The Airacobra was well armored in vital areas with homogenous steel plate, face-hardened steel plate, and, as mentioned, armor glass. Armor was installed around the propeller reduction gear box, the bulkhead between the gun bay and the pilot, and in front of the windshield. Armor was also installed on the turnover structure while more armor protected the oil tank.

Second Lieutenant James C. Robertson of the 39th Pursuit Squadron, 39th Pursuit Group, waves at the cameraman during a night mission from Nachitoches Airport, Louisiana, during 1941 war games exercises. Airacobra is a P–39D. Aircraft is camouflaged in Olive Drab and Neutral Gray with Black designators. Red cross behind the engine exhausts was a marking for the war game. (USAF/22844)

The P–39C and P–39D were pressed into service as quickly as they came off the Bell production line. The Army was desperate for new fighters and the Airacobras were looked upon as being deliverance from the primitive aircraft with which they had been operating. This was a fighter, the Army hoped, that could compete with the best European fighting machines. Unfortunately, the officials did not know just how wrong they were.

The first outfit to receive the Airacobra was the 31st Pursuit Group who immediately put their new machines to work by taking them to the huge First Army war game that took place in the Carolinas during September 1941. (It should be noted that the rather curious designation of Pursuit was dropped during May 1942 for the more descriptive term of Fighter.) The 31st Pursuit Group was activated on 1 February 1940 and its first aircraft was the Airacobra. Commanded by Col John R. Hawkins, the 31st contained three squadrons initially; the 39th, 40th and 41st Pursuit Squadrons. The pilots were pleased with their new

mounts and, since they only had more obsolete Army aircraft to compare the P–39 with, initially thought that the Airacobra was quite a machine, although they were soon to learn the hard way that it was not.

The giant war games that took place during September through November were to prove that America was not ready for the war engulfing the rest of the globe. However, the games did bring to light the fact that a considerable amount of the Army's textbook tactics – both in the ground and in the air – were completely out of date and revisions were undertaken to correct the problems and to lay down a solid foundation of tactics which would prove to be of use once America entered the war.

During the war games the Airacobras of the 31st Pursuit Group, flying with the 'Blue Forces', roared into the air on countless missions to support Army troops, intercept 'enemy' bomber formations, and tangle with opposing fighters. During these three months certain unsettling facts concerning the P–39

began to appear. Firstly, it became quickly obvious that the P–39 would not be capable of fighting above 12,000 ft due to the lack of a turbosupercharger on the Allison. Secondly, the Airacobra was prone to a number of maintenance problems including a weak nose gear that would quite often give way when operating off unprepared fields. Thirdly, it became obvious that the performance of Bell's fighter – even under 12,000 ft – was not all that sterling and the P–39 would be badly pressed by a quality fighter such as the Messerschmitt Bf 109. The armament of the P–39 was substantial and the aircraft was pleasant to fly, being described by one pilot as 'a good high-performance sport plane for a wealthy civilian pilot'. However, at this point the Army was stuck with the Airacobra since they had nothing else besides the P–40 to fall back on.

The British and French, during their frenzied aircraft buying missions prior to the start of World War Two, investigated the new product from Bell with considerable interest. On 13 April 1940, the British Aircraft Purchasing Commission decided that – based on figures issued by Bell – the Airacobra would make an ideal fighter for the Royal Air Force and a

contract was placed that called for the delivery of 675 Airacobra Mk Is, as the type would be designated in RAF service. However, the British soon found out that several 'mistakes' had been made when ordering the aircraft. All performance data had been based – and not very conservatively based – on the highly polished, low-weight prototype rather than the P–39D to which the Airacobra Mk I was basically identical. Originally having the name Caribou, the Airacobra Mk I differed from the P–39D in having British radios, gunsight, and detail differences. Also, the hard-hitting 37 mm cannon was replaced by a 20 mm Hispano M1 with 60 rounds. The RAF had experience with this weapon and selected it instead of the 'unknown quality' Oldsmobile weapon.

Bell made a great deal of publicity over the RAF order and posed camouflaged examples for press cameras to show how America was supplying its ally with the latest in aeronautical technology. After the Airacobra Mk Is were test flown, they were disassembled, carefully crated and shipped to Britain where the first example was erected and flown on 6 July 1941. Arrivals of crated Airacobras began to

increase and the first RAF unit to equip with the type was No 601 (County of London) Squadron, an auxiliary unit that had been activated with the start of the war. The Airacobra, used to the US Army's beautifully prepared long concrete runways, was not going to react well to the standard RAF field which was grass and short and would have been classified by American pilots as 'unprepared'. The Airacobra Mk I was a bit of a ground lover and RAF pilots transitioning to the type must have had their share of thrills as they saw the hedges at the end of the runway rapidly approaching while the Airacobra seemed to have other ideas on its mind beside flying. The Air Fighting Development Unit at Boscombe Down, responsible for testing and setting up tactics for new fighting aircraft, found the Airacobra Mk I to be woefully inadequate but the aircraft was duly issued to No 601 Squadron who, with considerable misgivings, gave up their trusty Hawker Hurricanes.

By September 1941, No 601 Squadron was ready for a 'press day', an event which meant that the Airacobra Mk Is would be lined up in impressive rows with the pilots and ground crews standing around looking 'smart' for the propaganda photographs and probably hoping Jerry would not send a bombed-up intruder over to disrupt the event.

The Squadron immediately had maintenance problems with the Bell fighters, including landing gear problems while operating from muddy grass fields. If mud got inside the wheel wells of the Airacobra during takeoff then,

quite often, the gear would not want to come down for landing. This would result in belly landings if all gear legs were jammed in the up position or, if one or two gear legs came down and the others did not, the pilot would simply jettison the car doors and take to his parachute. No 601 Squadron established itself at the historic Duxford aerodrome near Cambridge (today the site of the huge collection of vintage aircraft belonging to the Imperial War Museum) and, on 9 October, began flying reconnaissance missions over Dunkirk and other areas of the French coast, and attacking targets of opportunity. However, the pilots hated the aircraft and the Airacobras began breaking down with such frequency that squadron serviceability rates began dropping to the zero mark, an embarrassing situation for the hard-pressed mechanics. The Airacobra was withdrawn from RAF operational use

during December, examples in England being shuttled off to the Russians whom the British felt would take anything, while a few examples were retained for mundane test work. The remainder of the contract was rejected, leaving the US Army with the type.

A bit over 200 Airacobra Mk Is were eventually shipped to Russia while 179 were taken over by the Army as P-400s. These aircraft usually retained standard RAF day fighter camouflage and serials but had American national insignia. Some P-400s were retained in the training role while the majority were shipped off to Australia where the need for fighting aircraft was desperate after 7 December 1941. One pilot commented that 'the P-400, like the rest of the Airacobra series, was pleasant to fly, but we felt more comfortable with that big 37 mm up front rather than the puny 20 mm that the Brits had installed.'

USAAF armorers load up a P-39D with .50 caliber bullets. However, the people in this staged photograph were going to run into some problems since they were trying to load the .30 caliber wing guns with .50 caliber shells! This view also shows good detail of the Curtiss Electric propeller which was finished in a silver anodized color. (USAF/21744)

*B*ell P–39D–1–BE equipped with the 20 mm nose gun. With the P–39D series a small dorsal fin fillet was added.

*E*ngine run-up for a well-worn P–39D–1–BE. The long barrel of the 20 mm cannon is evident. The belly fuel tank has been modified with the rear portion sectioned off, perhaps as a non-standard napalm bomb. (Bell)

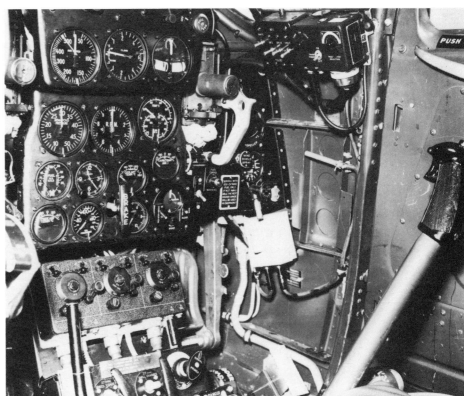

A training school group of P–39D–I–BEs. Stateside training aircraft could be identified by the large numbers painted on the fuselage. (USAF/22521)

*C*ockpit of a P–39D. The Airacobra's cockpit was designed for a 5 ft 8 in pilot who weighed 200 lb with parachute and full flight gear. For larger pilots the cockpit was definitely on the cramped side but the roll down windows helped a bit when the aircraft was on the ground. (USAF)

We knew that if we hit something with the 37 mm that it was going to be heavily damaged if not destroyed.'

The Airacobra was deployed to the vital Canal Zone in Panama before the outbreak of the war to bolster the weak defenses. The fact that defenses for the Canal were weak came upon the Army like a bolt of lightning when they realized that a co-ordinated attack by Japanese and German submarines could spell doom for the Free World's important transportation route. The Army decided to double the number of pursuit aircraft at the Canal in August 1939, and Curtiss P–36s and Douglas B–18s were sent to Albrook Field which was in the throes of rapid expansion. By the end of 1939 and the start of 1940, it was evident to the American government that the Germans, who had strong connections in Latin America, were stirring up trouble and anti-American feelings. On 17 June 1940, the Canal Zone and the Hawaiian Territories were alerted against the possibility of immediate attack by German forces in the Canal and by the Japanese in Hawaii. This alert, although proven inaccurate but prophetic in many ways, served as another order for more aircraft for the Canal's dozen airfields. Twenty-four P–39Ds were dispatched to the Canal Zone along with a larger

number of P–40s. These aircraft helped modernize the area's defenses which were also bolstered by the addition of an early radar unit.

Operating out of the more primitive Canal airfields, the Airacobra ran into the same enemy that the RAF had encountered: landing gear failure. Between 1941 and 1942, eight P–39Ds suffered accidents during landing, another 20 were victims of gear failure, while 16 crashed into the sea or jungle. The original batch of Airacobras was supplemented by further aircraft sent from the States to constantly replenish the diminishing number of fighters. Units of the 6th Air Force which operated the P–39 in the Canal Zone included the 43rd, 24th, 31st, 52nd, 53rd, and 51st Fighter Squadrons. The P–39s are not recorded as having seen any action during their assignment in the Canal Zone although some of the antiquated B–18 Bolo bombers slugged it out with the U-boats which they found on the surface and, in a couple of instances, the B–18 crews found themselves floating in life rafts on the surface of the Atlantic watching the U-boat sail away and wondering where they went wrong. Pilots of the Airacobras that went down at sea were faced with the possibility of becoming a meal for the sharks which abounded in unpleasant profusion while those that went down in the jungle had the possibility of becoming the main course for the equally unpleasant native population. Several times it was suspected that natives had done away with pilots who had been forced to bail out of malfunctioning Airacobras. One pilot commented: 'When one of our boys went missing with the possibility of having been killed by the natives, our squadron would mount an "unofficial" mission against native encampments where the firepower from the guns and the effects of 500 lb bombs leveled several villages whose inhabitants were taken by surprise from our low-flying Airacobras.' Although probably satisfying for the pilots participating in these revenge missions, they certainly did nothing to improve the natives' disposition the next time they saw a white devil

The Airacobra had to prove itself during an extensive series of war games held in the Southern States during the later part of 1941. These aircraft are from the 31st Pursuit Group which, with its 39th, 40th and 41st Pursuit Squadrons, flew in support of Army units that were maneuvering in the field. These factory-fresh aircraft did not carry nose guns. (USAF)

floating to the jungle in his parachute. Since chances for combat were slim, pilots blew off steam by 'rat racing' down the many rivers in the area while trying to pick off alligators with the 37 mm cannon.

As 1941 continued, P–39s were rapidly reaching USAAF squadrons and, after the 31st Pursuit Group, the 58th Pursuit Group received its Airacobras. The 58th, consisting of the 67th, 68th, and 69th Pursuit Squadrons was activated on 15 January 1941, and served as a replacement training unit for pilots until 1943. The Group operated a mixed bag of aircraft that included P–35s, P–36s, P–40s, and P–39s.

By the time of 7th December 1941, some P–39s had been transferred to Hawaii but most were destroyed or damaged on the ground during the Japanese raid. The mass confusion following the Japanese attack had every fighter unit in the Pacific clamoring for more aircraft. Frantic shipments began from American West Coast ports as crated parts and aircraft were shipped around the clock. With

such frenzy and poor intelligence reports coming from areas under attack, it was not uncommon for aircraft to arrive at their destinations lacking vital parts to make them airworthy. The first unit to have the distinction of taking the Airacobra into combat was the 8th Pursuit Group. This historic unit was, in December 1941, part of the aerial defense force for New York City but was quickly moved to the Pacific in the early part of 1942 with headquarters at Brisbane, Australia. Once arriving in Australia, the Group immediately began assembling their aircraft and deploying them to forward operating bases in New Guinea. The 8th PG was joined by the 35th Fighter Group (carrying the new Fighter designation) during July of that year with more Airacobras and the 39th, 40th, and 41st Fighter Squadrons which had originally been attached to the 31st FG, the first USAAF unit to operate the P–39.

The Airacobra pilots detached to the airstrips in the steaming jungles of New Guinea were to face problems that were totally alien to the average American airman. First, they were

n an area where America had never been and the few available maps were so riddled with inaccuracies that they were virtually useless. Secondly, intelligence reports were so wildly inaccurate that the pilots really did not know what they would be facing; rumors ran rife. Thirdly, the USAAF pilots had come to realize that the Airacobra was a dog and that they would be opposing Japanese warplanes whose reputation had made them seem invincible.

The P–39s operating in this area were a mixed bag that included P–39Ds and Airacobra Mk Is from the cancelled British order. Parts and maintenance manuals were in short supply as the ground crews labored to prepare as many P–39s for combat as possible. Not only were the pilots faced with the possibility of flying fighters that could not be adequately maintained, they were also faced with the harsh reality of flying over stretches of water where, if forced down, chances of rescue were remote. Such was the fighting spirit of the American pilots and the desire to strike back at the enemy that the dangers were forgotten as

Airacobras bravely ventured across the ocean to new forward bases and onto sweeps, attacking Japanese shipping or targets of opportunity.

The 347th Fighter Group was activated at New Caledonia on 3 October 1942, with a mixed bag of P–400s and P–39D–1–BE Airacobras which were also equipped with the 20 mm cannon. Detachments of this Group, which was attached to the 13th Air Force in January 1943, were sent to Guadalcanal where they flew protective patrols, supported ground forces, and attacked shipping. The 67th Fighter Squadron, attached to the 347th FG, shot down a Zero on 22 August – one of the earliest victories to be scored by an Airacobra during those dark days. Heat, humidity, poor maintenance, and disease all took their toll on the American pilots who operated from crude airstrips under the most primitive of conditions.

Back at the Bell factory in New York, work was carried out on further versions of the Airacobra even as reports came in challenging the usefulness of the design. The designations P–39F and P–39G were assigned to aircraft essentially similar to the P–39D–1 and P–39D–2 but equipped with the Aeroproducts constant-speed hydraulic three-blade propeller rather than the Curtiss Electric propeller. Most of the different versions of the Airacobra, as seen from the specifications tables, were created by engine, propeller or minor equipment changes. The final versions, the P–39N and P–39Q, were built in the most numbers of any Airacobra. These aircraft were mostly supplied to Russia via the Lend-Lease program.

31st Pursuit Group P–39D, carrying the guns in the nose and wing, was assigned to an umpire to help keep score during the war games. UMP was painted on the side of the fuselage in large white letters. The 31st's shield consisted of 'per bend nebule Or and azure, in chief a wyvern, sans legs, wings endorsed of the second'. Motto is 'Return with Honor'. Note the multi-colored spinner and short barrel for the 37 mm cannon. (USAF)

Russia had a huge appetite for aircraft and seemed to take anything they could get. A wartime press release from Bell gives an idea of the manner in which 1940s America regarded their ally:

'Buffalo-built Bell Airacobras are proving the ideal plane for Russian winter fighting. This was explained in a report received by the British Information Services from official London sources. The Russians call the P–39 the "Flying Cross."

'It was mid-winter of last year when the Airacobra first flew in Russia, but the first authentic reports are just filtering through. Indications are that the approaching Soviet Winter will find the P–39s operating in the same fashion as last year. Explaining how the Airacobras had to be assembled in sub-zero temperatures, the British report continues:

'"The aerodrome runways were of snow, rolled hard enough to support the weight of an aircraft, the surface anything up to three feet above the level of the ground underneath. The Airacobra is the right aircraft for these conditions as it cannot ground-loop nor turn over on its nose. [Note: like the performance specifications for the RAF's Airacobra I, these statements are not exactly true!] Judgment of

***H**igh-angle view of 31st Pursuit Group Airacobras undergoing maintenance during the war games. These aircraft were painted in the standard Olive Drab and Neutral Gray camouflage scheme with the national insignia in four positions. (USAF)*

landings is also rather harder on snow and once again the nosewheel undercarriage scores. Also it was found almost unnecessary to use brakes after landing on snow while the take-off was only slightly lengthened.

'"The squadron re-equipping with the Airacobras collected the aircraft and began a few weeks of intensive training. The Airacobra was christened 'The Flying Cross' and the two things which the Russians chiefly praised were the armament – for obvious reasons – and the metal propeller which they said was preferable to wood when ramming."

'Explaining how the planes are assembled, the report adds:

'"The mechanics were divided into erection gangs, each of which was responsible for the complete erection of an aircraft. As soon as the aircraft is allotted to a gang, it sets to work on it with eagerness, their one aim being to send it on its way to the front as soon as possible. First, all the loose items of equipment are carried into the hangar where they are guarded as personal property. Next a tractor is attached to the fuselage cradle and it is dragged into its erection bay. Finally a labor gang is called and the wings are lifted and carried into the hangar. It must be admitted that the labor gangs are unskilled and the wings get rather roughly handled but the Airacobra is tough and damage was rarely serious.

'"The erection mechanics work with a will. They have been trained the hard way with too few tools and too little equipment; their skill with the tools to which they are accustomed is striking. They have very great ability at impro-

visation. They quickly appreciate the object of the special purpose tools but unfortunately the efficient use and handling of such equipment is outside their experience.

'"Sooner than expected, a new Airacobra with red stars stands out in the snow, its sleek lines emphasized by the stubby I–16 fighter which stands beside it."'

Production of the P–39N and P–39Q totalled 7,000 units and virtually all of this group was transferred to the Soviet Union where the fighters were put to good use attacking tanks and ground targets. The Russians particularly liked the damage that the 37 mm cannon could do to German armor. In the air, the P–39 was no match for experienced *Luftwaffe* fighter pilots who blasted them out of the air with alarming regularity. Germany's greatest ace, Erich Hartmann, recalls attacking Russian Airacobras: 'I got behind the Airacobra, closed

right in, and after a short burst the enemy fighter went down and crashed with a tremendous explosion ... I was happy to get this Airacobra down.' Hartmann destroyed at least 33 Airacobras but admits that the type could be dangerous when in the hands of a very experienced pilot. The Soviets had a unit of Airacobras flown by their top aces, called the 'Red Guards', and the Germans realized that this was a very dangerous group.

The ultimate version of the P–39, the Q Model, had all wing guns deleted and replaced with a pod under each wing that held one .50 caliber machine gun. On many Qs, even this reduced armament was eliminated – relying strictly upon the nose guns. Many pilots felt that the weight loss aided performance a bit and, at that stage, the overweight Airacobra needed every bit of help it could find. Only 75 P–39Qs were retained by the USAAF and passed on to the 332nd Fighter Group in Italy

during February 1944. The pilots of this unlucky unit probably could not believe that they would receive such an outmoded fighter so late in the war but, fortunately, the Airacobras were replaced in a couple of months with P–47 Thunderbolts.

Probably the strangest model of the Airacobra was the XP–39E. Only three models of this aircraft were manufactured and it was intended as a test vehicle for the new Continental V–1430–1 engine. The XP–39E featured a laminar flow wing and various other modifications. Each aircraft had its own modified stabilizer of different shape and configuration. The XP–39E never flew with the Continental since that engine was not ready so Allison V–1710–47s were installed. Intended to be put into production as the P–76 with an order for 4,000 aircraft, the 'new' fighter was wisely cancelled during May 1942.

The use of the Airacobra in the Pacific

40th Pursuit Squadron Airacobras deployed during 1941 war games. Note the white crosses painted on the fuselages to designate that the aircraft were assigned to the games. When operating from unimproved strips during war time, a fault in the landing gear system quickly became evident. The nose gear was particularly weak and would collapse under difficult circumstances. Mud getting into the wheel wells would prevent the landing gear from locking when they were extended. (USAF)

spread during 1942 and 1943 and the USAAF and USN fought a desperate battle against superior forces with excellent equipment. The pilots of the outmoded and outperformed Airacobra were pressed into inventing tactics by which they could lure the Zekes down to low altitude where the P–39 stood a better chance of survival. Wishing not to dogfight with the enemy, a decision that would have been fatal, the P–39 pilots would try to make one high speed pass at the enemy and then escape at full throttle. If they could hit anything during this

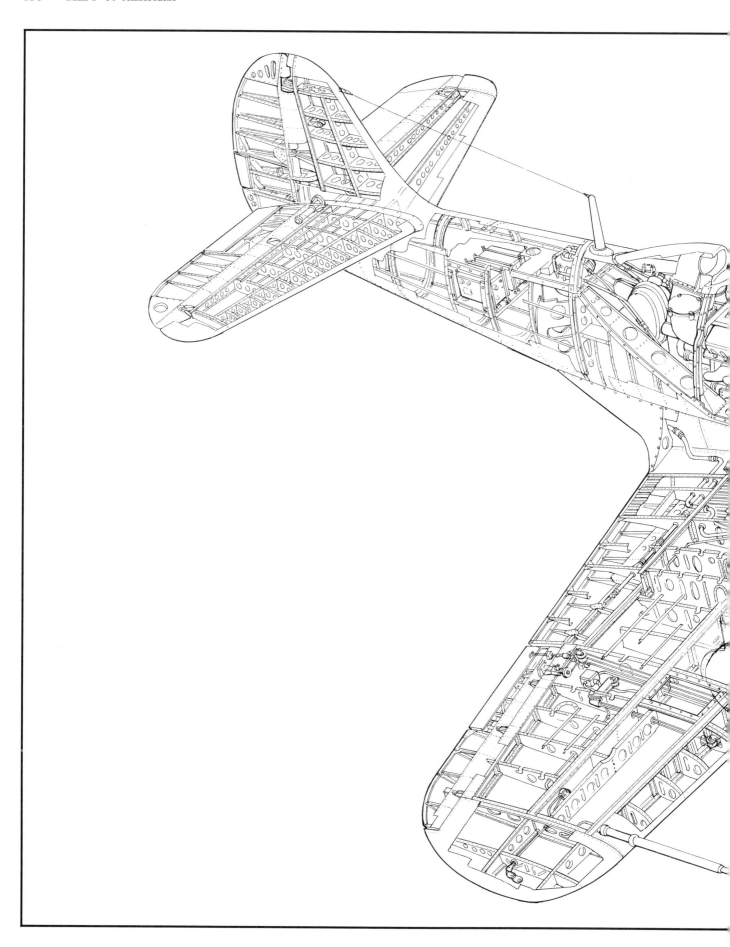

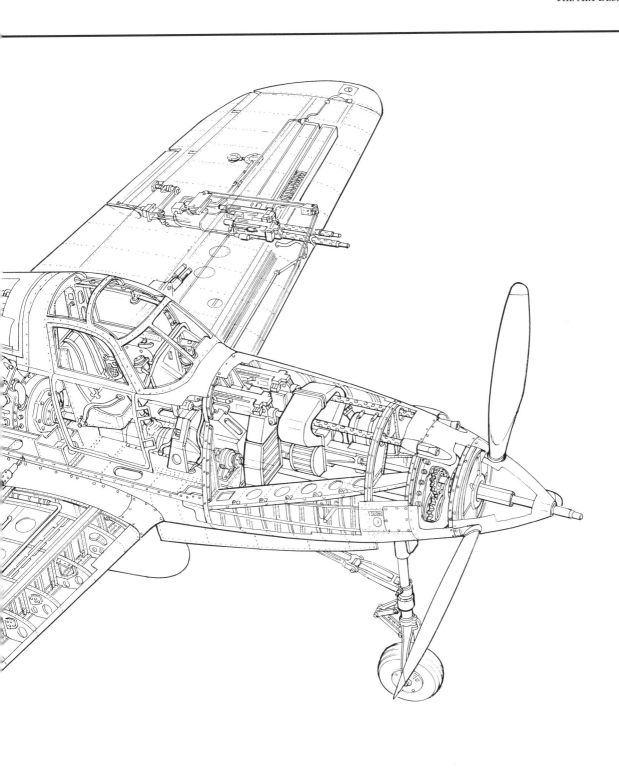

Bell P–39D–2 Airacobra

pass, destruction of the lightly built Japanese aircraft was almost assured. One pilot recounted that, during a head-on pass with a Zeke, a shell from the 37 mm cannon slammed into the Japanese fighter which instantly disintegrated. During combat more flaws with the Airacobra began to reveal themselves. One of the most discussed was the mysterious 'tumbling'.

A virtual mythos has been built out of the question of whether the Airacobra went through a peculiar aerodynamic maneuver which was given the name tumbling. The tumble was taken to be an inadvertent maneuver which was so unconventional that

Airacobras everywhere: elements of the 31st Pursuit Group undergoing maintenance during war games. Most of the systems in the Airacobra were easily accessible via large panels that could be taken off the airframe. (USAF)

there was no known recovery method. During this maneuver the Airacobra was reported to tumble tail over nose. The only recommended procedure was to get out of the aircraft as fast as possible since it would be dropping like the proverbial iron brick. Interviewing surviving Airacobra pilots leaves the tumble with part of its mystery still intact. Many pilots have flatly denied that this strange maneuver could take place while others recall that they 'heard about it' from other pilots but even fewer state that they have actually done it. Usually the tumble would come about during aerial combat when the Airacobra pilot would be entering a very tight maneuver and high-speed stall the P–39. It was thought because of the unique mid-engine installation of the P–39, which had much of the weight centered around the middle of the airframe, that the high-speed stall would throw the aircraft into the end-

over-end tumble. The problem, or the rumor of the problem, became so severe that Bell sent a field representative to the South Pacific to help iron out the trouble. Lt Col Richard Kent recalls the problems of tumbling: 'Another deadly factor in the P–39 was also due to the short wings and resultant airflow. When performing aerobatics at altitude or in ship-to-ship combat that resulted in an unco-ordinated turn or too tight a turn, the plane was said to stall without warning and tumble end over end. Several pilots have told me this happened to them and it took 15,000 ft to recover. This tumbling characteristic was debatable – it never happened to me and, intentionally and unintentionally, I stalled the plane in almost every conceivable situation but at high enough altitude to recover. Perhaps I was just lucky to stall it in such a way to avoid the tumble. These stalling factors, however,

caused many pilots to avoid flying the P–39 whenever possible and contributed to its reputation as a dangerous plane to fly.'

Edwards Park recalls tumbling in his *Nanette*, one of the finest and most evocative books written on World War Two aerial warfare: 'When you flipped on all three gun switches and fired your entire arsenal, there was a great roaring noise – *braaaaap* – and the cockpit filled with smoke so your eyes ran, and your airspeed dropped off a little. All this weight of armament tended to compensate for the engine being mounted amidships. But after you'd spent some ammunition the center of gravity would slide back, and the plane could do some strange things. It could tumble, for example. That means somersault, nose and tail swapping places as it drops out of the sky. No plane ought to do that.

'I did it once, practising acrobatics in Florida. I was on my back ("... and there I was on my back with nothing on but the radio ..." – fliers' joke back then) and managed to stall out, and she tumbled once, the sun swinging down past the nose, and then the earth, while we fell 12,000 ft. Absolutely terrifying.'

Lack of range, poor maintenance reliability, and the mentioned poor performance gave Airacobra pilots nightmares in the South Pacific. Fighting alongside equally outmoded P–40s, USAAF pilots had to face formations of Japanese bombers well protected by Zekes and Oscars. Japanese bombers, especially the Betty, were well-armed and quite fast but they suffered the fatal flaw of all Japanese combat aircraft – lack of armor and self-sealing fuel tanks. Ben Brown recalls interception missions against the Bettys: 'If the bombers had the slightest lead on us the pilots would firewall the throttle and run away which was a bit

embarrassing for fighter pilots. Once the old P–39 got up around 300 mph, it would shake and make a terrible racket like an old dowager protesting a ride in a fast car. The Jap gunners with their 20 mm cannons in the tail were good and we would have to be careful approaching the Bettys if and when we could catch them.'

Pilots of 35th Fighter Group valiantly went out on several missions each day to intercept Japanese raiders. Results of these air battles were usually rather inconclusive, with both sides taking losses. The aerial defense of Australia and New Guinea took place from primi-

Conditions in the Aleutian chain were often less than ideal. These unfortunate pilots are being driven out to their P–39Fs as the squadron dog faithfully tags along on the rain-soaked ramp. This photograph was taken on 3 November 1942 at Adak. (USAF)

disastrous results. The toll of physical problems with the pilots was also high – jungle fever, malaria and dysentery running wild in the unimproved jungle camps. Still, daily missions were flown against the enemy. Pilots began to realize that having the engine behind them was not all that valuable. The Japanese pilots had been trained to shoot at the wing roots of American aircraft – quite often the location of fuel tanks – but would usually miss and the bullets would thud into the engine and accessories compartment. The lack of an engine up front meant that the pilot would have little to protect him in case of a crash landing in a rocky or wooded area. A plus factor was the fact that the Airacobra's rounded belly seemed to be ideally suited to water crash landings. The aircraft would gently skip like a rock and then settle down on the surface of the ocean, giving the pilot a chance to crawl out and take to his life raft, not like the later P–51 which would violently dig into the water because of its belly scoop and be on its way to the bottom within a few seconds.

The dogged responsibility felt by American pilots in defending Australia meant that their attacks on the Japanese bomber formations were savage and determined. The Japanese were startled by this showing and had to regroup and lick their wounds. The P–39s, P–400s, and P–40s of the 49th, 35th and 8th Fighter Groups began attacking Japanese ground targets as well and it was discovered that the Airacobra made a stable dive bomber. Field modifications were undertaken and the P–39s were able to handle a 500 lb bomb on a center section rack under the fuselage. The usual tactic was to dive quite low and release the bomb with a sharp pullout to escape the blast effects and to get away from anti-aircraft fire. Two squadrons led by the redoubtable Buzz Wagner arrived in New Guinea during April of 1942 and immediately put their Airacobras to work attacking anything that looked even vaguely Japanese. Air bases were attacked, ships were strafed and fuel dumps were blown up. The enemy soon begun to develop a healthy respect for the punch of the Airacobra.

Airacobras flew daily air patrols over Port Moresby, hoping to catch Japanese raiders before they could drop their bombs. It was hard, gruelling work with little in the way of thanks. The military realized the plight of the Airacobra pilots and began to take measures to replace the P–39 as soon as possible. Lockheed P–38s were shipped to the Pacific as fast as they could come off the production line to replace Airacobra equipped units but the unlucky 347th Fighter Group did not give up their Airacobras until August of 1944, by which time they were doing mainly ground

Pilot and crew chief strike a casual pose amidst the squalid living conditions at Kodiak, Alaska, on 7 August 1942. The P–39F is parked on a dirt revetment with belly drop tank and bombs stored nearby. (USAF)

The distinctive wolf's head insignia marked this P–39F as belonging to the 57th Fighter Squadron at Kodiak, Alaska. Photographed on 7 August 1942. Note belly tank installation. The P–39F was equipped with the Aeroproducts propeller built by General Motors. (USAF)

tive air strips that took a toll on both aircraft and pilots. The Airacobras were constantly suffering from mechanical problems, their Allison engines overheating almost as soon as they started. It became common practice to tow the Airacobras to the end of the runway rather than taxi them. This way the coolant would not overheat in the high jungle temperatures. The pilot would then start the Allison, perform the briefest of engine run-ups, and then get the aircraft into the air as quickly as possible. This lack of run-up quite often meant that engine problems would not surface until the P–39 was in the air – often with

*T*his P–39F was assigned to the Training Command's Central Instructor's School. Note the red bordered national insignia. (USAF/28072)

P–39L 42–4558 belonging to the 93rd Fighter Squadron, 81st Fighter Group, in Tunisia during 1943. Aircraft had a very patched-up Olive Drab paint scheme and carried the name The Pantie Bandit on the nose along with the painting of a cartoon animal.

P–39N–1–BE undergoing an in-the-field engine change somewhere in North Africa during 1943. The P–39N was fitted with an Allison V–1710–85 driving an Aeroproducts propeller.

P–39N with the characteristic heavy grey exhaust stain of the Allison engine on the side of the fuselage. 42–8896 carried the name III Winds on the nose section. Photograph taken 28 June 1943

at Gray Field, Washington. Aircraft was assigned to the 353rd Fighter Squadron. (USAF/25404)

*T*he Russians received the majority of the 4,905 P–39Q Airacobras built. This example is seen at Praha during May 1945. The P–39Q had fittings for carrying an optional two .50 caliber machine guns under the wings but this example does not have them fitted. The Russians were fond of painting patriotic slogans on their aircraft, as can be seen from the inscription above the exhaust stacks.

P–39Qs of the 333rd Fighter Squadron, 318th Fighter Group, at Bellows Field, Hawaii, in 1943. The 333rd FS operated the Airacobra from 1942 to 1944. (J. Maita)

Line-up of P–39N–I–BE Airacobras at a Stateside training base. A large number of the 2,095 N Model Airacobras was sent to the Russians. (USAF)

support work and letting the aerial fighting go to the newer aircraft.

Many Airacobras were shipped off to the Aleutians Island in Alaska to help fend off the threat of Japanese invasion. Some of the Aleutians were actually invaded and occupied by Japanese who immediately began building bases for aircraft and ships. The conditions in the Aleutians were as bad as the South Pacific except instead of the terrible heat everything was cold – very cold. Airacobra pilots quickly discovered that the heaters in their aircraft were totally unsuited for the cold weather at the top of the world and they attempted to do everything possible to keep warm. Every panel line was taped over, newspapers were stuffed inside the nose to plug air leaks, and pilots dressed in as many layers of clothing as possible. Weather conditions contributed to the destruction of many P–39s, strong cross-winds caused the P–39s to go out of control, heavy fogs and low cloud banks would hide airfields, ocean landings would result in almost instant death because of the freezing water and, on top of all this, the Japanese were busy attacking the Americans whenever possible.

The enemy felt that a foothold in the Aleutians could be the basis for future incursions into Canada and eventually the United States. Submarines could be replenished and sent south to attack the important Pacific shipping lines.

USN aerial units and the 54th Fighter Group attacked the enemy on Kiska Island whenever possible. Airacobras strafed and bombed enemy supply dumps and airfields, also shooting up Japanese float planes that would be tied up in the harbor. The P–39s destroyed 20 enemy aircraft during their time in the Aleutians – losing one pilot in aerial combat, the commanding officer of 42nd Squadron. Many Airacobras, however, were written off in accidents – usually caused by the poor weather conditions or by mechanical problems. Once again, the Airacobra – although outclassed – helped stem the threat of a Japanese victory.

In Europe, the USAAF's Airacobra-equipped units suffered the same fate that had befallen the other squadrons in the Pacific and Aleutians. The 31st Fighter Group had been reorganized with the 307th, 308th, and 309th Fighter Squadrons and sent to England in July of 1942. The squadrons were quickly pushed into action but one sweep into Europe with 12 Airacobras – and the loss of six – quickly convinced the American military to pull the Airacobra out of the arena of combat in Western Europe. The 31st Fighter Group re-

equipped with Spitfires and enjoyed much more combat success. The only other P–39s to operate with the USAAF in Europe saw action in Italy. Other units went to North Africa where the 81st and 350th Fighter Groups operated in the Operation Torch landing. In these theaters the Airacobra was used as a ground support aircraft and was usually protected by medium- and high-cover fighters. The 81st and 350th Fighter Groups saw heavy action as they followed the Allied advances in Italy, attacking German armor, supply depots, and troop concentrations.

Foreign air forces also used the Airacobra. Beside Russian and British use, the P–39 saw service in Portugal where examples that had been forced to land while on ferry flights were impressed and used as interceptors. The Portuguese eventually got their hands on 18 Airacobras, which they purchased from America after the end of the war. The American pilots that had been flying these aircraft were interned but usually managed to 'escape' back to England or to North Africa via merchant ships. The Portuguese *Arma da Aeronautica* were more than pleased to have what they considered modern aircraft.

The Airacobra also saw service in the markings of the Royal Australian Air Force. The RAAF operated a mixed bag of P–39Ds and Fs, amounting to an original batch of 22 aircraft serialled A53–1 through A53–22. Several others were given to the RAAF by local USAAF units and the aircraft were pressed into service when the threat of invasion from Japan was at its strongest. When the prospect of invasion decreased following several Allied victories, the surviving Airacobras were returned to the USAAF.

The French had been first to order the Airacobra but the fall of that country prevented any machines from being delivered. However, France eventually did receive about 200 Airacobras when the USAAF began to supply Free French units in North Africa. The French were pleased to get the aircraft, many of which were distinctly tired, but were less than thrilled with their American instructors. The French, apparently still smarting from American attacks on French naval and air units and along with the typical French intransigence toward foreigners, made life miserable for the American fighter pilots that had been assigned to teach the French the finer points of flying the Airacobra. The French would only acknowledge the presence of the Americans during flying instruction and then retire to their tents or bars to pretend that the Americans did not exist. The French were eager for any aircraft that could attack the Germans and they put their machines to good use attacking German armored units and providing ground support for troops. The French were probably the last to keep the Airacobra in service, retiring the type in 1947.

After the capitulation of Italy, America quickly began building up that country's air force to help battle with the stubbornly retreating Germans. After training, a number of Italian P–39Q equipped squadrons began operations against the Germans on 18 September 1944. These aircraft made some sorties but contributed little to the Allied victory in Italy.

Thus the Bell Airacobra, originally intended as America's premier fast climbing interceptor, found itself as an overweight and underpowered aircraft that could not fight above 12,000 ft. The Airacobra's greatest achievement was the fact that it was there and ready to use when an ill-prepared America found itself thrust into a strange and foreign war. Today, two flying examples of the Airacobra are operated by the Confederate Air Force and Kalamazoo Air Zoo where they are admired as rare examples of America's fighting aircraft from the darkest days of World War Two.

P–39Q 'Tarawa Boom De-Ay' with underwing gun packs at Oahu Field in Hawaii during the Spring of 1944. Note the three Japanese kill marks under the windshield. (USAF/65220)

A P–39Q on its way to Russia. Airacobras being sent to Russia were ferried from the United States over Canada to Alaska where they were picked up by Russian pilots. The Russians liked the 37 mm cannon for attacking armor. (E. Deigan)

P–39Q *in the lead with two P–39Ns in the background. These aircraft were assigned to a training school. Note the underwing gun pods on the P–39Q. (USAF)*

*P*ossibly the ugliest fighter aircraft modification during World War Two was the TP–39. Converted from small batches of Fs and Qs, the TP was a dual control trainer that put the second seat in the nose section where the armament would have gone. The TPs were not armed and had additional dorsal and ventral fins added for stability.

*Q*uite often it is what is in the background of a photograph that is more interesting than the main subject. Behind this P–47 Thunderbolt are part of the Navy's collection of F2L–1K Airacobras. These machines, still in Army paint but with Navy painted on the nose, were to have been used as targets but it is not known if they were radio controlled as Navy records are sketchy.

INTRODUCTION TO THE AIRACOBRA
By Ben L. Brown

Spoiled by the sparkling performance of the P–51C, Ben Brown found the Airacobra a disappointment.

My introduction to the Bell Airacobra came about in a rather pedestrian manner. I had gone through flying school in Texas with the Royal Air Force rather than the USAAF. The RAF method of teaching was considerably different and quite rigorous. The top ten students in my class were treated with a few hours in a factory fresh P–51C from the North American plant in Dallas. That was some machine compared to the trainers we had been flying and it was an experience I will never forget. Since I was number two in class standings I was able to get in a few more minutes flight time in the Mustang.

At the RAF school we flew 80 hours in Stearmans and then went directly to the AT–6 for 140 hours of flight time. The basic stage with the BT–13 trainer was completely eliminated. Our top ten students comprised four Americans and six Britons. The location was at Terrill, and it was the first such school in the United States that the British had talked the Americans into creating. Other schools were established in Lancaster, California, two in Oklahoma City and one in Florida. We had a terrific navigation program that was as comprehensive as the USAAF's navigator school. We also got to fly long cross-country missions along with plenty of low-level training and night flights.

After graduation we were sent to Las Vegas, Nevada, for fighter indoctrination training. The base had a number of mixed variants of P–39s for us to learn on and we were given three or four days of ground instruction before being allowed to fly the aircraft. The situation was much more casual than it is today because the aircraft that we flew were not multi-million investments but rather worn out obsolete fighters. The P–39 was an easy aircraft to fly and we quickly piled up the required number of hours. Some of our aircraft had 37 mm cannons while others were equipped with the 20 mm unit. The 37 mm cannon was fun to fire but a problem arose because the slow firing cannon had a completely different missile trajectory to the machine guns so it was very hard to get all the guns hitting the same target.

When we completed training we went to San Francisco and were put upon one of the deluxe pre-war cruise ships that had been converted to a troop carrier and steamed away to Honolulu. From Hawaii we went to Townsland, Australia, and that is where the USAAF had a forward strip. The base was equipped with P–40s and P–39s and we were not too pleased to be back with the Airacobra because even at that early date in the war the pilots realized that the Airacobra was a dog but we just did not have anything else at the time. We quickly began flying missions against the Japanese – going after their shipping, supply

Ben Brown flew P–39s for two and a half months in action against the Japanese from Townsville, Australia. He commented: 'The P–39 was a lot of fun to fly if you did not have to worry about somebody shooting at you or, conversely, if you had to try to shoot at somebody. It was a nice looking airplane but, on final summation, it was a bad aircraft – a dog that could not do the job for which it was designed.'

depots and bombers. The Airacobra's lack of range would mean that on many occasions we would have to deploy to primitive forward bases. The Airacobra had some trouble at these bases if mud got inside the wheel wells during takeoff. This would quite often cause the landing gear to not lock when lowered, resulting in a crash landing.

I always flew the Airacobra down low since it was really worthless above 12,000 ft. The South Pacific climate meant that you wore the least amount of clothes under that plexiglass hot-house. I just wore shorts, parachute, Mae West and a baseball cap. I never wore an oxygen mask because it was just too uncomfortable at low altitude. I also wore just the standard headset without any other form of ear protection which I now regret since the Airacobra was extremely noisy inside – it produced a noise unlike any other aircraft and the effect on the ear-drums was permanent. One nice feature was that we could roll the windows down in flight to get some extra air. This had to be done at lower speeds because at higher speeds a suction would be created inside the cockpit that would swirl everything around.

A typical mission in the Airacobra would involve getting up in the morning, going to the briefing, going to the airplane, getting in it and taking off. I never even once looked over the aircraft, never even kicked the tires, just got in and flew the thing if the crew chief said it was ready to go. Of course I was only 20 years old and stupid. After the war when I continued flying I would very carefully check out the aircraft before taking it up. Survival makes one more cautious.

Starting the Airacobra was always a thrill. The thing would buck, gasp and snort and feel like it was tearing itself into a million pieces. All those gears and long drive shaft contributed to a feeling that the P–39 was going to tear itself apart until you got the revs up to about 1,200 rpm and then the damn thing would smooth out. For starting we had to be towed out to the runway because, with the high jungle temperatures, the Airacobra would overheat very quickly on the ground. Once we started the engine we were on our way after a very brief run-up. This, of course, would lead to problems and several times during takeoff pilots found themselves in gliders when the engines quit. I remember watching several P–39 'gliders' go crashing through the jungle at the end of the strip, tearing off both wings, ripped off the tail section and finally sliding to a stop as a complete ruin. The pilots would open the car door and casually stroll away as if nothing had happened.

Once airborne we would stay low and head out for our assigned target. Quite often we would run into enemy aircraft and if they did not want to tangle with us they would simply open the throttle and outrun the Airacobras. We had a bad time with the Betty bombers that we would try to catch for they were fast and if they had a head start we would be hard-pressed to catch them. Once the P–39 got a bit over 300 mph it felt it was going to fall apart – shaking, vibrating and making the most god awful noise. Actually, we were probably lucky that we did not engage the enemy more often. If we had some height and were intercepted by Zekes we would dive away for the Airacobra went down like a rock and no Zeke could keep up with it and those that did usually did not live to tell the story for the Zeke's most vulnerable position with the P–39 was in a dive – especially if there were several of us and one of the Airacobras could get behind the Zeke while in the dive and blow him out of the air with a squirt from the cannon.

Our missions were usually short because of the range of the P–39 and we would return to base, execute a fighter break over the airfield and come in to land, switching off the Allisons as soon as possible to prevent overheating. The mechanics would then take the aircraft, go over them, reload the guns and prepare them for the day's next mission. In the meantime we would go to our tents and attempt to relax and play cards.

Our missions took us to such delightful places as Biak, Finchaven, Port Moresby and other tropical paradises. The coastwatchers would tell us about Jap ship movements and off we would go. Without our belly tank we only had a two hour range so we would use the tank on the way out and then drop it before attacking the enemy. We liked going after the shipping as the cannon would make a nice hole in the Jap ships. The cannon was slow firing and there was a built-in delay switch so that the gun could not be fired too quickly and burn up the barrel.

I did just about every maneuver that I could think of in the P–39 except for spinning the aircraft. Even at that young stage of my life I was smart enough not to attempt spinning a fighter aircraft. I had heard about 'tumbling' but it never happened to me. The P–39 was a lot of fun to fly if you did not have to worry about somebody shooting at you or, inversely, if you had to try to shoot at somebody. My crew chief had painted a shark's mouth on the nose of my Airacobra along with the inscription *Mabel's Boy*, my mother's name. It was a nice looking airplane but, on final summation, it was a bad aircraft – a dog that could not do the job for which it was designed. After two and a half months of flying the Airacobra we were very relieved to receive brand-new P–38s. Now we could do some damage to the Japs.

COBRAS TO ALASKA
By Ben L. Brown

To keep the Russians supplied with combat aircraft, an aerial highway was created between the United States and Alaska.

The *Wehrmacht* was knocking on the door at Stalingrad during 1942. US aircraft deliveries to Russia had bogged down. To remedy the problem, F. D. R. Roosevelt gave top priority to the shipment of aircraft to the Russians, and the 7th Ferrying Group of the Alaskan Division of the Air Transport Command was given the task of getting the planes to the Russians.

In all, 6,000 aircraft were delivered to the Russians via Great Falls, Montana, north to Fairbanks, Alaska, and on to Russia. I was one of the 7th Ferrying Group pilots who delivered these aircraft. As I review and recall these incidents that happened over 30 years ago, I realize what a great chapter in my life took place. Few pilots in our armed forces ever had such a great opportunity to fly all types of aircraft to so many places in the world. As all former ATC pilots will agree, this was one great time and it will never happen again. It was fantastic in so many respects that I, and many of the oldtimers like myself, wish that we could do it all over again for just a few days.

The ATC was a giant operation. Beside the ferrying division, it operated aircraft transporting VIPs, parts and supplies, medical evacuees, and all types of military personnel, and, at the time, was probably the largest airline in the world. It trained and retrained personnel constantly. Ground crews went to school to learn their jobs and later returned to school to learn about new aircraft. All pilots coming into the ATC were sent to various schools for retraining. Even airline pilots and former civilian instructors were sent to training schools. Former combat pilots and new pilots right out of flying schools were checked out in various aircraft or sent to instrument schools. The ATC made the best effort of any branch of service to train everyone to do his best at his particular job. I was happy to have been a part of this organization.

Ferry pilots were a colorful group of characters; many were former instructors, airline pilots, combat pilot and crop dusters. These men had a lot of experience and know-how in flying the unusual in all types of weather and situations. A pilot had to be versatile because he never knew what type of aircraft he would be ferrying next. Some pilots were single-engine fliers, others were strictly twin-engine, and those that loved to fly them all were called Class 5P pilots and they flew in any type of weather. Many of us had 'green' instrument cards that put us up in some of the roughest weather that one can imagine ... this was long before ILS and GCA.

A typical trip from Great Falls, Montana, would take us away from our base for 35 to 45 days. It would run something like this: Go to Seattle, pick up a B–17G and take it to Elgin Field, Florida. From there, hop a commercial airline (ATC pilots had a top priority rating which guaranteed them a seat even if a paying passenger had to be removed) and head for Farmingdale, Long Island. There, pick up a P–47D and ferry it to Oakland, or perhaps head for Nashville and pick up a B–24 for Sacramento. Then, pick up a P–51D and head for Newark, go to Buffalo and take a P–39 or a P–63 to a training base in the South. Eventually you were re-routed back to your home base to pick up your pay and *per diem* and get your mail, have a few days rest and then head for the north country. They might keep you on the Alaskan run for a month and then back again on the road in the States or South America. In three years of this type of flying I managed to check out and fly over 55 various types of military aircraft.

My first assignment north was greatly anticipated and I looked forward to it because it sounded so different according to all the stories I had heard from other pilots. My home base was Gore Field, Montana, an enlarged commercial field taken over by the Army. It was situated on top of a plateau overlooking Great Falls, about 800 ft above the city. Located ten miles east of Great Falls was another field called East Base where all aircraft going north were processed and winterized.

Here we encountered the Russians – not many, but a chance to see a few. The Russian purchasing commission had a delegation of civilian and military personnel stationed there to observe and count the aircraft they were going to get. They were unusual in that they never socialized with us and never ventured out alone but always in groups with one acting as interpreter. Several admitted they spoke English and all carried a small translation book. Later on I managed to get friendly with some of them but they maintained a very reserved atmosphere at all times. In the mess halls they sat by themselves and when they would go into Great Falls for a movie or a visit to a bar they would stick together like glue.

On one occasion I was invited over to their big table at the Silver Dollar Saloon to help them order some food and drink. After they chatted in Russian they finally began asking a few guarded questions about America. My answers were what any American would give about our customs, cars, people, homes, living conditions, etc. They were shocked to see the number of cars in the streets, especially in wartime, and when I began asking similar questions about their country they became very quiet and suddenly forgot their English. One man usually carried the money to pay for everything and what a roll of greenbacks he carried! It seemed they were always loaded with money.

Later on I did some of the checkout work and gave cockpit checks to some of their pilots when a new or updated aircraft came through. My personal thoughts were that these pilots were rough and showed no flying *finesse* at all. Overall, I would judge them to be poor and men I would have washed out.

The closest I came in contact with the Russians was having two Russians assigned to fly along with us from Great Falls to Fairbanks in a new B–25J. They were to observe and also to get some time and experience in the Mitchell. They spoke English quite well and had been in combat on the Eastern Front flying various Russian fighters and using our P–39s to knock out German tanks. They were going to be used as navigator pilots flying their group in B–25s from Fairbanks back to bases in Russia. It seemed that they did loosen up a great deal once they were away from Great Falls and were on their own. They talked more freely than ever and did a great deal of drinking when on the ground.

In Fairbanks we had no contact at all with the Russian crews that flew in to pick up their aircraft except for a cockpit check and some ground school sessions with interpreters. The Russians would fly in on C–47s and in a few days perhaps 35 to 50 pilots would be ready to take back all the aircraft that had accumulated over the past few weeks. Then there would be a great assembly of pilots and aircraft with a mass departure. The B–25 was used as the navigator ship and all aircraft would end up flying a loose formation and just follow him back to Russia. Later in the war we saw a number of women pilots who were sent along to do the flying and they flew anything that was on the ground and ready to go.

I began flying P–39Qs late in 1943 and after the usual ground school for flight review, routes, radio frequencies, emergency procedures, we were issued our flight equipment for the Alaska flight. It consisted of a backpack parachute, a .45 caliber automatic and a special pillow-type cushion we sat on that contained all our emergency food rations, extra ammo, and flares. Not much to take with you if you had to jump. In winter, we had big flying boots, parkas, hats, and gloves – all furlined and it was a hell of a job getting into and out of a 39 or 63 while enclosed in all this bulk.

Radio equipment was primitive with LF ranges but later on, VHF came into use. Most aircraft had ADF or loop-type ADFs which were fairly accurate but the further north you flew the worse the radios operated. The major air bases along the route were at Whitehorse and Edmonton. The other refuelling stops at first were dirt strips with tents. Later they were updated with hangars and black top and the usual tarpaper shacks and pot-bellied stoves. At first, maps were inaccurate with many major landmarks often shown 15 to 20 miles from their actual positions and many of the peaks were higher than shown. The Canadian Rockies were always to our left and we followed the Alaskan Highway, or had it in view for about 900 miles out of the 1,935 mile route from Great Falls to Fairbanks.

When ferrying fighters we flew in better weather since we had no wing de-icers and we would always fly 500 ft on top if the weather was poor and would make a flight plan only if our destination was open. But with the other type aircraft we flew in any kind of weather. With luck we made 800 miles the first day, other times we would fly only as far as good weather would allow. A typical trip in Kingcobras would be to leave Great Falls in the morning, land at Edmonton for fuel and lunch and then take off for Fort St John. We would stay overnight there and in the morning we would clear for Whitehorse, refuel and go on into Fairbanks. Sometimes we made the trip in two days but that was rare. After making our delivery to Fairbanks we would catch a C–47 flight back to Great Falls, flown by Western Airlines pilots under contract to the Army.

Weather was our greatest enemy and one problem which we could not control. Summer was the best time from May through October when most days were clear and only the usual summer rain and thunderstorms were seen and avoided. But the winter months were horrible. At times temperatures went to 55 below and many air bases would sock in zero-zero within three minutes and aircraft would not start until the bush pilots taught us about diluting the gas with oil. When the temperatures were low, aircraft were put into hangars and started inside. Then the doors would be opened quickly and you taxied out and called the tower as you rolled along for takeoff instructions. Many of our ferry flights took two weeks because of bad weather and sometimes you would be weathered in for a week at one base.

Getting down to the business of flying, P–39s and P–63s were where the action was. The similarity of the two aircraft was apparent when you got into the cockpit. Both aircraft were mainly electrical in operation; the gear, flaps and the props were General Motors Aeroproducts units that were linked with the throttle. Some P–39s came through with Curtiss Electric props. The 63 was a bigger aircraft

The Russians received the majority of the P-63 Kingcobras produced yet they never paid for them, ignoring the terms of the American Lend-Lease contract.

in all departments and a great improvement over the 39. The fuel arrangement was similar and both carried about the same quantity of fuel. The 63 had 68 gallon tanks in each wing and 75 gallon auxiliary tanks under each wing. The 39s had 60 gallon tanks in each wing and early models carried a big 175 gallon belly tank between the main landing gear and it was a handicap in flying, affecting airspeed and flight characteristics.

The major improvements that Bell made with the P-63 were the laminar-flow wing, four blade propeller and two larger coolant radiators to overcome the ground heating problem that the 39 had. As a rule, the 63 encountered no ground heating problems at all unless it was extremely hot and there was some traffic delay in getting off the ground.

The early model P-63s had a 1,325 hp Allison and later on they installed the new 1,510 hp Allison in the C model. The 63 could climb to 10,000 feet in a shade over two minutes while the 39 took about three minutes to do the same. The 63 was about 25 to 30 mph faster than a 39 in both cruise and top speeds. On ferry flights we cruised the 63 at about 250 mph IAS versus 230 mph for the 39. The 63 grossed 8,800 lbs on takeoff and the 39 grossed out at 7,700 lbs, which made a great deal of difference in takeoff, climb and general flight operations. On our ferrying

flights no oxygen was carried so we limited our flights to 10,000 ft or below. A few times, in order to get above weather we encountered en route, we had to get up to 15,000 ft or higher for short periods and then come back on down again. But usually we stayed down around 5,000 ft above the terrain and on many trips we cruised at 500 ft or below and flew low the entire leg of that part of the trip just to sightsee. As we approached our landing destination we would pull up to around 1,000 ft and make the usual traffic pattern.

Of course, the tricycle landing gear was the best part of flying 39s, 38s, and 63s. You could taxi faster, had greater ground visibility and the landings and takeoffs were simple compared with the conventional type of landing gear. Ferrying the aircraft with auxiliary tanks under each wing was not too pleasant for many reasons. If you had engine failure on takeoff you could not or did not hardly have time to release the tanks and in flight they slowed you down about seven to ten mph and you were not supposed to exceed about 275 IAS with the tanks attached. However, we exceeded this airspeed on many occasions and few tanks ever popped off. But they could be released electrically if necessary by hitting the wing tank switches and pressing the top button on the stick. The P-63 had delightful flight characteristics. Using 54 inches manifold pressure for takeoff, accelerating rapidly, and with proper trim, the Kingcobra would fly itself off the ground. Torque was no problem, or at least not as bad as in the P-51, but right

rudder had to be used in most takeoffs to ensure a good straight pattern.

Back to the Alaska ferry flights. Fairbanks is where the fun began and the excitement really made the adrenalin flow. Crews were assigned from Gore Field on the day before the flight. Anywhere from three to 15 pilots were sent over to East Base for briefing and aircraft assignments. The size of the flight depended on how many aircraft were ready to go and how many qualified pilots were available. Usually the flight was made up of five to seven aircraft. The flight leader ran the show. He was a pilot who had five or more trips to Fairbanks and he was given a secret flight number for the trip as aircraft numbers were never used en route. So the flight leader designated who was to fly number two, three, four, etc. As an example, the flight number might be 150 and each pilot was designated 150A (Able), 150B (Baker) and so forth. The takeoffs and landings were a set procedure throughout the trip. Formation flying was a must and any pilot who later turned out to be poor in formation flying was usually relegated to some other type of flying. At this point none of us realized that our flight tactics would later be the same ones that the Blue Angels and other flight demonstration teams use in their operations.

The pilots were driven out to the planes took their usual pre-flight walk around their aircraft and got seated and ready to start engines. On a signal from the flight leader, all engines were started after the flight leader got his going. The flight leader handled all radio transmissions to the tower, range stations, etc. After permission to taxi was given, the flight leader began to taxi and each wing man followed out to the run-up area at the end of the active runway. After all run-ups were completed the flight leader got clearance for all members of the flight to taxi onto the runway. The leader was in the center with each wing man staggered to his right and his left. After all flight members were on the runway and holding, the flight leader began his takeoff roll. After he broke ground he continued a normal climb straight out for a longer than usual period and then began a shallow turn to the left. As he broke ground, the number two man started his roll, and as he broke ground number three began his roll and this took place until all flight members were airborne.

The last man usually had to make a quickie left turn shortly after takeoff to catch up with the rest of the flight. After all members joined up on the leader in an echelon formation, the leader made shallow turns to get us all lined up for a flight over the field on the heading we were to take toward our first ground reporting station. After we left the area the flight broke up into a loose formation and we followed the flight leader from station to station until we approached our first refueling stop. Now the important part of formation flying was that many times we took off in good weather and then had to climb up through a solid overcast from 100 ft to 500 ft thick to get 500 ft on top, and likewise we had to regroup to make it back down through an overcast before landing. So we held a tight formation going up and coming down through the stuff. Our takeoff and landing minimums for fighter aircraft were usually 1,000 ft overcast and three mile visibility. The C–47s could be flown with 300 ft and one-half mile for takeoff and 500 ft and one mile for landing.

About ten miles from touchdown, the flight leader would call us all in for a close-in right or left echelon formation depending on the field and runway we were going to use. He would call the tower and request a straight-in approach. ach. Our usual tactic was to barrel in across the field at 400 to 500 ft and make a tactical peel-off and pull up to about 1,000 ft, drop the gear, and each wing man would space himself accordingly. The flight leader would land on the left side of the runway, number two would land on the right, and so on until all members had landed, usually three aircraft were on the runway at one time completing their landing

and getting off onto a taxi strip. Now, where some of the crazy weather came into play up in this part of the country was that the temperature and dew point were close so much of the time that the fields would sock in within two minutes, and sometimes the last man to land could hardly see the field. On several occasions the last man did not make it and pulled up and climbed back up through the overcast and circled, staying up there until someone came up to guide him back down and make an instrument approach when the field opened up a bit. We usually carried enough extra fuel to go on or return to the first emergency strip nearby which was open or had better landing minimums. You could get back up easily but it was getting down that was tough, and many times the older pilots had to help out a new man.

After a few trips north, we began to get to know most of the personnel at the various air bases en route and knew just about what we

could get away with regarding aerobatics, buzzing, and low altitude antics. Edmonton, Whitehorse and Fairbanks were big and you did not fool around at these fields, but the others were usually more relaxed and most anything was acceptable. Places like Watson Lake, Northway, Fort St John, Grand Prairie and Snag were small enough where you could get away with a lot of clowning around. A number of times we would be weathered in at one of these primitive strips and if we could not continue for a day or two, many of us would just takeoff and fly around the area and scout the countryside, put on little airshows, buzz the hell out of everything in the area, lakes, animals, and just have fun.

Many pilots would not do any of this and just stayed on the ground and would not break any rules. Some fields, in spite of the location and facilities, offered good food and had lots of recreation material. If a number of flights were all going north at once we would all agree to

*L*t Ben Brown outfitted for a spot of cold weather flying in a Russian P–63. The area over which the P–63s were ferried was, in many parts, uncharted and being forced down could spell doom for the pilot. (B. L. Brown)

Above

Bell P–63 Kingcobras are given a final check at the factory before being allocated to ferry pilots who would begin the long flight to Alaska. The ramp at the Bell factory is literally covered with the red-starred machines. (Bell)

Above right

Another Kingcobra work of art was produced with Little Marge, a P–63C–5–BE. It is interesting to speculate exactly what the rather conservative-minded Russians had to think about all the scribbling on their new fighters. (B. L. Brown)

Above centre

This P–63C carries some more of Lt Brown's artwork. The car door entry and exit system on the P–63 was almost identical to the early Airacobra. (B. L. Brown)

Right

To help relieve the boredom of the long ferry flights, the pilots would chalk markings and messages on the Kingcobras. Lt Brown added his mother's name and a shark's mouth on 42–70763. On the original print the designation block under the pilot's door can be seen to read: 'US Army Air Forces USSR', giving an indication of the aircraft's Lend-Lease identity. (B. L. Brown)

stop at a certain base for a big party. Everyone carried liquor and did some bootlegging on the side and one of the big sports we enjoyed was playing poker. Everyone usually had plenty of money and the stakes were plenty high. Thousands of dollars were on the table during a day and each pot was easily worth a hundred or more. Crap shooting was also a favorite. Most of the pilots were on good terms with the base personnel but I did witness a few disputes that came to blows.

USO shows came through at times. No top entertainment but they made a good effort. Of course, many of the men were interested in the ladies who were in the show but they were nothing to get excited about as a rule and most of the base personnel had not been away from their girl friends or wives for too long a time so they were not too excited over the whole thing. I remember landing at Snag on one trip and the men on the field had no liquor or beer at all and were anxious to buy most anything. I auctioned off several fifths of average liquor I had for $60 a fifth (that's the most I ever received) with the usual price being $25 to $30.

The route to Ladd Field, Fairbanks, was designed to be about as safe as possible under wartime conditions. Radio facilities improved each month and by the end of the war the trip was very pleasant. We flew over vast areas of flat terrain and the huge Canadian Rockies on our left were beautiful to see and one never tired of looking at them. Many times the ground below was obscured by an overcast but the Rockies were always sticking above everything, and snow-covered. We used to fly over to them as they were quite close at certain places along our route and we liked to fly around the peaks and down into the valleys where we would see many types of deer, moose, antelope, bear, horned sheep, and even see eagles cruising around at various altitudes. At times geese by the hundreds would be spotted flying at 3,000 ft.

One of the most amusing and exciting incidents took place at Watson Lake. Several flights were weathered in for over a week and life was pretty boring. You can do just so much drinking, gambling, eating and sleeping. It was spring and the lake was still frozen. Several of the pilots with lots of energy decided to get some rifles and scout around, maybe shoot a rabbit or something. They started walking out across the field toward the trees and paralleling the lake when they literally ran into an Alaskan brown bear with a cub. In their excitement to get away, one of the pilots fell down and his gun accidentally discharged. The big mother bear became enraged and charged, chasing one of the pilots across the field. She nearly caught up with one pilot and

when another pilot fired off a shot slightly wounding the bear that only made matters worse. They headed for a small shack at the edge of the field and went inside, only to have the bear continue on right into the shack. They went out the back door in a great rush, the bear slowed down and tired out, let matters stand and limped back to her cub.

In the three years of operation of flying aircraft to Alaska, over 20 pilots were killed and many were forced down due to weather or mechanical difficulties, and I believe that only five never made it back. One pilot took about six weeks to walk out but he made it. Survival was questionable in winter and everyone who flew prayed his aircraft would not malfunction until he was close to a field or emergency strip. Some fields were so small and had so few RCAF personnel manning them that if you got caught in bad weather or at night, you had to buzz the field in order for them to turn on the lights.

Of the 40-plus trips I made north, I had only two close situations. One was lucky – we had just passed over Grand Prairie and had made our position report and were just about out of sight of the field when I noticed my oil pressure needle was slowly going down to zero. I immediately called the field for an emergency landing and peeled off to the left, my flight of five P–63s following me on in and by the time I hit the runway for a quickie cross-wind landing, the needle was on zero and I had to be towed in to the ramp. My flight continued on later in the day by tagging onto a flight that was passing by and I stayed a couple of days until the leak was repaired and then I took off and tagged along with another flight north.

The roughest situation was later on when I took off with a flight leaving Watson Lake. I sprung a coolant leak on takeoff and at 800 ft had no place to go. I could not make it back to the field at all, trees were everywhere and the engine froze and stopped. I soon found out that a fighter goes nowhere without that big prop turning. This is where the emergency procedures came into use. I merely pulled the emergency door handle, the door fell off and I rolled out the right side and away I went into the blue. When faced with a no-choice situation, you soon learn what to do real quick. My small 24 ft chute opened up quickly and I came down without any problem, except with my winter equipment increasing my weight I hit pretty hard in the trees and fell right on through down to the ground. Luckily the Alaskan Highway was a few miles away and I hiked over to it and started back to the field. After an hour or so from the time I hit the silk, some of the base personnel came rumbling down the stone and dirt highway and picked me up. Rescue was unknown up in that

country and we were told that your chances of getting found in winter were practically nil. It would have been great if we had helicopters at that time for that is the only thing that would have been able to get any of us out.

Another sidelight was having some female ferry pilots go north with us on some trips. They were known to all as WASPS and were very good pilots. I had met many of them while flying throughout the country. They flew mostly fighters but some were checked out in twin-engine as well. Many of the WASPS were stationed at Dallas or Long Beach. On one trip, two WASPS flew P–63s north with us. One of these girls was a Chinese-American who was later killed while landing at a field in the States. The WASPS proved to be a real asset and made the trip more enjoyable.

By the early summer of 1945, deliveries of Russian Lend-Lease aircraft came to a virtual halt. The war had ended with Germany, the defeat of Japan was near, and no further aid was needed. It seemed odd to see the air bases kind of dry up. By late summer many pilots and ground personnel were now being discharged if they had enough 'points'. Everyone was leaving or being transferred. Those of us who stayed in continued to ferry aircraft within the States, picking up planes from various air bases that were closing down and ferrying them to storage centers. The big storage bases then were Kingman, Arizona; Walnut Ridge, Arkansas; and Muskogee, Oklahoma. All kinds of aircraft imaginable were being flown to these bases; many were being stored and thousands of others were busted up for scrap value. By the winter of 1945, the bases in Montana were almost entirely closed. Gore Field was closed and personnel were either discharged or transferred; the big East Base was kept for future use.

In early 1946, the big storage bases were bursting at the seams with aircraft. It is a sight I shall never forget. One cannot comprehend the sight of thousands of beautiful aircraft of all types just sitting there in the sun and going to waste. I flew aircraft that had only 50 hours on them to these bases where they were pushed out into the field to sit and die. I had half seriously thought of flying a P–51 or a P–63 to my home and hiding it somewhere. I do not think anyone would have ever noticed that it was gone. They never would have missed it. This was the end of an era, one that will never exist again. We who lived and participated in those years never knew how wonderful it was until we got home and found out as time went by that now again we wished we could make just one more trip north. No other generation will ever experience a situation exactly like ours. It was great while it lasted.

BELL P–39 AIRACOBRA VARIANTS, SERIAL NUMBERS AND SPECIFICATIONS

Variants

XP–39 Prototype. Allison V–1710–17. No armament. One built.

XP–39A Proposed YP–39 fitted with V–1719–31 high-altitude powerplant. Not built.

XP–39B Prototype reconfigured with NACA and Army modifications.

YP–39 Service test aircraft. Fitted with 37 mm cannon and two .30 and two .50 caliber machine guns in the nose. Allison V–1710–37. Thirteen aircraft built.

P–39C First production variant. Originally to be designated P–45 because of changes from prototype. Armed with 37 mm cannon and four nose guns. Twenty built and three shipped to Britain via Lend-Lease. Allison V–1710–35 engine.

P–39D Fitted with self-sealing tanks and extra armor plate. Provision for carriage of drop tank or 500 lb bomb. D–2 armed with 37 mm cannon, two .50 caliber nose guns and four .30 caliber guns in the wing. D–1 fitted with 20 mm cannon in place of 37 mm weapon. The D–3 and D–4 were ground attack versions with extra armor plating. Total of 923 constructed. Allison V–1710–35.

Airacobra Mk 1 RAF variant. Same as the P–39D except for substitution of 37 mm cannon with a 20 mm cannon. Allison V–1710–E4 (export version of –35). Eventually rejected by RAF; 675 ordered with 212 diverted to USSR (54 lost during U-boat attacks on convoys), and 179 aircraft taken over by USAAF after 7 December 1941 as P–400.

XP–39E Three early production P–39Ds modified to flight test the new Continental V–1430–1. Modified with laminar flow wing and different tail configurations on each aircraft. Never flown with the Continental and instead powered with Allison V–1710–47. Eventual production as P–76 planned but cancelled. Three aircraft were used for test work with the new P–63.

P–39F Same as P–39D–1 with Aeroproducts propeller instead of the Curtiss Electric unit. Some modified as P–39F–2 with ground attack and recon. duties. Total of 229 built.

P–39G Same as P–39D–2 but with Aeroproducts propeller. However, aircraft not built under this designation (*see* P–39K–1, P–39L).

P–39K–1 First 210 aircraft of the P–39G order. V–1710–63 engine and Aeroproducts propeller.

P–39L Total of 250 built from P–39G order with Curtiss Electric propeller.

P–39M Total of 240 built. Allison V–1710–83 with Curtiss Electric propeller.

P–39N Allison V–1710–85 and Aeroproducts propeller with 11 ft 7 in diameter. Later production Ns had reduced internal fuel capacity. Total of 2,095 built.

P–39Q Two .50 caliber machine guns carried under wings in pods but these were deleted on many aircraft. Retained 37 mm cannon and two .50 caliber machine guns in nose. Some fitted with four-blade Aeroproducts propeller. Most sent to Russia under Lend-Lease. P–39Q–10 and above had propeller setting linked to the throttle for automatic adjustment. P–39Q–21 and 25 fitted with four-blade propeller. Allison V–1710–85. Total of 4,905 built.

TP–39Q Dual control indoctrination trainer modification of P–39Q.

A–7 Radio controlled target drone conversion of Airacobra. Apparently not built.

Serial Numbers

XP–39	38–326
YP–39	40–027 through 40–039
XP–39B	38–326
P–39C	40–2971 through 40–2990.
P–39D	40–2991 through 40–3050, 41–6722 through 41–6841, 41–6842 through 41–7052, 41–7057 through 41–7058, 41–7080 through 41–7115
P–39D–1	41–28257 through 41–28406, 41–38220 through 41–38404, 41–38563
P–39D–2	41–38405 through 41–38562
XP–39E	41–19501 through 41–19502 and 42–71464
P–39F	41–7116 through 41–7344
P–39J	41–7053 through 41–7056, 41–7059 through 41–7079
P–39K	42–4244 through 42–4453
P–39L	42–4454 through 42–4703
P–39M	42–4704 through 42–4943
P–39N	42–4944 through 42–5043, 42–8727 through 42–9126
P–39N–1	42–9127 through 42–9726, 42–18246 through 42–18545
P–39N–5	42–18546 through 42–19240
P–39Q–1	42–19446 through 42–19595
P–39Q–5	42–19596 through 42–20545
P–39Q–10	42–20546 through 42–21250
P–39Q–15	44–2001 through 44–3000
P–39Q–20	44–3001 through 44–3850, 44–3859 through 44–3860, 44–3865 through 44–3870, 44–3875 through 44–3880, 44–3885 through 44–3890, 44–3895 through 44–3900, 44–3905 through 44–3910, 44–3915 through 44–3919, 44–3937 through 44–3940
P39Q–21	44–3851 through 44–3858, 44–3861 through 44–3864, 44–3871 through 44–3874, 44–3881 through 44–3884, 44–3891 through 44–3894, 44–3901 through 44–3904, 44–3911 through 44–3814, 44–3920 through 44–3936, 44–3941 through 44–4000
P–39Q–25	44–70905 through 44–71104
P–39Q–30	44–71105 through 44–71504
Airacobra Mk I	AH570 through AH739, AP264 through AP384, BW100 through BW183, BX135 through BX434

The following serial numbers are of interest to the Airacobra chronicle:

XFL–1	Highly modified Naval version of the Airacobra. One aircraft built, BuNo 1588.
F2L–K	Airacobras obtained by the Navy for use as drones. It is not known if the aircraft were radio controlled. Seven aircraft obtained, including BuNo 91102 and 91103 (102 was P–39Q–10–BE/42–20807, 103 was P–39Q–5–BE/42–19976). The other five aircraft carried BuNos 122447 through 122451.

Specifications

XP–39

Span	35 ft 10 in
Length	28 ft 8 in
Height	11 ft
Wing area	200 sq ft
Empty weight	3,995 lb
Loaded weight	5,550 lb
Max. speed	390 mph
Cruise speed	n/a
Ceiling	32,000 ft
Rate of climb	3,800 fpm
Range	n/a
Powerplant	Allison V–1710–17 of 1,150 hp

XP–39B

Span	34 ft
Length	29 ft 9 in
Height	11 ft 10 in
Wing area	213 sq ft
Empty weight	4,530 lb
Loaded weight	6,450 lb
Max. speed	375 mph
Cruise speed	310 mph
Ceiling	36,000 ft
Rate of Climb	2,800 fpm
Range	600 miles
Powerplant	Allison V–1710–37 of 1,090 hp

YP–39

Span	34 ft
Length	30 ft 2 in
Height	11 ft 10 in
Wing area	213 sq ft
Empty weight	5,042 lb
Loaded weight	7,235 lb
Max. speed	368 mph
Cruise speed	257 mph
Ceiling	34,500 ft
Rate of Climb	2,700 fpm
Range	600 miles
Powerplant	Allison V–1710–37 of 1,090 hp

P–39C

Span	34 ft
Length	30 ft 2 in
Height	11 ft 2 in
Wing area	213 sq ft
Empty weight	5,070 lb
Loaded weight	7,275 lb
Max. speed	379 mph
Cruise speed	274 mph
Ceiling	33,200 ft
Rate of climb	n/a
Range	500 miles
Powerplant	Allison V–1710–35 of 1,150 hp

P–39D

Span	34 ft
Length	30 ft 2 in
Height	11 ft 10 in
Wing area	213 sq ft
Empty weight	5,462 lb
Loaded weight	8,200 lb
Max. speed	368 mph
Cruise speed	213 mph
Ceiling	32,100 ft
Rate of Climb	2,720 fpm
Range	800 miles
Powerplant	Allison V–1710–35 of 1,150 hp

XP–39E

Span	35 ft 10 in
Length	31 ft 11 in
Height	11 ft 10 in
Wing area	236 sq ft
Empty weight	6,936 lb
Loaded weight	8,918 lb
Max. speed	386 mph
Cruise speed	205 mph
Ceiling	35,200 ft
Rate of climb	2,800 fpm
Range	500 miles
Powerplant	Allison V–1710–47 of 1,325 hp

P–39K

Span	34 ft
Length	30 ft 2 in
Height	11 ft 10 in
Wing area	213 sq ft
Empty weight	5,658 lb
Loaded weight	8,400 lb
Max. speed	368 mph
Cruise speed	213 mph
Ceiling	32,000 ft
Rate of climb	2,800 fpm
Range	750 miles
Powerplant	Allison V–1710–63 of 1,325 hp

P–39N

Span	34 ft
Length	30 ft 2 in
Height	12 ft 5 in
Wing Area	213 sq ft
Empty weight	5,657 lb
Loaded weight	8,200 lb
Max. speed	376 mph
Cruise speed	n/a
Ceiling	32,000 ft
Rate of climb	2,600 fpm
Range	750 miles
Powerplant	Allison V–1710–85 of 1,200 hp

P–39Q

Span	34 ft
Length	30 ft 2 in
Height	12 ft 5 in
Wing area	213 sq ft
Empty Weight	5,645 lb
Loaded weight	8,300 lb
Max. speed	385 mph
Cruise speed	n/a
Ceiling	35,000 ft
Rate of Climb	2,700 fpm
Range	650 miles
Powerplant	Allison V–1710–85 of 1,200 hp

Weight vs Horsepower

Many of Bell's problems with the Airacobra can be related to rapidly escalating weight which was not backed up by more engine power. This list gives a quick idea of the performance problems that beset the series.

	Max. Weight	Max. Horsepower
XP–39	5,550 lb	1,150 hp
XP–39B	6,450 lb	1,090 hp
YP–39	7,235 lb	1,090 hp
P–39C	7,275 lb	1,150 hp
P–39D	8,200 lb	1,150 hp
XP–39E	8,918 lb	1,325 hp
P–39K	8,400 lb	1,325 hp
P–39N	8,200 lb	1,200 hp
P–39Q	8,300 lb	1,200 hp

Armament

XP–39	None
XP–39B	None
YP–39	37 mm cannon/two .50 caliber MGs/two .30 caliber MGs
P–39C	37 mm cannon/two .50 caliber MGs/two .30 caliber MGs
P–39D	37 mm cannon/two .50 caliber MGs/four .30 caliber MGs
Airacobra Mk I	20 mm cannon/two .50 caliber MGs/four .30 caliber MGs
P–39D–1/D–2	20 mm cannon/two .50 caliber MGs/four .30 caliber MGs
P–39Q	37 mm cannon/two .50 caliber MGs/optional two .50 caliber MGs in wing